THE COMPLETE BOOK OF
UNICYCLING

by Jack Wiley, Ph.D.

THE COMPLETE BOOK OF UNICYCLING

by Jack Wiley, Ph.D.

FIRST EDITION

Ninth Printing

Copyright © 1984 by Jack Wiley

A portion of the material in this book is from *The Unicycle Book*,
Copyright © 1973 by Jack Wiley.

Printed in the U.S.A.

Library of Congress Catalog Card Number: 84-50464

ISBN 0-913999-05-9

Solipaz Publishing Company
P.O. Box 366
Lodi, California 95241

CONTENTS

INTRODUCTION

It has been eleven years since I wrote **The Unicycle Book.** During this time I have collected extensive new material on the subject of unicycling. Not only that, but unicycling has changed dramatically during this time. My original idea had been to simply revise and update **The Unicycle Book,** but there was so much to add and change that this was no longer practical. What was needed was essentially a complete new book, using only a portion of the material from the original book. I have also changed the title to **The Complete Book of Unicycling.**

The emphasis of the new book is on learning to ride unicycles and then on learning to do all kinds of things on unicycles once basic riding has been mastered. The history and development and records and feats are covered in the final chapters.

I first became interested in unicycling when I was in the seventh grade. A friend showed me the remains of a unicycle that had belonged to his uncle, a former professional stage performer. I was immediately fascinated by the idea of riding on one wheel, even though I had no idea about how to go about it. I purchased the unicycle and, with the help of a man at a bicycle shop, built the unicycle back up. I learned to ride it by trial and error. Back then, other unicycle riders were rare. I don't recall ever having seen anyone ride one outside the professional realm.

By the time I wrote **The Unicycle Book,** unicycling was beginning to emerge as a recreational activity and sport. Since that time, the popularity of unicycling has accelerated. There are now numerous unicycle clubs and riding groups, national and international organizations devoted to unicycling, and national and international competition. The skill level of many amateur riders has increased dramatically in recent years, and many unicyclists are now performing tricks that I would not have thought possible when I first started out or even when I was writing my first book on the subject. The attempt here is to bring the material contained in the first book up to date and cover what might be considered as modern unicycling. This is no simple task, since unicycling seems to have made more progress, at least at the amateur level, in the last ten years than in all the other approximately one hundred years since the invention or discovery of the unicycle.

The information contained in this book really comes from a number of sources. First, my own experiences. Unicycling has been an important part of my life for 34 years now. Second, my research into the subject. I have tried to follow not only the development of unicycling in my own time, but also to go back to the historical aspects of how it all might have began. And third, the help of others, both directly and by inspiration.

This book is dedicated in memory of William M. Jenack, who spent many years of his life promoting and teaching unicycling and was in my opinion the foremost authority in the world on the subject of unicycling. He contributed tremendously to the original **The Unicycle Book.** We continued to exchange letters up to near the time of his death on February 24, 1982. Bill Jenack was a remarkable person. He was the torch that lit the flame of modern unicycling.

1

Many other people contributed to making this book and/or the original **The Unicycle Book** possible. Special thanks is extended to Al Hemminger, John Foss, JeanPaul Jenack, Kenneth Fuchs, Paul Fox, Jim Moyer, Franz Karrenbauer, Joseph W. Stegen, Jr., Kit Summers, John Held, Monica C. de Hellerman, Dr. Miles S. Rogers, Charlotte Fox Rogers, Peter Hangach, Jim Smith, Bernard Crandall, Hans Born, Bert Sikorsky, David Metz, Fred D. Pfening, Dr. Roland C. Geist, Frank S. Malick, Fred Teeman, William B. Laighton, Jr., Ralph Hanneman, John McPeak, Steve McPeak, Jack Painter, Nicholas S. Gatto, Herman Yung, Alvin Drysdale, Father James J. Moran, and the many other people who freely shared their ideas, techniques, and experiences with me.

Chapter 1

ON ONE WHEEL

If you had never seen or heard of anyone riding a one-wheel pedal cycle, you might well think it would be impossible. It looks much more difficult than it actually is. Of course, almost everyone today has seen someone ride a unicycle, but this has not always been the case.

When I first started unicycling in 1949 at the age of 13, I had seen unicycling in circus and stage acts, but I don't remember having seen anyone ride on the streets.

The situation is now dramatically different. A person riding a unicycle on the street, while it will still draw admiration from those watching, is no longer an uncommon sight in many parts of the United States. In fact, there are now thousands of unicyclists in this country (no one seems to know exactly how many, but some estimates place the figure at over 40,000). There are also many unicyclists in Great Britain, Europe, Japan and other parts of the world.

Today there are not only thousands of amateur riders, but also numerous unicycling clubs and parade riding groups, a national organization, an international organization, and national and international unicycling competition.

The background and history of this phenomenal increase of interest in unicycling as a recreational activity and sport is covered in Chapter 14.

REASONS FOR POPULARITY

Unicycling is a wholesome and challenging recreational activity, sport, and performing art for young and old alike (Fig. 1-1). Within reason, almost anyone who wants to can learn to ride a unicycle. Youngsters and teen-agers of both sexes readily take to this activity. Children, both boys and girls, as young as three have learned. At least one 66-year-old man learned. Several blind persons have picked up the skill.

The cost of unicycles, while not cheap, is in a price range that many people can afford. Essentially all you need to get started is a basic standard unicycle, which presently are available new in a price range from about $75 to $125. It's even possible to reduce this cost by purchasing a used unicycle, building your own, or using a "club" unicycle.

Unicycling is a fun activity. Perched on one wheel there's a unique freedom. You can go forward or backwards. You can turn on a dime or make wide sweeping turns.

Unicycling is good exercise. Cycling is one of the best forms of physical fitness exercise. The unicycle requires vigorous use of the leg muscles; in fact, at an equivalent speed, more than when on a bicycle. The unicycle is not freewheeling. In most cases there is a one-to-one gear ratio. Thus, it requires one full turn of the pedals to make one full revolution of the wheel. Not a very efficient means of transportation, but good exercise.

Unicycling offers a challenging activity for all ages, male or female, and all levels of skill. Learning does not end when ten yards, or even a block, can be covered on a standard unicycle. At any skill level, from the beginner to the most advanced, there's always one more stunt to learn, always a skill that can be done better. For some, just learning to ride is

Fig. 1-1. Unicycling is now a popular recreational activity, sport, and performing art.

enough, but other people want to do artistic skills, ride in parades, enter competitions, or perform on the stage.

Unicycling is good training for other sports, especially those requiring balance and agility, such as skiing and skating.

Unicycling is an ideal urban activity. It lends itself to small confined quarters such as small apartments, offices, sidewalks, play areas, and even hallways. You can't ride a bicycle around an office, but you can a unicycle.

Unicycling is fascinating. It's amazing that it's possible to maintain balance on one wheel. It is this enchanting quality that attracts many to this activity.

Unicycling is an excellent social activity. Of course, it can be done alone, but it's also ideal for groups. What better way is there to get to know each other than by sharing an activity?

Unicycling offers a means of artistic expression. There's unlimited opportunity for creativity, as is the case in dancing or painting a picture.

Unicycling can be a means to adventure. Some will want to use the unicycle for a unique journey, such as a journey around the world (someone actually did just this; see Chapter 15).

Unicycling also offers things that are difficult to define and classify. One family, for example, took up unicycling because it was something they could all do together. For one boy it was a means of proving himself when he found out he was too small for any success in the typical school sports. For others, it's just something that they want to do.

UNICYCLES

Over the years up to the present time a variety of unicycle types, sizes and designs have developed. For our purposes here, a "unicycle" is defined as a one-wheel cycle that has the center of gravity of the rider and cycle when ridden above the center of the wheel. Another type of one-wheel cycle is often called a "monocycle" and has the rider inside the wheel with the center of gravity of the rider and cycle when ridden below the center of the wheel (see Chapter 14).

Unicycles are divided into two basic groups: standard and giraffe.

Standard Unicycles

The basic standard unicycle is the most common and popular type in use today (Fig. 1-2). This unicycle has an axle that is fixed to the hub with the crank arms in turn fixed to the axle. The axle turns in blocks or bearings that are mounted on the ends of the fork prongs. A saddle is mounted on the stem end of the fork. Typical wheel diameters are 20-inch, 24-inch, and 26-inch, although wheel sizes from about 16-inch to 27-inch are often considered to be "regular-size" standard unicycles.

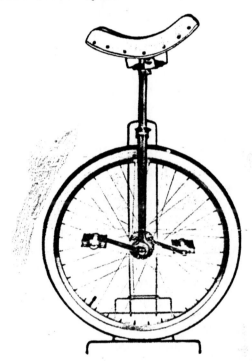

Fig. 1-2. A standard unicycle (courtesy Oxford International Corporation).

Standard unicycles make use of a range of wheel sizes from quite small (10-inches or less in diameter) to very large (56-inches or more in diameter). Figure 1-3 shows a small-wheel unicycle with a standard-size frame for an adult rider and a small-wheel unicycle with a reduced frame size. Small-wheel standard unicycles with corresponding small frames are sometimes called "midget" unicycles. For a very small child, however, such a unicycle may be "standard" size. For our purposes here, a midget unicycle is defined as one that is small relative to the size of the rider.

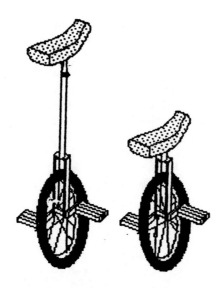

Fig. 1-3. Small-wheel unicycles with regular and reduced frame sizes.

Standard unicycles with unusually large wheels are often called "big-wheel" unicycles. A unicycle in this category is shown in Figure 1-4. Records for the largest wheel unicycles ridden are covered in Chapter 15.

There are many novelty variations for the upper configurations of standard unicycles (Fig. 1-5). A standard unicycle with handlebars instead of a saddle is a very old variation and was possibly used before unicycles with saddles. Another variation on this theme is a model with both a saddle and handlebars, which was probably in use before unicycles with saddles alone. Still another variation uses a post instead of a saddle or handlebars. A novelty variation is to use an animal or bird form, such as a horse from a rocking horse or the figure of a roadrunner, in place of or mounted to the unicycle saddle.

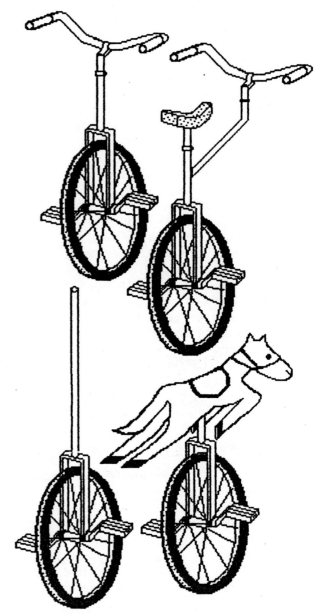

Fig. 1-5. Standard unicycles with variations in upper configurations.

Fig. 1-4. Big-wheel unicycle.

Novelty wheel and crank arm variations include a wheel with feet, double parallel wheels (also called "dicycle"), and kangaroo, which has the crank arms extending in the same direction from the axle and parallel to each other (Fig. 1-6). All of these novelty wheel and crank arm variations can be constructed with regular saddles, handlebars, saddles and handlebars, posts, and animal forms (see Fig. 1-5). All of these cycles can in turn be constructed with regular, small, and big wheels, giving many possible combinations.

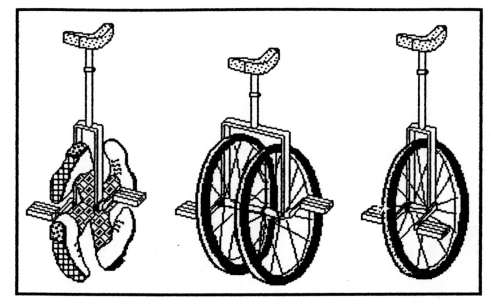

Fig. 1-6. Novelty wheel and crank variations: wheel with feet; double parallel wheels; and kangaroo.

Regular standard unicycles and all variations described above including all upper configurations and all wheel types and sizes can be constructed with off-centered and/or out-of-round wheels, including a "square wheel" (Fig. 1-7). This gives hundreds of possibilities.

A standard unicycle wheel with axle, crank arms and pedals (Fig. 1-8), but no frame or saddle, is often called an "ultimate" wheel. While a standard unicycle wheel assembly can be used, ultimate wheels are often specially constructed so that the pedals are closer to a plane in the center of the wheel than is typical on a standard unicycle. These can be constructed in a variety of

wheel sizes, including large wheels.

Closely related is an ultimate cycle with two parallel wheels (Fig. 1-9), which is much easier to ride than the single-wheel model.

Ultimate wheels can also be constructed with feet wheels. All wheel types described above can also be constructed with off-centered and out-of-round wheels in a variety of wheel sizes.

Tandem unicycles that have characteristics of both standard and giraffe unicycles (Fig. 1-10) have been built. This tandem unicycle operates similar to a standard unicycle except that it has chain-drives similar to those used

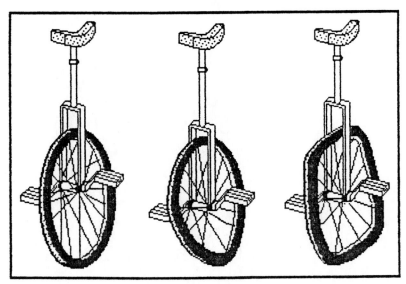

Fig. 1-7. Variations in wheel shapes: off-centered; out-of-round; and square.

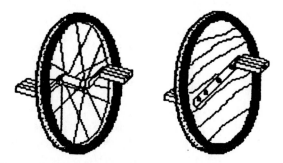

Fig. 1-8. Ultimate wheels.

Fig. 1-9. Ultimate cycle with parallel wheels.

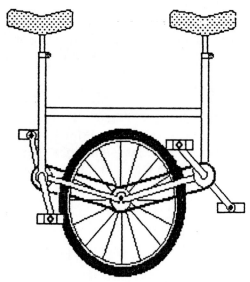

Fig. 1-10. Tandem "standard" unicycle.

unicycle and handlebar unit (Fig. 1-13), a unicycle with saddle and unicycle with handlebars (Fig. 1-14), and a unicycle with saddle and unicycle with handlebars and saddle (Fig. 1-15) are variations.

At least two different versions of motor-driven "standard" unicycles have been invented and ridden. These unicycles are detailed in Chapter 14.

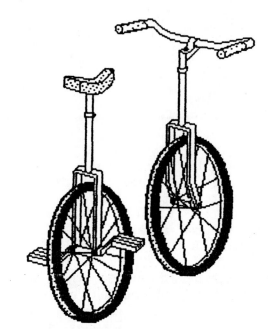

Fig. 1-11. Handlebar unit for use with standard unicycle.

Fig. 1-12. Unicycle and handlebar unit connected to form "bicycle."

on many giraffe unicycles. Other designs are also possible.

A handlebar unit (Fig. 1-11) is a device that can be used with a standard unicycle. These are sometimes connected to a standard unicycle (Fig. 1-12) to form a "bicycle" that can also be ridden with the front wheel off the ground as a unicycle. Brake-apart bicycles that form a

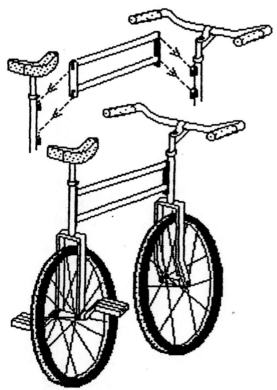

Fig. 1-13. Brake-apart bicycle that forms unicycle and handlebar unit.

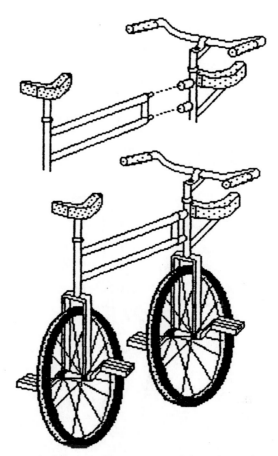

Fig. 1-15. Brake-apart bicycle that forms saddle and handlebar and saddle unicycles.

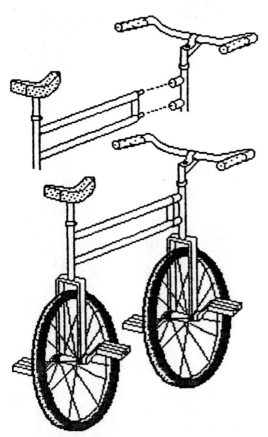

Fig. 1-14. Brake-apart bicycle that forms saddle and handlebar unicycles.

Machines that have legs and feet that walk when pedaled are sometimes considered to be in the category of standard unicycles. These machines are covered in Chapter 14.

Giraffe Unicycles

The other major class of unicycles are the giraffe unicycles (Fig. 1-16). These are sometimes called "chain-driven" unicycles, but many tall unicycles have other types of drives, such as wheel to wheel. For this reason, we will use the term "giraffe" to refer to this type of unicycle in this book.

A basic giraffe unicycle is about five or six feet from the ground to the saddle when the unicycle is upright. Variations include shorter and taller models (Fig. 1-17). The shortest models have the crank axle located just above the wheel. Giraffe unicycles have been constructed and ridden that are over 100 feet tall (see Chapter 15).

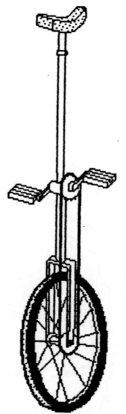

Fig. 1-16. Basic giraffe unicycle.

Handlebar units have been constructed for use with giraffe unicycles (Fig. 1-18).

A popular variation is a giraffe unicycle with a tiny wheel (Fig. 1-19). Small-wheel giraffe unicycles generally have a larger chainwheel at the crank than at the sprocket at the hub, which gives a pedal action similar to that of a basic giraffe unicycle with a larger wheel. Information about the records for the smallest wheel giraffe unicycles ridden is given in Chapter 15.

A variety of giraffe unicycles have been constructed with zigzag frames (Fig. 1-20). A number of different zigzag configurations have been used. Double connected sprockets are often used at the bends and separate chains are used to link each straight section from the wheel to the crank.

Multi-wheel giraffe unicycles are another popular variation of the basic giraffe unicycle. One type has a chain drive, with the extra wheels turning for decorative purposes (Fig. 1-21). Another type has the wheels turning each other without a chain drive (Fig. 1-22). If three

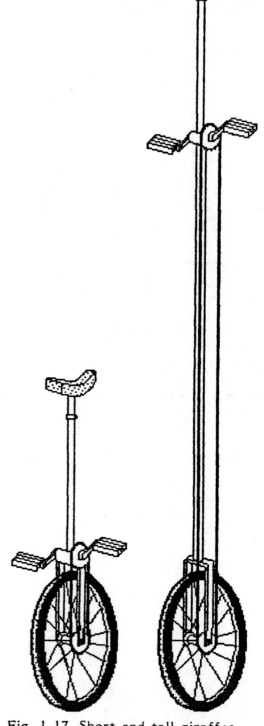

Fig. 1-17. Short and tall giraffes.

or five or some other odd number of wheels are used, the direction the crank turns is the same as the direction the bottom wheel turns. The upper section of this type of unicycle is basically

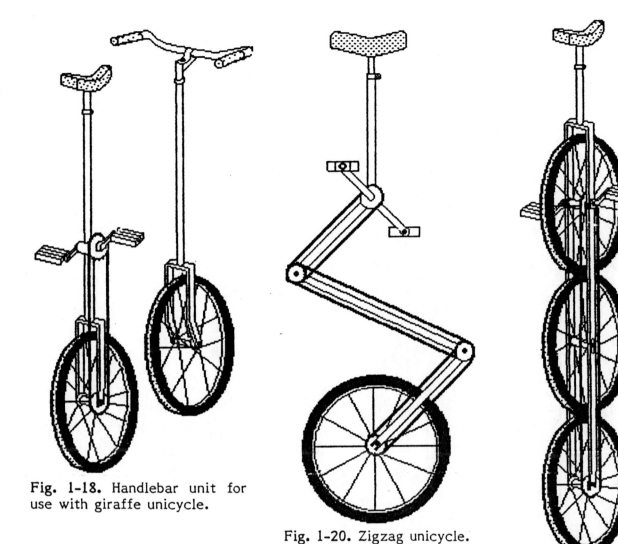

Fig. 1-18. Handlebar unit for use with giraffe unicycle.

Fig. 1-20. Zigzag unicycle.

Fig. 1-21. Multi-wheel giraffe with chain drive.

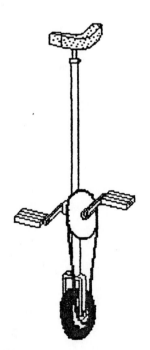

Fig. 1-19. Giraffe with small wheel.

a standard unicycle. The three wheels can be the same or different sizes. If the upper and lower wheels are the same sizes and the center wheel is smaller, the gear ratio remains one-to-one. The lower and upper wheels can be of different sizes, which changes the drive ratio.

Similar unicycles are constructed with two (Fig. 1-23) or four or some other even number of wheels. These unicycles are difficult (but not impossible; see Chapter 10) to ride because the bottom wheel turns in the opposite direction of the crank. Two-wheel models with a reversing gear at the cranks to give the normal pedal direction have also been constructed (Fig. 1-24).

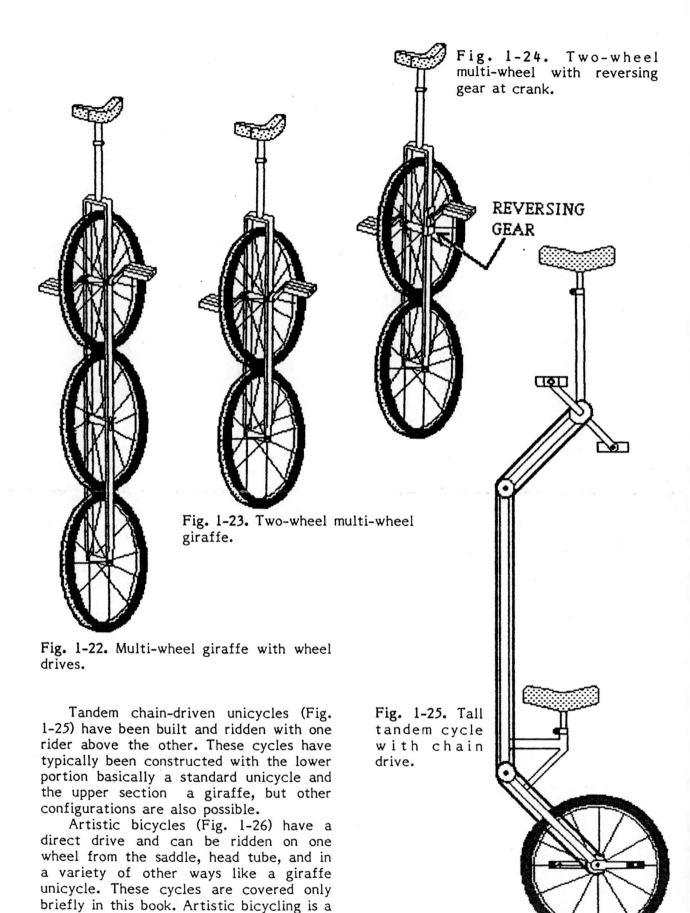

Fig. 1-24. Two-wheel multi-wheel with reversing gear at crank.

REVERSING GEAR

Fig. 1-23. Two-wheel multi-wheel giraffe.

Fig. 1-22. Multi-wheel giraffe with wheel drives.

Tandem chain-driven unicycles (Fig. 1-25) have been built and ridden with one rider above the other. These cycles have typically been constructed with the lower portion basically a standard unicycle and the upper section a giraffe, but other configurations are also possible.

Artistic bicycles (Fig. 1-26) have a direct drive and can be ridden on one wheel from the saddle, head tube, and in a variety of other ways like a giraffe unicycle. These cycles are covered only briefly in this book. Artistic bicycling is a highly developed competitive sport in Europe.

Fig. 1-25. Tall tandem cycle with chain drive.

12

Fig. 1-26. Artistic bicycle.

HOW TO GET STARTED

The usual procedure is to begin with a standard unicycle for learning basic riding. The following chapters detail how to go about this, from selecting a first unicycle and taking your first pedals on one wheel, through basic and intermediate unicycling to some of the most advanced skills being performed today.

Chapter 2

MECHANICS

Before attempting to learn to ride a unicycle, it is helpful to first understand the mechanics that make it possible to keep balance on one wheel. The basic purpose here is to relate some of the laws of physics to unicycling. Or, in simpler terms, to show how it is possible to ride a unicycle. I should point out that only limited scientific study has been done on the subject of unicycling.

MONOCYCLING

Mechanically speaking, the simplest one-wheel cycle has the rider inside the wheel with the center of gravity of the rider and the cycle when the cycle is being ridden below the center of the wheel (Fig. Fig. 2-1). First, however, we will consider the wheel only. If rolled, the wheel generally remains balanced until it stops rolling.

While the wheel is rolling, two types of motion are involved: linear and angular (Fig. 2-2). In linear motion, a body moves in a straight line, with all parts moving the same distance, direction, and speed. A bullet is an example of this type of motion.

In angular motion, one part of the body, the axis, remains fixed in relation to some other part. The hands on a clock demonstrate this type of motion.

A rolling wheel displays both types of motion. A point in the center of the hub moves in a linear fashion; a point on the rim is in angular movement to the axis in the center of the wheel. If the wheel is perfectly balanced as regards alignment and weight, the center of gravity (the point at which the effective weight of the body is centered) will be in the exact center of the wheel and on the axis.

Gyroscopic action also enters into the picture, but since this is of great complexity, no attempt will be made to show this principle here. However, it should be noted that this explains in part why the wheel tends to remain balanced while it is rolling.

Fig. 2-1. A monocycle has the rider inside the wheel.

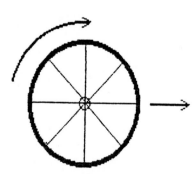

Fig. 2-2. Linear and angular motion simultaneously in rolling wheel.

When the rider is placed inside the wheel, the effect of the force of gravity (which is represented by a constant acceleration of, for all practical purposes, 32 ft/sec^2) must be considered. Even though the rider is generally on a platform that rolls on a track on the inside of the wheel rim, for practical purposes he can be considered as a body hung from a fixed point in the center of the wheel in such a way that he can swing to and fro under the combined forces of gravity and momentum. Placing the rider inside the wheel serves to lower the center of gravity and thus make balance even easier. In fact, if the center of gravity is placed below the lowest point on the wheel, as is the case with the unicycling clown shown in Figure 2-3, balance is no longer a problem because the center of gravity is actually hanging from the wheel.

The rider inside the wheel remains at the bottom of the wheel because of the force of gravity. The pedal action keeps the wheel in motion (rolling). Thus, keeping balance is relatively simple. The same principles apply to motor-driven monocycles. Stopping (braking), however, becomes a considerable problem. The

braking is, in effect, a friction between the riding platform and the wheel. If the friction becomes too great, the rider becomes part of the wheel and starts somersaulting as though inside a clothes dryer. Attempts to overcome this problem have involved adding additional wheels that come in contact with the ground whenever the rider starts to rotate with the wheel.

Turning of a monocycle can be accomplished to a limited extent by leaning, but this is not entirely satisfactory. Maneuverability is extremely limited.

UNICYCLING

Unicycling differs from monocycling in that the unicycle rider is above the wheel (Fig. 2-4). This adds considerably to the difficulty of keeping balance. Nevertheless, it is an additional factor that makes riding a unicycle possible. The unicycle is not freewheeling. By means of the pedals, the rider is in direct control of the wheel. Without this control, balance is extremely difficult (only a few advanced riders have managed coasting on a unicycle with their feet off the pedals, and this has been limited to short distances). Whereas a rolling monocycle will keep balance by itself without a

Fig. 2-3. Because the center of gravity is below the string, this toy clown has no problem keeping balance.

Fig. 2-4. On the unicycle, the center of gravity is above the wheel.

rider, a rolling unicycle, once released, quickly falls.

Then how is it possible to ride a freewheeling bicycle on the rear wheel, as children frequently do on banana-saddle bicycles? First of all, even though the bicycle will coast when pedaling is stopped, the bicycle is not completely freewheeling. There is still considerable friction involved. Second, the rider pedals at a rate where the wheel is not freewheeling, i.e., faster than the wheel is turning. The front wheel is being pulled toward the ground by gravity. Power is being applied to the rear wheel by the pedaling action to move the rear wheel toward the front wheel to exactly overcome the falling action of the front wheel. Sustained wheelies done with the rider coasting (not pedaling) are extremely difficult, similar to coasting on a unicycle.

In unicycling, the basic mechanism involved in keeping the rider above the wheel is the direct control that the rider has over the wheel. All that is required is the ability to speed up or slow down (brake) the wheel and, in extreme cases, reverse the pedaling direction. For equilibrium (balance) to exist, the center of gravity of a body must fall within its base. The base of the unicycle is a small area of the tire, so small in fact that stationary balance with no movement is extremely difficult, if not impossible. With a hard flat spot on a wide tire, however, stationary balance becomes easier.

In motion everything becomes easier. If balance is lost forward while riding forward, recovery can be made by increasing the pedal speed (Fig. 2-5). If the center of gravity falls behind the base of support while riding forward, decreasing the pedal speed will bring the center of gravity forward over the base of support (Fig. 2-6). Or to put it another way, to ride forward, the saddle and thus the rider, must be in linear motion with the axle of the unicycle. However, considerabale correction is possible by changing the pedal speed. If the axle gets ahead of the saddle, slowing the pedal speed (braking) will allow the saddle (and rider) to catch up. Or if the saddle gets ahead of the axle, speeding up the

pedaling will allow the axle to catch up.

The same principle can be applied to maintaining balance in one spot with forward and backward pedal motions. If the saddle starts to fall forward,

Fig. 2-5. When balance is lost forward while riding forward, correction is made by increasing speed of forward pedaling.

Fig. 2-6. When balance is lost backwards while riding forward, correction is made by slowing down or reversing the pedaling.

correction is made by pedaling forward. If the saddle starts to fall backwards, correction is made by pedaling backwards

When riding a unicycle forward, a forward lean (of the saddle and rider) is used. The forward pedaling tends to rotate the saddle backwards. The principle can be demonstrated by balancing a pole that is leaning by moving the base of support under it (Fig. 2-7). The amount of lean when riding a unicycle depends on the speed of riding. They must correspond closely if balance is to be maintained. The required lean increases as the speed increases.

Another way of looking at the same thing is to consider the center of gravity (of the unicycle and the rider) and the base of support (the part of the wheel in contact with the riding surface). Whenever the center of gravity falls outside the base of support (that is, if a plumb line were suspended from the center of gravity and it did not fall in the area where the tire contacts the ground), the base of support must be moved toward (and under) the center of gravity if balance is to be restored.

Maintaining balance in the forward/bacward direction is accomplished mainly by movement of the unicycle wheel rather than by movements of the rider,

such as leaning the upper body or moving the arms. In fact, many experienced riders feel that keeping the body in line with the unicycle frame is extremely important for easy riding. Trying to maintain balance by wild arm and body motions is something like trying to balance a wet noodle on your finger.

The same principles apply to riding backwards. When balance is lost backwards, correction is made by increasing the speed of backward pedaling (Fig. 2-8). When balance is lost forward, correction is made by slowing down the backward pedaling or changing the pedal direction to forward (Fig. 2-9).

For both forward and backward riding, balance to the side presents little difficulty as long as balance in the forward/backward direction is maintained.

The same balance principles also apply to turning, which is a form of correction for being off balance to one side. If the unicycle and rider are off balance to one side, a twisting action can be used to turn the unicycle in that direction so that the wheel can be pedaled under the center of gravity. Turning can be accomplished by leaning in the direction of the desired turn and

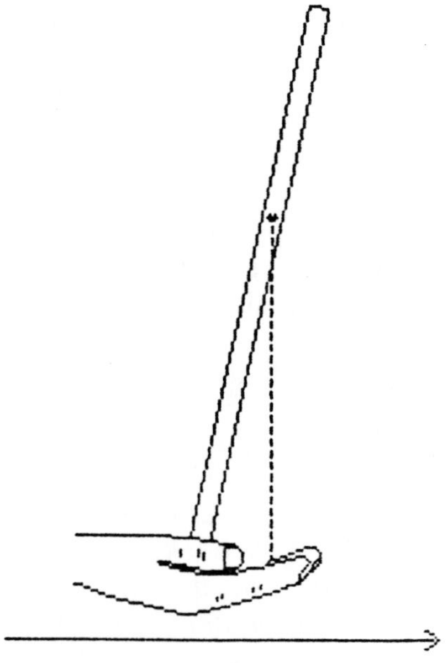

Fig. 2-8. When balance is lost backwards while riding backwards, correction is made by increasing the speed of backward pedaling.

Fig. 2-7. Balancing a leaning pole by moving hand under it.

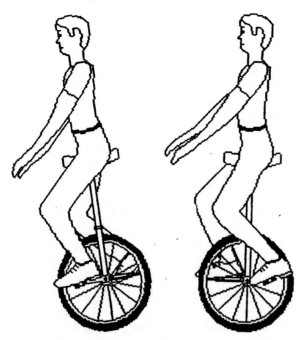

Fig. 2-9. When balance is lost forward while riding backwards, correction is made by slowing down or changing direction of pedaling.

regaining balance as detailed above.

The above discussion has focused on a rolling wheel that can change the speed and stop and change the direction of rotation. Often overlooked is the fact that the unicycle wheel and crank arms and pedals act as a base of support with the friction between the tire and the riding surface resisting turning so that the rider can shift the unicycle forward or backwards in relation to the unicycle hub. For example, if the unicycle is stationary and the rider has the pedals frozen in a horizontal position with one pedal forward and one back, the center of gravity can be shifted backward by applying greater pressure on the forward-positioned pedal to shift the body backward. This can be done while still keeping enough pressure on the back-positioned pedal so that the unicycle wheel does not rotate. These shifting actions can take place even when the unicycle wheel is rotating, and I now believe that these shifting actions play a major role in unicycle riding.

Turning can be done in smaller and smaller circles until the unicycle is being ridden in a circle smaller than the

diameter of the unicycle wheel.

Twisting is basically turning that is done in one spot. There are two basic types of twisting that can be done on a unicycle: action-reaction twisting that does not produce any total angular momentum and pirouetting, which involves total angular momentum.

At this point it is important to understand Sir Isaac Newton's Laws of Motion, as they are fundamental to twisting on a unicycle. Newton's First Law (Law of Inertia) is: "Every body continues in its state of rest, or of uniform motion in a straight line, except in so far as it may be compelled by impressed forces to change that state."

This means that a force is necessary to get anything to move. Once moving, it travels in a straight line and a further force must be applied to slow it down, stop it, speed it up, or change its direction. A ball rolling along level ground would continue to roll in a straight line if it were not for ground and air friction. The same applies to angular motion. A pirouetting ice skater would go on spinning forever if it were not for friction.

Newton's Second Law (Law of Acceleration) states: "The rate of change of momentum is proportional to the impressed force, and the actual change takes place in the direction in which the force acts." This means that any change in velocity (positive or negative) will be directly proportional to the amount of force used and inversely proportional to the object's mass.

Newton's Third Law (Law of Reaction) states: "To every action there is an equal and opposite reaction; or the mutual actions of two bodies in contact are always equal and opposite in direction."

In the case of the unicycle, there is friction (a friction surface between the ground and unicycle tire). However, this friction is limited. Action-reaction turning without developing any total angular momentum can be done by extending the arms outward and twisting the upper body rapidly in one direction. The lower body and the unicycle wheel will have an opposite and equal reaction in the opposite direction. This can be demonstrated by standing on a turntable that has very little friction, such as a twist exercise platform. If the arms and upper body are rotated in one direction (Fig. 2-10), the feet and body turn in the opposite direction. However, when the motion of the arms and upper body stop, so does the motion of the feet and lower body. No total body angular momentum has been established. What has been demonstrated is an action and opposite and equal reaction among the parts of the body itself. No total angular momentum has been established in relation to the ground. However, because there is considerable friction in the bearings between the ground and the twist platform (and usually even more between a unicycle tire and the ground) the body can be turned to the new direction of the feet by moving the arms and upper body slowly to the new position. However, using twist platforms that have very little friction, even this is difficult. If there were no friction, even a slow motion return to the original body position would bring the platform back to the original position.

In the case of the unicycle, however, the friction is great enough that the unicycle can be turned by this type of action-reaction twisting without developing any total angular momentum. A series of such turning actions can be done to turn the unicycle all the way around. However, the amount of turn possible from each individual action-reaction movement is quite limited, usually less than one-half turn.

When total angular momentum is established, the body continues to revolve even when all motion of the body is halted. The axis of the revolving body is a straight line, itself at rest in the body, about which all other parts rotate in a plane at right angles (Fig. 2-11). In the case of the pirouetting unicycle and rider, the motion is a horizontal or near horizontal plane about the vertical or near-vertical axis, which passes through the center of gravity and the point of support (where unicycle tire is spinning on the ground).

Since it has been demonstrated that action-reaction motions within the body itself will not result in total angular momentum, the angular momentum must be established in some other way, such as pushing against an external object or from being spun by a partner or converting linear motion forward or backwards of the unicycle or angular momentum of the turning of unicycle wheel into total angular momentum. Once total angular

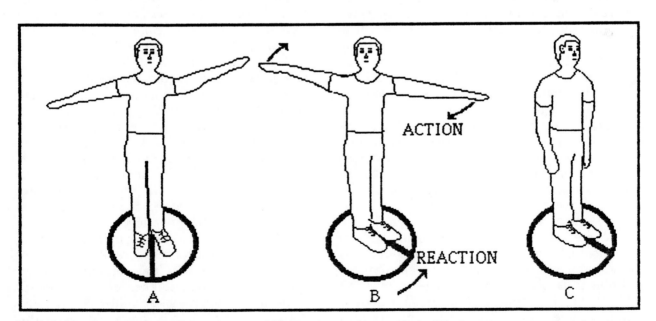

Fig. 2-10. Action-reaction turning: (A) Arms are extended; (B) Arms are rotated (action) and turntable rotates in opposite direction (reaction); (C) Arms are brought to sides and body is rotated toward new direction of feet.

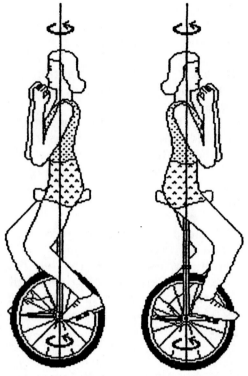

Fig. 2-11. True spinning or pirouetting involves total angular momentum about an axis.

momentum has been established, the twisting speed can be changed. This can be demonstrated on the twist platfrom. With someone standing on the platform with the arms extended outward, another person can set this person in motion (give the person total angular momentum). The person on the platform is then turning without body movement. The person can then pull the arms in close to the body and the twisting speed is increased. In turn, it can be slowed by putting the arms back out. By holding heavy weights in the hands, the experiment is even more convincing. If there were no friction present (in turntable, air, etc.), the same angular momentum would continue until some outside force stopped it.

I am now convinced that a number of unicycle riders can establish total angular momentum in the open without any contact with a partner or other object. While it is difficult to determine how this total angular momentum is established, it would have to develop from some already established linear or angular momentum, such as the forward motion of the

unicycle or the angular momentum of the turning wheel, or from an action-reaction between the unicycle wheel and riding surface. Further study is needed to determine the skills and techniques for best establishing total angular momentum while unicycling in the open.

The basic mechanics for the performance of basic unicycle balance, riding, turning, and twisting have been discussed in simplified form. While many sport skills have been mechanically analyzed, only a limited amount of work has been done relating to unicycling. One study was done relating to forward and backward balance, which suported the mechanics detailed above. Further study is needed, especially regarding turning and twisting and other advanced aspects of unicycling.

On special unicycles, such as a tall chain-driven giraffe unicycle, the principles are basically the same. Having the center of gravity higher doesn't appear to make balance any more difficult, and some riders think it is easier. However, other factors, such as fear, can enter the picture.

Another possible approach to studying the mechanics of unicycling is to find out what part of a unicycle is needed to make riding possible. Wheels with only pedal arms and pedals can be ridden (see Chapter 10), so the unicycle frame is not absolutely necessary, although it definitely makes things easier. The so-called "ultimate wheel" is extremely difficult to master, but many advanced unicyclists have accomplished this feat. A review of the mechanical principles given above show that nothing additional in the way of mechanics is required. Correction to maintain forward and backward balance are the same, only much more difficult to execute. A wider wheel makes riding considerably easier. In any case, balance is primarily maintained by speeding up or slowing down the pedaling.

However, try riding a unicycle that is complete except for crank arms and pedals with the feet free of the wheel on footrests attached to the fork. For power, a push or coasting downhill is allowed. While a few people have demonstrated some ability to maintain balance on such a cycle or a regular unicycle with the feet free of the pedals (coasting) or a wheel without crank arms or pedals by placing the feet on an axle that is fixed with the wheel hub, these skills are extremely difficult. Ten years ago I thought such delicate balance would be impossible, but I have now seen a few riders manage this to limited degrees. However, some type of direct control of the wheel appears to be required for most unicycling.

Being able to physically move the wheel over the ground seems to be another requirement. An attempt to ride a unicycle on bicycle rollers will quickly demonstrate this. Once balance is lost forward or backwards, there is no way to bring the unicycle back in balance. Some unicyclists have managed to maintain limited stationary balance with the unicycle on the ground without noticeable body movement, but this is extremely difficult. A flat spot (and the larger the better) on the wheel helps considerably here.

Frank Malick's motor-driven unnicycle (see Chapter 14) demonstrates the basic mechanics of the pedal-driven unicycle. In the case of the motor-driven unicycle, the rider stays balanced by means of a hand control. When starting to fall forward, additional speed is required to speed the wheel so that it is driven under the rider. Starting to fall backwards calls for braking, which moves the rider forward over the wheel. These adjustments are made on demand by a thumb-positioned slider, which in turn controls an electromagnetic friction brake and an electromagnetic friction clutch.

Finally, it must be pointed out that biological laws also, in addition to mechanical laws, apply to unicycling. If the correct motion is made at the proper time, that is, the mechanics are correct, then the unicycling skill can be successfully done. This assumes, however, that the rider is able to perform the correct mechanics. For various reasons, such as lack of strength, poor coordination, fear, and so on, the rider may not be able to do this. As the unicycling skills become more difficult, the biological requirements become more critical.

Many people already have adequate strength and other physical fitness requirements for basic riding. If not, special exercises, such as with weight machines, may be helpful. Advanced riders may well be able to benefit from special exercise programs to improve strength, endurance, flexibility and other fitness parameters (see Chapter 5).

Chapter 3

UNICYCLES AND OTHER EQUIPMENT

A number of manufactured standard and giraffe unicycles are now available. You can also have these cycles custom built for you or build them yourself. Most other types of unicycles are not presently being manufactured; you will need to have these custom made or make them yourself. Construction of unicycles is covered in my book **How To Build Unicycles and Artistic Bicycles** (available from Solipaz Publishing Company, P.O. Box 366, Lodi, CA 95241).

Also covered in this chapter are care and repair of unicycles, clothing and protective devices, and props and related equipment.

MANUFACTURED UNICYCLES

A number of companies (both domestic and foreign) are presently manufacturing standard-type and/or giraffe unicycles or have manufactured them in the past but have stopped production. Since it is difficult to determine at any given time which brands and models are in production, some of the unicycles covered below may be currently out of production. Even if a particular unicycle is not presently being manufactured, you may be able to purchase them used, and some stores may still have new ones in stock.

Standard Unicycles

Standard unicycles are and have been manufactured in two basic classes. The recommended unicycles are built in a manner similar to quality bicycles. These unicycles feature sturdy bearings mounted securely to the unicycle frame, an axle fixed to the hub, crank arms securely attached to the axle (these can be of the cotter or cotterless type of bicycle design

and construction), and an inflated tire with a tube and are often called "professional model" unicycles, although this is the type also recommended for use by "amateur" riders.

The second major class of manufactured standard unicycles are constructed along the lines of tricycles or have some combination of both tricycle and bicycle design and construction. My experience has been that these unicycles are a waste of money. While they may hold up for a time with small children, their lack of precision makes them difficult to ride. For adults, they are not only difficult to ride, but also of inadequate strength. These unicycles generally have a much lower price tag than do "professional models," but they are generally poor economy. These unicycles will not be treated further in this book. My advice is that if you want to take up unicycling, get a "professional model" unicycle.

Almost all unicycles of present and recent manufacture have special curved unicycle saddles (see Fig. 3-1). Some earlier models were sold with racing-type bicycle saddles. These saddles are generally unsuitable and should be replaced with unicycle saddles.

The following are descriptions of some of the quality manufactured standard unicycles that I'm familiar with (some of these are not presently in production, but you may be able to purchase these used and possibly even new).

Schwinn® (Schwinn Bicycle Company, Chicago, Illinois) has probably manufactured and sold more standard unicycles in this country than any other domestic manufacturer. At the time of this writing, these unicycles are not in production because the factory is moving to new facilities, but hopefully these unicycles will be back in production again soon. In any case, many Schwinn bicycle stores still have a supply of these unicycles in stock.

The Schwinn standard unicycles (Fig. 3-1) feature adjustable seat posts, sealed crank bearings, nylon cord tires, tubular rims, and chrome plated forks. The Model U20 has a 20-inch wheel and the Model U24 has a 24-inch wheel. The U20 weighs 14 pounds and the U24 weighs 15 pounds. Both models feature professionally designed unicycle saddles.

Figure 3-3. They are available with 20-inch (Model 0020) and 24-inch (Model 0024) wheels. It is my understanding that these unicycles are not presently in production, but are included here because I recently saw new ones for sale in a bicycle shop, you may be able to purchase used ones, and they are high quality, well-constructed unicycles. I used Columbia unicycles in a YMCA program in the mid-1960s with excellent results.

Matthews unicycles (Fig. 3-4) are made by LRV Industries, South El Monte, California. Available with 20-inch (Model 1080) and 24-inch (Model 1480) wheels, the unicycles feature one-piece, polished

Fig. 3-1. Schwinn 20-inch and 24-inch wheel unicycles (courtesy Schwinn Bicycle Company).

Columbia unicycles (Fig. 3-2) made by the Columbia Manufacturing Company, Inc., Westfield, Massachusetts, feature forged steel forks, pneumatic inner tube tires, adjustable seat posts, three piece ball bearing crank assemblies, triple-plated chrome wheels, and flamboyant royal blue baked-on enamel forks. The frame, hub, crank, and saddle-post assemblies are shown in

Fig. 3-2. Columbia unicycle with 24-inch wheel (courtesy Columbia Manufacturing Company, Inc.).

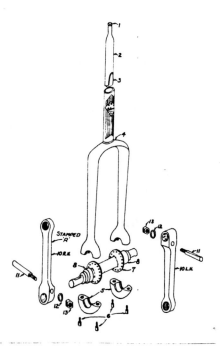

Fig. 3-3. Assembly of Columbia unicycle (Courtesy Columbia Manufacturing Company, Inc.).

chrome-plated forks with special design to combat side sway, aircraft quality bearings that never need lubrication, adjustable seat posts, and deluxe saddles.

A number of standard unicycles made in Japan are imported to the United States. The Oxford International Corporation in Highland Park, Illinois, imports quality models with tubular reinforced forks, industrial type bearings, and adjustable seat post. The Model P20 has a 20-inch wheel and the Model P24 has a 24-inch wheel. The 24-inch wheel size is shown in Chapter 1, Figure 1-2.

Miyata unicycles are well-designed unicycles that are manufactured in Japan by the Miyata Company and readily available in the United States. They offer three sizes in painted models, a 16-inch wheel, a 20-inch wheel, and a 24-inch wheel with cottered type crank assemblies. The 16-inch is the only quality manufactured unicycle that I know of that is available with this wheel size. These unicycles are ideal for children who do not yet have the leg-length for riding a 20-inch wheel unicycle. The Miyata is also available in chrome-plated models with 20-inch and 24-inch wheels with cotterless type cranks. The Miyata

Fig. 3-4. Matthews unicycle (courtesy LRV Industries).

unicycles have the best designed and shaped saddle that I have seen on any manufactured unicycle. There is also a wire spring encircling the saddle that gives protection should the unicycle be dropped.

A variety of other quality standard unicycles made in Japan have been imported to this country, including the Sturdee (Fig. 3-5) and American Eagle brands.

24

Fig. 3-5. Sturdee unicycle with 20-inch wheel.

DM Engineering in Dorset, England, manufactures quality standard unicycles with 18-inch, 20-inch, 24-inch, and 28-inch wheel sizes with plastic coated or, at extra cost, chrome plated frames.

Standard unicycles are also made in Europe, but not many of these have been imported to this country. For a number of years, Bauer standard unicycles with 26-inch wheels were made in Germany, but these are no longer being produced. This same company was once also a leading manufacturer of artistic bicycles.

Giraffe Unicycles

The selection of manufactured giraffe unicycles is more limited than that of standard unicycles.

The Schwinn Bicycle Company introduced their Model U-72 giraffe unicycle in 1977. The cycle is of high quality construction and is about 6-feet tall, with the actual height depending on the setting of the saddle. The cycle has a 20-inch wheel, a one-piece steel crank, and a Schwinn unicycle saddle. At the time of this writing, these unicycles are not in production because the factory is moving to new facilities, but hopefully these unicycles will be back in production again soon. In any case, some Schwinn bicycle stores still have these unicycles in stock.

The Cycle Components Company in El Monte, California, introduced their Penguin model giraffe unicycle in 1977. This cycle is about 4-1/2 feet tall and has a mag wheel.

Oxford P21 Hi-Boy Unicycle (Fig. 3-6) is a six-foot, chain-driven unicycle with a 20-inch wheel. It's made in Japan and imported to the United States by the Oxford International Corporation in Highland Park, Illinois.

DM Engineering in Dorset, England, offers a 5-foot chain-driven giraffe unicycle with a 20-inch wheel and can be supplied with either a single or double chain drive.

Where to Buy

Quality unicycles, such as those detailed above, are available from bicycle shops, chain stores, and mail order firms. A list of suppliers is included in the Appendix.

Used manufactured unicycles can be found at secondhand and thrift stores, garage sales, and from classified ads in newspapers.

Assembly

In many cases, manufactured unicycles can be purchased from bicycle shops fully assembled, but an extra charge is sometimes made for this. In most cases, when you purchase a unicycle in the shipping carton, all of the major jobs, such as spoking and aligning the wheel, have already been done at the factory.

Fig. 3-6. Oxford P21 Hi-Boy Unicycle (courtesy Oxford International Corporation).

The remaining assembly is usually easy. Figure 3-7 shows the components of a Sturdee unicycle (made in Japan) that were taken from the shipping carton. No assembly or other instructions were found in the shipping carton (this is an exception to the rule; most manufactured unicycles come with assembly instructions). However, assembly was easy. A hex key was provided for the bearing block bolts. These were removed, the blocks fitted over the bearings, and then the bolts were fastened in place. The saddle post was then slipped inside the frame and fastened in place by tightening the bolt on the clamp. The saddle was then slipped over the other end of the saddle post and the bolt tightened.

The pedals were marked "R" and "L" for right and left. It is important to make sure that the pedal is threaded to match the crank arm. This threading arrangement is used so that under

ordinary riding conditions of forward pedaling the pedals will tend to tighten rather than loosen the threaded attachments to the crank arms.

The final task was to inflate the tire. When this was done the tire did not seat properly, but after it was deflated and broken free of the rim all the way around and inflated again, it did seat properly. The saddle height and angle were then adjusted for the rider (see Chapter 4). The saddle was angled upward slightly to the front. A check was then made to see that all bolts were firmly secured. The unicycle was then ready to ride. Figure 3-5 shows the assembled unicycle.

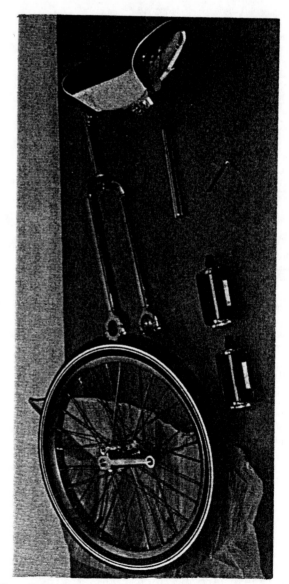

Fig. 3-7. Components of Sturdee unicycle as received in shipping carton.

Assembly of the Schwinn standard unicycle differs somewhat in that the fork is in two pieces. The saddle post with a series of adjustment holes fits between the two fork sections and a bolt is used to hold the assembly together.

Giraffe unicycles have a chain that is fitted between the crank and wheel sprockets. The wheel should be adjusted so that the sprockets are in line, the chain is tight, and the hub and crank axles are parallel to each other. The shorter the distance between the sprockets, the more critical this alignment becomes. Riding a giraffe unicycle without the chain properly aligned and adjusted could result in the chain breaking.

Chain-driven giraffe unicycles that have threaded on sprockets with safety nuts at the wheel hubs often slip. To help eliminate this problem, ride the unicycle with the chain and sprockets on the left side, opposite of that on a bicycle. If the unicycle has a front and a back, you will also need to reverse the saddle. In this manner, the greatest force on the hub sprocket, which usually comes from backward pedal pressure when mounting, will tighten the threaded sprocket rather than loosen it. Giraffe unicycles with keyed sprockets, such as the Penguin, do not have this problem and can be ridden with the sprockets and chains on the right sides like bicycles.

CUSTOM MADE AND BUILDING YOUR OWN

You can also have standard and giraffe unicycles similar to the manufactured models custom made, or you can build your own. If you want a unicycle or component of a type or size not manufactured, such as handlebar units, multi-wheel and zig-zag giraffe unicycles, kangaroo and big-wheel standard unicycles, and small-wheel giraffe cycles, you can have these custom made for you, or you can build your own or, in some cases, modify a manufactured unicycle to your requirements.

Sources for custom-built unicycles are given in the Appendix.

Plans and instructions for building a variety of standard unicycles (including small wheel, midget, big wheel, ultimate wheel, handlebar, off-centered wheel, and kangaroo models), handlebar units, giraffe unicycles (including small wheel, short, tall, multi-wheel and zigzag models), and artistic bicycles, are in my book **How To Build Unicycles and Artistic Bicycles** (Solipaz Publishing Company, P.O. Box 623, Stockton, CA 95201).

CARE AND REPAIR

Properly taken care of, most well-constructed unicycles will give long service with a minimum of maintenance. Especially important is to avoid dropping the unicycles. In fact, one of the first skills that should be learned is how to catch the unicycle when dismonting. If the unicycle is dropped, the pedal arms and saddle are particularly vulnerable to damage. It is sometimes helpful to cover the saddle of a unicycle with a heavy carpet material if the cycle is to be used for learning. Some unicycles such as the Miyata feature metal "bird cage" protectors that help protect the saddle if the unicycle is dropped. However, even if these devices are used, every effort should be made not to drop the unicycle.

Unicycles should be stored inside out of extreme weather conditions. This also helps to prevent the unicycles from being stolen.

Many manufactured standard unicycles have sealed bearings, so no additional lubrication is required. This type of bearings is lubricated and sealed at the factory. The manufacturer's instructions should tell you if any additional lubrication is required on the unicycle. Giraffe unicycles frequently require lubrication at both the crank axle bearings and the hub axle bearings. The chains should also be kept clean and oiled. This maintenance is essentially the same as for bicycles.

The unicycle should be kept clean and dry. Use a cloth to wipe off dirt and moisture. Wax should be applied at regular intervals to painted and chrome-plated surfaces.

Keep all bolts properly tightened. From time to time it may be necessary to align the wheel and adjust the spokes. You can have this work done at a bicycle shop if you do not know how to do it yourself.

Keep the tire inflated to the proper pressure. The range of pressures are generally given on the side of the tire. For a unicycle, the upper limit is generally used. Since rubber has a slight porosity, innertubes slowly lose air. A gauge can be used until the owner becomes familiar with the feel and look of the correct pressure in the tire. If the air hose at a gas station is used, care should be taken so as not to over-inflate the tire, which can cause a blow out. An under-inflated tire is sometimes used for learning to ride (see Chapter 4).

Many unicycle owners learn how to change tires and tubes and patch punctured tubes. After rmoving the wheel assembly from the unicycle, the same procedure as for removing and replacing a bicycle tire is used.

Tire life can be prolonged by rotating the tire position around the rim from time to time so that twisting and turning will be done on different areas of the tire. To rotate tire, deflate, rotate the tire around the rim to a new position, and reinflate tube. Always make certain that the valve stem is straight.

Spare parts are sometimes available from bicycle shops where the particular brand of unicycle is sold. Parts can also be ordered from manufacturers. Many bicycle shops are equipped to repair unicycles.

Some manufactured unicycles are sold with a guarantee for replacement of defective parts. Failure due to accident, abuse, neglect, normal wear, or improper assembly is generally not covered. In some cases, the buyer is entitled to take the unicycle in for a free checkup a certain number of days after purchase. This generally includes free replacement of any parts found to be defective and adjustment of all functional parts and assemblies.

CLOTHING AND PROTECTIVE DEVICES

Comfortable play and recreational clothing is ideal for unicycling. Boys and men often find it more comfortable to wear boxer shorts rather than briefs or an athletic supporter. For shows, parade riding, and competition, you may want special costumes, as detailed in later chapters.

Shoes should be worn. At first, shoes with heels are helpful. Later, most any athletic shoe with a flexible sole will be okay. Riding barefooted is not a good idea, as you may stub your toes or catch them in the spokes.

Some riders have the problem of hitting their ankles on the crank arms when riding. One solution is to turn the ankles slightly outward. Various types of ankle protectors can also be used. One type that works well can be cut from a motorcycle innertube (Fig. 3-8). This design fits snugly and stays in place. Various types of padding, such as foam rubber, can be placed under the rubber.

For some riders banging the ankles will not be a problem, in which case the protectors will not be needed.

Some beginners have attempted to pad other parts of the body, such as the knees and gluteus maximus, in an attempt to avoid injury from a fall. However, if

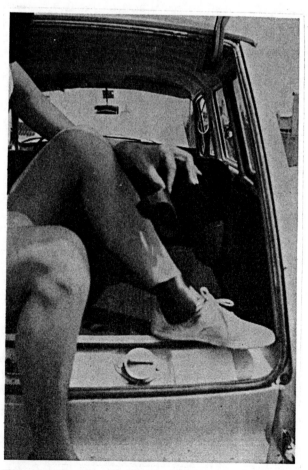

Fig. 3-8. Ankle protectors cut from motorcycle innertube.

the proper technique for learning is followed, as detailed in the next chapter, this padding will not be needed, although some unicycling teachers believe that knee pads are a good idea. Most other padding just gets in the way. An important exception to this is for competitive racing, where knee pads and other safety equipment are highly recommended (see Chapter 11).

PROPS AND RELATED EQUIPMENT

A variety of props and related equipment, such as stop-blocks, jump ropes, juggling balls, rings, and clubs, poles, spinning plates, hula-hoops, and plastic markers are detailed in later chapters. Sources for manufactured equipment are included in the Appendix.

TRANSPORTING UNICYCLES

Transporting unicycles in motor vehicles presents many problems similar to transporting bicycles. Some unicycles will fit in the trunks or back seats of some cars. Even larger unicycles will often fit inside vans.

Unicycles can also be carried outside motor vehicles on racks. Bicycle racks are frequently used for this purpose. They can be modified so that the particular unicycles can be securely attached.

Another possibility is to tow a trailer containing the unicycles. This method is ideal when a large number of unicycles must be transported, such as for parade riding groups.

Chapter 4

LEARNING BASIC TECHNIQUES ON A STANDARD UNICYCLE

I have seen many methods used for learning to ride unicycles. While most result in learning to ride, some work much better than others. Many people have learned to ride by trial and error, without any instruction. This method (or lack of method) often works, but it has a number of drawbacks, especially that it often isn't the safest way to learn, it can lead to bad riding habits that can be difficult to correct later, it can be damaging to unicycles, and it can take an unnecessarily long time.

The method detailed below in this chapter has proven to be efficient and result in good riding techniques.

HOW LONG WILL IT TAKE?

This, of course, depends on many things. It depends, for example, on the physical, mental, and emotional characteristics of the person attempting to learn. It depends also on the method used for learning.

I know of a few people who have learned to ride a unicycle to the point where they could solo with reasonable control in an hour or less. However, this is the exception and not the rule. A few days of practicing several hours a day is more typical. Some people have taken a month or even more. Certainly there are people who could never learn to ride a unicycle. But it has been my experience that nearly everyone in reasonable physical shape (and some who aren't) who has a strong desire to learn and who sticks with it can learn.

I know of one school that had riding a unicycle as a requirement for passing physical education. Every student (fourth to eighth grades, both boys and girls)

learned to ride. The time that it took them to learn, however, varied widely. Some took to it quickly, others took a long time. But every student there did learn.

As a general rule, young people seem to learn most readily, but even at relatively old ages it isn't impossible. As a case in point, a 63-year-old-philosopher decided that he could learn to ride a unicycle. Even though the salesman at the bicycle shop tried to talk him ot of it, the philosopher bought the unicycle and carried it home with him. It took him three months to get the knack of it, but he did learn. And this in spite of the fact that he did not know how to ride a bicycle. I know of a 65 year old man who learned to ride, and perhaps the "record" is even older than this.

However, the fact that others have learned may not offer much encouragement to a beginner holding a unicycle for the first time. The unicycle may look impossible at this point. It won't even stand up by itself. Of course, neither will a bicycle, but at least the bicycle only falls sideways. The unicycle takes its pick of directions.

Most people want to learn as fast as possible, but it's also important to consider safety and the development of good riding techniques. This will save time in the long run.

ADJUSTING THE UNICYCLE

For most people, I have found that a standard unicycle with a 20-inch wheel works best. The unicycle should be of the "professional" type (see Chapter 3). Small children sometimes learn best with a unicycle with a 16-inch wheel. Most teenagers and adults can also learn on a unicycle with a 24-inch or 26-inch wheel, but this can make learning a little more difficult.

Before actually starting, it's important to have the unicycle properly adjusted. The saddle height is correct when, mounted on the unicycle, your leg is almost extended to reach the pedal in the down position (lowest point in relation to the ground). This should be possible, however, without having to lean the body to that side in order to keep the ball of the foot flat on the pedal. The adjustment on most unicycles is made by loosening the saddle-post clamp, sliding the post up or down in the fork stem until the saddle is the desired height, and then retightening the clamp. On some unicycles, such as the Schwinn, the saddle-adjustment bolt passes through the unicycle frame and the saddle post. To adjust to a new height, remove the bolt and move the saddle post up or down in the frame to desired height. Then insert securing bolt. It may be necessary to move the post slightly to allow the bolt to pass through one of the adjustment holes.

Most manufactured unicycles now come with special unicycle saddles. Some of these saddles are shaped the same on both ends, making the front or back arbitrary. However, for proper riding, the end of the saddle that is used as the front should be angled slightly upward. If the unicycle saddle is shaped with a front and a back, it should be angled slightly upward toward the front for easiest riding. Most manufactured unicycle saddles allow for adjustment of the angle, but a few don't. Fortunately, these are usually mounted at suitable angles. If the saddle is not angled upward toward the front, it will tend to slip out from under the rider and steering and control will be difficult. The amount of upward angle is a matter of personal preference, but many riders find that having the front of the saddle from one to about three inches higher than the back to be about right.

To adjust the saddle angle on most unicycle saddles, loosen the clamp, tilt the saddle to the desired angle, and then retighten the clamp.

Some beginners start with a slightly under-inflated tire, which helps prevent twisting about a vertical axis. After getting the "feel" of the unicycle, the tire should be inflated to the correct pressure.

TRAINING AIDS

I have seen many different training aids used, including training poles, supporting ring that slides along an overhead cable, and spotting belts. I have tried these and other similar devices in my own teaching, but have concluded that they usually retard rather than aid learning at the beginning level, although they may be useful for learning more advanced skills (see Chapter 5).

Bob Gannon, Popular Science go-anywhere, do-anything reporter, found this to be true when he took up the challenge of the unicycle. He first tried a number of devices for learning. One of these was a rope suspended from the ceiling and tied to his belt at a height so he could not fall onto the floor, or so he thought. The result, part of the ceiling torn away and a bad spill. In the end he did learn, but only after he got advice from a pro and used essentially the methods described below in this chapter.

There are some learning aids that I have found to be helpful, however. First, you will need a 4 x 4 inch block of wood a couple of feet long to use as a stop-block or a curb from about four to six inches high located adjacent to a suitable riding surface that will serve the same purpose. Second, you will need two partners to assist you in learning. It is not necessary that they know how to ride unicycles.

A PLACE TO LEARN

Learn on a hard smooth surface, such as asphalt, concrete, or a wooden floor. You will need a large open space. In most cases, except perhaps in a recreation room, it's best not to try to learn to ride a unicycle inside a house, at least not if the floor, furniture, etc., are valued.

After learning to ride, it will no longer be necessary to be so selective as to where the unicycle is ridden. Experienced riders, for example, can ride on grass, but this is extremely difficult for a beginner and generally only serves to make learning more difficult.

Learn on the level or slightly downhill, but avoid an uphill grade. Again, an experienced rider can unicycle on varied terrain, but it is best to be selective for learning.

SAFETY AND PROTECTION OF UNICYCLE

In order to make learning to ride a unicycle a safe and enjoyable experience, it should be done one step at a time. Master each step before going on to the next one. It is extremely important to learn the correct techniques right from the start, including dismounting. Remember, dismounting is not falling. It's a controlled method for getting off a unicycle.

Learn to ride in an area that is free of automobile traffic and other hazards.

Don't forget about the "safety" of the unicycle. Try not to drop it, as this can damage and even ruin it. Learn the correct techniques for catching the unicycle by the saddle when dismonting, as detailed below in this chapter, right from the start.

LEARNING TO RIDE

While there are all degrees of being able to ride a unicycle, and it's possible to continue to learn new skills and techniques throughout a lifetime, we often say that a person knows how to ride a unicycle when he or she can ride solo with some degree of control and confidence.

In order to ride, a person must first mount the unicycle. The most important riding skill to master is the forward/backward balance. Once this is learned, side-to-side balance and making turns is usually fairly easy. Unicycling is possible basically because the rider has control of the wheel and thus the relationship between the wheel and unicycle frame. When the wheel gets behind the rider, the pedal action is increased so that the wheel catches up and is moved back under the rider. In turn, if the wheel gets ahead of the unicycle frame, the rider slows the pedal action so that the unicycle frame and rider catch up. Smooth forward riding is done by being slightly off balance forward

and pedaling forward so that the wheel moves forward at the same speed as the unicycle saddle.

One method of riding is to always be in either exact balance or off balance forward, but never off balance backwards. However, this method limits the rider to forward riding and stopping and does not allow regaining balance if balance is lost backwards or permit riding backwards.

In order to overcome these limitations, the rider needs not only to be able to pedal forward at varying speeds and to stop the pedal action, but also to be able to reverse the pedal direction and be able to pedal backwards at varying speeds. These actions greatly increase the control that the rider has in moving the unicycle wheel, and for advanced riding they are essential. It has been my experience that these techniques are best learned right from the start, before a forward-only-pedaling pattern has been learned.

In the above discussion, I have considered the unicycle frame and the rider to be a unit, but this is only true if the rider maintains good posture, with the body upright and the head and shoulders in line with the unicycle frame (Fig. 4-1). Balance is usually best controlled by pedal action rather than movement of the upper body or arms. This means that the rider is a fixed extension of the unicycle frame. This is the old principle of being easier to balance a broomstick than a flexible hose on your hand.

Fig. 4-1. Good riding posture with the body upright and the head and shoulders in line with the unicycle frame.

Learning with Two Helpers

To get started, you will need two assistants, a block of wood or curb for use as a stop-block, and a suitable riding surface. Place the unicycle wheel against the stop-block or curb (Fig. 4-2). Stand behind the unicycle on the curb or behind the block of wood and tilt the unicycle back toward you. Have one pedal back toward you so that placing weight on it will force the wheel against the curb or block. With the helpers at your sides, straddle over the unicycle saddle. Hold hands with the helpers and mount the unicycle by placing foot on the pedal that is back toward you. This will be the right foot if the pedal that is back is on the right side and the left foot if the back pedal is on the left side. One position or the other will probably feel most natural, and you can deliberately place the pedals in position for this.

Step the other foot from the ground to the free pedal and allow the saddle (with your weight on it) to come up to a position over the wheel. Keep most of your weight on the pedal that is toward the curb or block to prevent the wheel from rolling forward out from under you.

When mounted on the unicycle (Fig. 4-3), have the helpers stand directly to your sides. The helpers should support you with their palms upward and hold your hands out so that your arms are extended to your sides. The helpers should provide side-to-side support and keep you from twisting and turning. This will allow you to concentrate on learning the forward/backward balance, which is the key to learning to ride a unicycle.

Begin by leaning the saddle slightly forward and making a half-pedal revolution forward (Fig. 4-4). Strive to keep the saddle moving forward at the same rate as the wheel. A common mistake is to let the saddle lag behind. Take only a half pedal revolution until the crank arms are in the next horizontal position. Freeze the pedals in this position and stand up on the pedals with legs locked straight and unicycle saddle squeezed between your legs. This will make it easier for the partners to help you regain balance. The helpers should remain directly to your sides as you move along so that they can keep you from twisting and falling to the side.

After the first half-pedal revolution, regain balance and then make a second half-pedal revolution. Freeze with the pedals in the horizontal position, standing up on the pedals with the legs locked straight and the unicycle saddle squeezed between your legs.

Continue riding forward with this half-pedal then freeze pattern. Avoid trying to regain balance by rocking the pedals back and forth or upper body

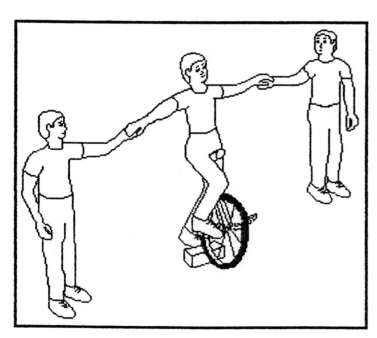

Fig. 4-2. Position for mounting unicycle with stop-block or curb and two helpers.

Fig. 4-3. Rider mounted on unicycle with helpers standing directly to sides.

Fig. 4-4. Riding half-pedal revolution forward with helpers.

motion, as this tends to confuse the helpers.

The freezing action should be done in the with the crank arms in a horizontal position. This makes it easy to start the next pedal action. Don't get stuck with one pedal down and one pedal up.

For dismounting (Fig. 4-5), come to a complete stop with one pedal in the down position. Release one hand from a helper and grasp the forward end of the saddle. Step the foot from the upper-positioned pedal to the ground behind the unicycle. As you dismount off behind the unicycle, hold the unicycle by the front of the saddle so that the unicycle does not fall.

Dismounting behind the unicycle is generally considered to be the most satisfactory method, although many beginners think coming off forward is

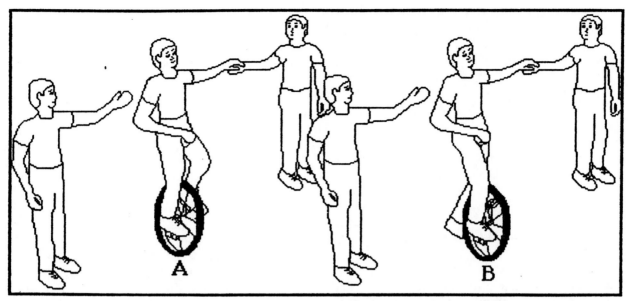

Fig. 4-5. Dismounting to rear: (A) Stop with one pedal in down position, release one hand from helper, and grasp saddle at front; (B) Step foot from upper-positioned pedal to ground behind the unicycle.

correct. I suggest that you learn to dismount toward the rear of the unicycle first. But also try coming off forward (Fig. 4-6) so that you know you can do it.

To dismount forward, come to a complete stop with one pedal in the down position. Release one hand from a helper and grasp the back end of the saddle. Step from the upper-positioned pedal to the ground in front of the unicycle. As you dismount forward, hold the unicycle up by the back of the saddle so that it does not fall to the ground.

Continue to practice mounting and riding forward with the help of two partners in the half-pedal and then freeze the pedal action pattern. Try to maintain good riding posture.

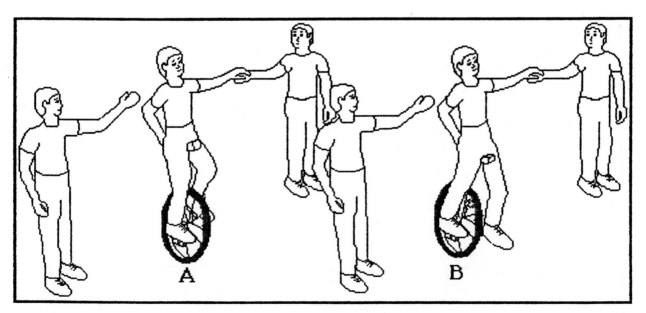

Fig. 4-6. Dismounting forward: (A) Come to stop with one pedal in down position, release one hand from helper, and grasp back end of saddle; (B) Step foot from upper-positioned pedal forward to ground.

Gradually decrease the length of time in the freeze positions. The helpers should remain at your sides. Use less and less hand pressure with the helpers. Their main function at this point should be to prevent you from twisting and falling to the sides so that you can concentrate on learning the forward/backward balance pattern.

It is important have the hub of the unicycle move forward at the same speed as the saddle. Maintain good posture so that your upper body is a fixed part of the unicycle. Learn to maintain forward/backward balance by pedal action rather than upper-body movement.

I feel that it is important even at this beginning stage to be able to make balance corrections not only by pedaling forward, but also by pedaling backwards. If you start to lose balance backwards when you are not moving, the correct action is to pedal in a reverse direction. If you have spent years pedaling a bicycle in the forward direction only, it will take some practice to get used to pedaling backwards.

Practice riding half-pedal revolutions backwards with two helpers, freezing the pedals in the horizontal positions as was done previously with forward pedaling (Fig. 4-7). Practice until you feel comfortable with the backward pedal action.

Then go back to forward riding, but from time to time work in some practice with backward pedaling. In this way, you will be learning both pedaling directions instead of forward only.

Continue practice with two helpers until you can ride forward with only light hand pressure on the two helpers. Also, make certain that you are maintaining good posture and making the balance corrections by pedal actions.

It may take less than an hour or a month or more of daily practice to reach this stage. Before going on to the next stage, you should also be able to mount and dismount backwards and forwards with only light hand pressure with the helpers.

Riding with One Helper

The next step is to repeat the above practice exercises, except this time with only one helper (Fig. 4-8). Continue to use the stop-block or curb for mounting, as was done previously (Fig. 4-9). For riding forward, the helper should stand directly to your side. This can be to your right or left, whichever feels the most

Fig. 4-7. Riding half-pedal revolution backwards with helpers.

comfortable to you.

Begin by mounting the unicycle with the aid of the stop-block (Fig. 4-9). Then ride forward, as was done previously. Maintain good riding posture and make forward/backward corrections by pedal action. When you are ready to dismount, dismount behind the unicycle, as detailed previously (Fig. 4-10). The helper should remain directly to your side. Use hand pressure only with the helper's palm

Fig. 4-9. Mounting with stop-block and one helper.

Fig. 4-8. Riding half-pedal revolution forward with one helper.

turned upward. Gradually decrease the hand pressure with the helper until you can solo. This may take less than an hour or a week or more of daily practice sessions.

Before going on to the next stage, you should be able to mount the unicycle with the aid of the curb or stop-block solo (without assistance from partner), ride with good posture and control for thirty feet or more, and then dismont to the rear of the unicycle with good control, catching the unicycle by the front of the saddle.

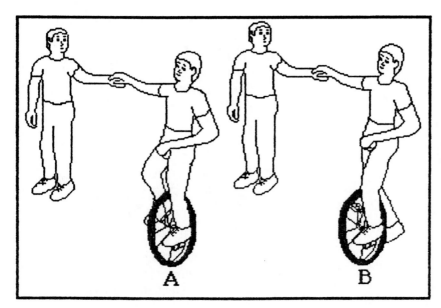

Fig. 4-10. Dismounting to rear with one helper: (A) Come to stop with one pedal in down position and grasp back end of saddle; (B) Step foot from upper-positioned pedal forward to ground.

From One Helper to Solo

The progression from using the one helper to riding solo should be gradual. After making half-pedal revolutions with freezing actions with the pedals in horizontal positions, try making full-pedal revolutions before freezing the action. Work up to the point where a number of pedal revolutions can be made continuously. When this can be done with only light hand pressure with the helper, try riding forward with brief hand releases with the helper (Fig. 4-11). Have helper keep hand in position for regrasping. Gradually work up to longer time periods of riding solo until you can ride with control for thirty feet or more (Fig. 4-12).

Use a similar procedure for learning to mount solo with a curb or stop-block (Fig. 4-13) and dismount solo to the rear of the unicycle (Fig. 4-14). The basic idea

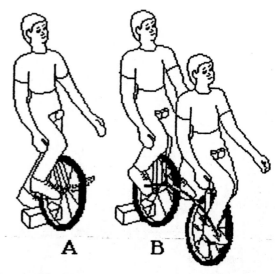

Fig. 4-13. Mounting solo with stop-block: (A) Position unicycle against stop-block with one pedal back; (B) Mount unicycle and ride forward.

Fig. 4-11. Riding forward with brief hand release from helper.

Fig. 4-12. Riding forward solo.

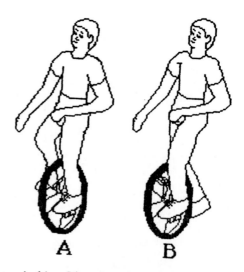

Fig. 4-14. Dismounting solo to rear: (A) Come to stop with one pedal down and grasp saddle; (B) Dismount to rear.

is to use the helper less and less until you can do the skills alone.

Also practice dismounting forward with one helper (Fig. 4-15), gradually using helper less and less until you can do it alone (Fig. 4-16).

You should also spend some time practicing backward riding with freezing actions after each half-pedal revolution with assistance from helper (Fig. 4-17).

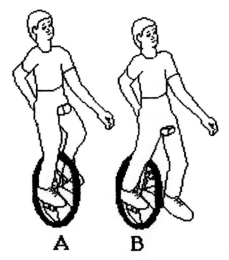

Fig. 4-16. Dismounting forward solo: (A) Come to stop and grasp back of saddle; (B) Dismount forward.

Fig. 4-15. Dismounting forward with one helper.

Fig. 4-17. Riding half-pedal revolution backwards with one helper.

RIDING LONGER DISTANCES FORWARD

Once you can solo, as detailed above, you will want to go on the further riding challenges. The next step is to ride for longer distances. If you have mastered basic riding as detailed above, this should not be difficult. Mount the unicycle using a curb or stop-block. Ride forward with a marker placed further than your previous record. This might be forty feet from the starting point. Ride with control to the marker, then dismount off behind the unicycle. Move the marker about ten feet further. Go back to the curb or stop-block and try for the new distance. Continue until you can ride for 100 feet or more. Try to maintain a moderate pace with good control. Do not try to "race" at this point. At first, the unicycle will probably tend to wobble with the pedal action, but with practice this can be largely eliminated.

By this time, you may be wondering where your arms should be when you are unicycling. When you were riding with two helpers, you had a place to put your hands. With one helper, you could put the free hand out like the one that went to the helper, or you could put it down at your side or somewhere inbetween. Riding solo, you have a choice of positions. To date, no arm positions have emerged as being "the correct" way to ride a unicycle, even for artistic competition. You may want to extend your arms outward like a tightwire walker, or place them casually to your sides, something like you do with natural walking. Some advanced riders have their arms at their sides, but slightly forward and without swinging them as they pedal.

TURNING

After learning to ride in a straight line (more or less), the next step is to make turns. Generally by this time some turning has already been done. The object now is to learn to turn when and where desired with good control.

Turning (Fig. 4-18) is basically leaning slightly in the direction you wish to turn and then twisting the unicycle slightly in that direction and pedaling forward so that the wheel of the unicycle is brought back under the center of gravity again. As a general rule, you should try to turn mainly by leaning, keeping action-reaction arm and upper-body movement to a minimum.

First, mount the unicycle with aid of curb or stop-block, as was done previously, and ride forward. Then make a 45 degree turn over a distance of several feet. Then repeat with a 45 degree turn over a distance of several feet in the opposite direaction.

Next, try 90 degree turns over a distance of several feet. Practice until you can make these turns in both directions with control.

Next, try half turns so that you reverse the direction of travel. The radius can be large at first, but gradually work down to a tighter turn. Then repeat with the turn in the opposite direction.

Always strive for complete control. Try to relax. Do not force the turns. Let a rhythmical lean do the work.

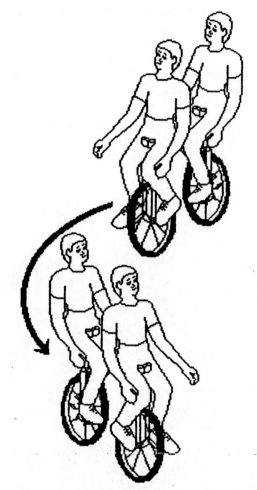

Fig. 4-18. Basic turning.

RIDING WITH A PARTNER

Once you have mastered basic riding, you are ready to try riding with a partner who has also mastered basic riding. It's even easier if your partner is a more advanced rider. In fact, an advanced rider can often substitute for a helper on foot for learning basic riding as detailed above in this chapter.

You can ride together with locked arms (Fig. 4-19) and holding hands (Fig. 4-20) with both riders facing the same direction. You will probably want to learn both ways.

Both riders can mount separately and then ride side-by-side before joining arms or hands. Once arms or hands are joined, you can ride together in a straight line and make turns. Try to maintain good riding posture. Riding with a partner is usually easy once basic riding has been mastered, as the riders serve to help each other maintain balance.

Fig. 4-19. Riding together with locked arms.

Fig. 4-20. Riding holding hands.

MOUNTING

After you are able to mount alone with the aid of a stop-block or curb, the next step is to learn to mount in the open. Begin with two helpers. Position the unicycle with one pedal back (Fig. 4-21).

Straddle over the saddle and place foot on pedal that is back. Hold hands with the helpers, who should be directly to your sides. Apply downward pressure on the pedal and step the other foot upward to the forward pedal, using the backward motion of the unicycle wheel to draw the unicycle saddle up over the hub. Continue the backward pedal action until the pedal that was down and back is forward and the crank arms are in a horizontal position. Freeze the pedals in this position so that the helpers can easily get you in balance. Then ride forward.

An alternate method of pedal action for mounting is to begin as previously, except when you step the last foot from the ground to the upper pedal, catch the pedal at the top of the cycle and immediately begin forward pedal action. However, I suggest that you learn with the continued backward pedal action first. Then with continued practice, you can use only the amount of backward pedal action required to get the unicycle in the desired balance.

Continue practice until you can gain control over the unicycle wheel after mounting. Gradually use less and less hand

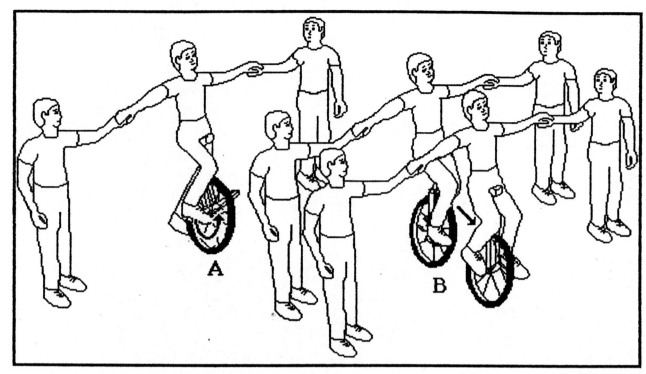

Fig. 4-21. Mounting in open with two helpers: (A) Position for mounting; (B) Backward pedal action is used to bring rider in balance on unicycle before riding forward.

pressure with the helpers. If when mounting you find that you are still off balance backwards when you reach the first horizontal pedal position, make an additional half pedal turn backwards to bring the unicycle into forward balance before riding forward. If you find that you are off balance forward when you

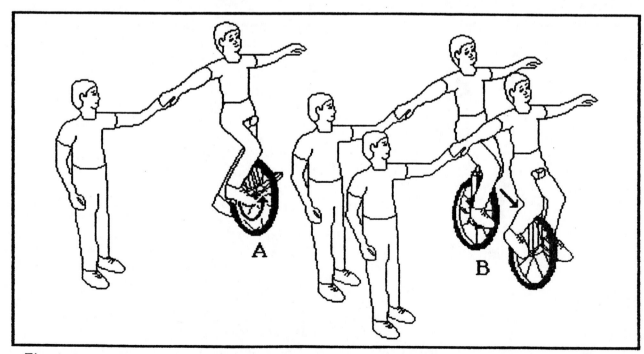

Fig. 4-22. Mounting in open with one helper: (A) Position for mounting; (B) Pedal backwards to first horizontal pedal position before riding forward.

reach the horizontal pedal position, start riding forward.

After you can mount with only light hand pressure from the two helpers, repeat the same practice exercises with one helper (Fig. 4-22).

Continue practice, gradually using the helper less and less, until you can mount solo (Fig. 4-23).

LEARNING WITH OPPOSITE-FOOT PATTERNS

In the above learning progression, it was suggested that you "place your best foot forward" for mounting and dismounting. This will serve well for most general and recreational riding. However, if you intend to go on to artistic riding, it is important to be able to do both mounting, dismounting, and half pedal actions with the feet in the reversed positions. For example, if you had the right pedal back and your right foot on the pedal for mounting previously, you will need to learn mounting with the left pedal back and your left foot on the pedal. The same thing applies to making a half pedal turn backwards after mounting and to dismounting both backwards and forward from the unicycle.

To learn these, go back and repeat the learning steps with the stop-block or curb and helpers with the new foot patterns. Continue practice until you can do the skills solo.

A LOOK AHEAD

With the above skills, you will be able to enjoy general and recreational unicycle riding. Some riders are satisfied to stop here at this basic level, but many desire to go on to more advanced riding skills, as detailed in later chapters. It is important to thoroughly master the skills detailed in this chapter before going on to more advanced riding.

Fig. 4-23. Mounting in open solo: (A) Position for mounting; (B) Back pedal; (C) Half-cycle forward; (D) Continue riding forward.

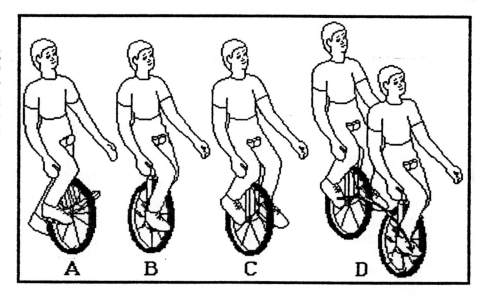

Chapter 5

TRAINING, TEACHING, AND COACHING TECHNIQUES

Many unicyclists do basic riding on standard unicycles, as detailed in Chapter 4, without giving much thought to things like warmup exercises, training exercises off unicycles, and organizing practice sessions to make the most of the practice time. However, if you desire to go beyond the basic level, these things become more important. For competition, especially as the standards and caliber of performance increase, training is an important consideration for anyone who aspires to become a champion.

Some people desire to teach or coach others in the art and sport of unicycling rather than learn to ride themselves or in addition to learning to ride themselves. The need for skilled teachers and coaches of unicycling has increased tremendously with the spread of unicycling as a popular recreational activity and competitive sport in recent years.

TRAINING TECHNIQUES

For the most part, the training techniques used for learning to unicycle, especially beyond the basic level, are still quite primitive in comparison to a sport like gymnastics. It is still possible, although becoming more difficult, to do quite well in national artistic unicycling competition with relatively little training or even much thought about serious training. A similar effort in gymnastics would probably not get anyone beyond the local level.

If we compare unicycle racing competition with track and field competition, the differences are probably even more dramatic. Very few good athletes have even tried unicycling, much less spent much time training for this

activity. However, there are many signs that all this is rapidly changing.

Workouts

Practice sessions for activities like unicycling are often called "workouts." Basically, this is the time that is used to try to improve your unicycling, whatever your ultimate goals may be, such as merely to learn to ride a little better, to ride in parades, to perform for others, or to enter competition.

As a general rule, the higher your aspirations, the more time that you will need to devote to practicing. However, practice time alone will not make you a champion performer or even improve your riding skill. Equally important is the quality of the workouts or how you use the practice time.

No matter how much natural ability one may have, unicycling still requires practice for improving ones skill level. To be effective, this must be above a certain minimum level, although this is difficult to determine precisely, and is probably different for each individual. There is probably a maximum effective amount of practice too. We have all heard of "burntout" athletes. However, in the case of artistic unicycling, it is probably possible for some top level performers to benefit from eight hours or more of daily practice, as is the case in figure skating. Not all of this time would be spent on the unicycle, just as the figure skater does not spend all of the practice time on ice. The amount of training time required for speed and endurance racing would probably be much less than for artistic riding.

As a general rule, each workout or

practice session should begin with a warmup. The main purpose of the warmup is to get the body ready for unicycling, to go from a resting state to the point where the body and mind are prepared for vigorous exercise; namely, to loosen up and get the blood flowing. After a warmup, the body should be ready to perform at a higher level and with less chance of injury.

In a class or group situation, the warmup may be led by an instructor, but even if you workout on your own, you should still warmup.

I suggest that you begin with exercises not using the unicycles. You might, for example, begin with rhythmical exercise. Start by walking, then easy jogging. Use arm swinging exercises. Gradually increase the intensity of the exercises. Then do stretching exercises. These serve not only as a warmup, but to some extent to increase flexibility. These exercises may also serve to help prevent muscle pulls and other related injuries during the body of the workout.

The actual workout will depend on the level of ability of the unicyclist and the purpose for unicycling. Generally, for artistic unicycling it begins with easy skills on unicycles and progresses to the more difficult. Most unicyclists will want to further perfect stunts and routines that have been learned previously, and work on new stunts and routines. For speed or endurance racing, you will probably want to not only work on your riding skills and techniques, but also practice for speed and/or endurance.

It is generally considered best to taper down gradually after a vigorous workout, rather than to stop abruptly. It is a sort of warmup in reverse, with vigorous exercise gradually tapering down into easy movements. This is usually followed by a shower.

Special Training Exercises

You may also want to do special training exercises off the unicycles, either during the regular workouts or during special sessions. The purpose of these training sessions might be for improving flexibility, strength, endurance, and other parameters required for unicycling. Working out with weight

training machines has many possibilities for for developing strength and muscular endurance for unicycling.

Training Equipment and Devices

I feel that unicycling is still in a primative stage as far as training equipment and devices are concerned. Possible training equipment and devices that have been used with varying degrees of success or lack of success include curbs and stop-blocks (see Chapter 4); a training pole carried by a person not on a unicycle for use by a person on a unicycle (Fig. 5-1); two training poles carried by the person on the unicycle and used for support against the ground (Fig. 5-2); training wheels similar to those used on children's bicycles except arranged so that the unicycle can fall only a certain distance in any direction without one or

Fig. 5-1. Training pole carried by person not on a unicycle.

Fig. 5-2. Two training poles used by person on unicycle.

Fig. 5-3. Using tennis-net cable as training support.

more wheels preventing it from falling any further; poles, railings, or walls used by the unicyclist for support (Fig. 5-3); platforms on wheels that are held onto by unicyclists as they ride or practice new skills; suspended ropes or cables with rings, pulleys, or other devices used to help support the unicyclist or prevent falling; and spotting belts and safety harnesses. Some of these devices may prove useful to you in their present stage of development, and others will probably be invented in the future. A number of training devices have been developed for artistic bicycling that are used by almost all top-level competitors, and similar devices may be used in the future for unicycling.

Stationary unicycles mounted on stands, stationary exercise "bicycles," weight training machines, and other similar devices may be used or developed to simulate certain aspects of unicycling. For example, I have made use of stationary exercise "bicycles" to improve leg strength for pedaling with one leg forward and backwards and for idling (pedaling with half or full pedal revolutions in alternate directions). If you use a bicycle ergometer that has a speedometer, you will need to disconnect it before pedaling backwards on many cycles to avoid breaking the speedometer cable.

TEACHING AND COACHING

The line between teaching and coaching is admittedly difficult to draw.

For our purposes here, teaching will be considered to be for classes; whereas coaching will be for developing unicyclists for demonstrations, parade riding, performing on stage, or competition.

There are a number of outstanding past and present unicycling teachers and coaches, and this is expected to be a growing endeavor in the future. Some of these people have been skilled unicyclists, but others have not been able to ride a unicycle themselves.

There are many different ideas about how teaching and coaching should be done, and successful teachers and coaches use such a variety of approaches that no meaningful rules can be given for successful teaching or coaching. For example some successful teachers and coaches seem to be foes of their students, tearing them down constantly. Other equally successful teachers and coaches treat their students on an open and friendly basis. While I prefer the latter, I realize that the former often works just as well in practice. Also, success may be in spite of the methods used, not because of them. And what is meant by success? Teaching a beginner to ride? Coaching a person to win competitions? There are many possible important factors. Perhaps many teaching and coaching methods used are inherent in the personalities of the teachers and coaches.

It is my belief, however, that it is helpful, if not essential, that a unicycling teacher or coach be well grounded in the mechanical aspects of unicycling, be something of a creative artist, and enjoy working with people.

Teaching unicycling classes requires organization. In most cases, it seems to work best if each person has a unicycle, but I have seen successful classes with ratios of one unicycle for each two or three students. With more students per each unicycle, there can be too much waiting between practice turns on the unicycles.

Many teachers make effective use of those who have already learned to ride in teaching beginners. This often involves dividing a class up into small groups.

Ideally, I suppose, coaching would be on a one-to-one basis (one unicyclist for one coach). This, however, is seldom practical. In most cases, a unicycle coach will be working with a number of unicyclists. This requires organization to make effective use of workout times.

Chapter 6

SOLO ARTISTIC RIDING ON STANDARD UNICYCLES WITHOUT PROPS

After learning basic riding, as detailed in Chapter 4, many riders want to go on to further challenges. This chapter details elementary, intermediate, and advanced artistic riding skills on standard unicycles without props. After learning the basic riding techniques detailed in Chapter 4 and some of the skills in this chapter, you can also begin the progression for learning solo riding on standard unicycles with props and partner and group riding on standard unicycles, as detailed in following chapters.

Solo artistic riding without props means that there is just you, a standard unicycle, and an open riding area. This, of course, is after you have learned a particular skill. In a number of cases helpers and/or training aids are used on initial attempts at new skills before they are done solo.

The basic skills detailed in Chapter 4 should be thoroughly mastered before beginning the progression detailed below.

Artistic riding is normally done on standard unicycles with 20-inch, 24-inch, or 26-inch wheels. Youngsters who do not have the necessary leg length for a 20-inch wheel can use a unicycle with an 18-inch or 16-inch wheel. Some of the stunts can also be done on standard unicycles with other wheel sizes (see Chapter 10).

ELEMENTARY SKILLS

Some of the skills covered here were introduced in Chapter 4. These should be further refined and perfected for artistic riding. While an attempt has been made to place the skills covered below in a progressive order of difficulty, this is somewhat arbitrary, and you may want to

modify this somewhat to fit your particular situation.

Regular Mounting

Regular mounting (Fig. 6-1) in the open is the method that is most often used for "getting aboard" a standard unicycle. The unicycle is positioned with one pedal down and back, as shown. The rider straddles over the saddle and places foot on rear positioned pedal. Downward pressure is applied to pedal with continuing backward pedal action as other foot is brought up to other pedal. The backward motion of the wheel is used to bring saddle and rider's body up over unicycle wheel. Backward pedal action is continued until pedal that was down and back at start is in a horizontal position forward. Foot that was stepped up to

Fig. 6-1. Regular mounting with backward pedal action: (A) Starting position; (B) Backward pedal action continues through vertical position; (C) Backward pedal action stops at horizontal position.

other pedal is then on pedal in horizontal position to rear. The rider is then in position to ride forward, ride backwards, or rock back and forth in one place (backward riding and rocking back and forth in one spot are covered later).

An alternate mounting technique is to continue the initial backward pedal action only until the starting-foot pedal is in approximately the down position (Fig. 6-2). The foot that is stepped from the ground contacts the other pedal near the top of the cycle and immediately starts a forward pedal action. This mounting technique is sometimes considered a separate skill from that shown in Figure 6-1. More advanced riders often do something inbetween, back pedaling as required to place the unicycle in the desired position for the particular riding that is to follow.

Regular mounting should be learned both with right pedal down and back with right foot on right pedal; and with left pedal down and back with left foot on left pedal. One side will probably feel easier than the other, but it is important for learning more advanced skills to be able to mount both ways. I suggest that the beginner concentrate on the side that feels most natural, but also spend some practice time trying the other side until it can be done too.

Methods for learning regular mounting

on a stardard unicycle are detailed in Chapter 4. At first, the mounting may be hit or miss, but with continued practice you will probably be able to do it consistently and with good control. Many advanced riders seldom if ever miss a regular mount on a standard unicycle.

The hands and arms can be in a variety of positions for regular mounting, including extended out to the sides at shoulder level, extended forward, or at the sides. The mounting is usually done with the hands free of the unicycle (Fig. 6-3), but it is also possible to mount holding onto the saddle with one (Fig. 6-4) or both hands. It is also possible to grasp the wheel forward of the fork when starting the mount, although this method is usually reserved for "big wheel" unicycles (see Chapter 10).

Fig. 6-3. Starting position for mounting standard unicycle with hands free of the unicycle and arms extended outward and slightly forward.

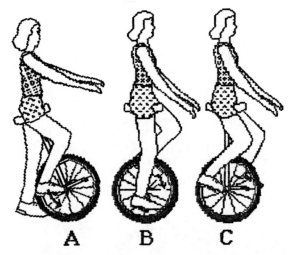

A   B   C

Fig. 6-2. Alternate method for mounting: (A) Starting position; (B) Backward pedal action continues only to vertical position; (C) Forward pedal action to horizontal pedal position.

Fig. 6-4. Mounting while holding onto front of saddle with one hand.

Riding Forward

Riding forward with control and good posture is fundamental to all artistic unicycle skills (Fig. 6-5). For artistic riding, the forward riding should be with a continuous pedal action, without pauses in the horizontal pedal positions. The riding should be in a straight line with a minimum of side-to-side wobble from the pedal action, which tends to cause action-reaction motions to the sides during the pedal revolutions.

Practice forward riding in a straight line by riding between two lines placed two feet apart on the riding surface. When this can be done, try the same thing with the lines placed one foot apart. Finally, try riding on a single line marked on the riding surface. Think of this line as a tightwire.

Riding forward can be done with a variety of hand and arm position, such as extended to the sides, extended forward, at the sides, or with the hands on the hips. No single position has yet emerged as being the best for artistic riding, so you may want to do some experimenting here.

Dismounting to Rear

The fundamental dismount for artistic riding is to the rear of the unicycle (Fig. 6-6). While mounted on the unicycle, the rider comes to a stop with one of the pedals in the down position. The front of the saddle is grasped by one hand and the foot on the upper-positioned pedal is stepped off backwards to the riding surface. The unicycle frame should be leaning slightly toward the rear when this action is started. When the first foot is on the ground, the other foot is moved off the down-positioned pedal and the unicycle held up by the front of the saddle so that it does not fall.

Fig. 6-5. Riding forward with control and good posture is fundamntal to all artistic unicycle skills.

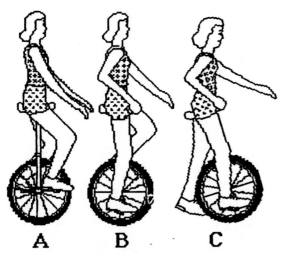

Fig. 6-6. Dismounting to rear: (A) Forward riding; (B) Pedal action stops in vertical position with unicycle slightly off balance backwards and saddle is grasped; (C) Foot is brought from upper pedal to ground.

The techniques for learning dismounting to the rear were detailed in Chapter 4. For artistic riding, the dismount should be refined so that it presents a smooth, controlled action. The dismounting should appear as a deliberate action rather than giving the appearance of the rider being saved from a fall. For artistic riding, it is important to be able to do dismounting to the rear on both sides. I recommend that you concentrate mainly on the side that feels most natural at first, but spend some time practicing the other side too.

Dismounting Forward

Dismounting forward (Fig. 6-7) is the method employed by many beginners, especially those who learn "on their own." Artistic riders generally prefer dismounting to the rear, as it gives a better impression. However, dismounting forward should also be mastered.

To dismount forward from riding, the unicyclist comes to a complete stop with one pedal in the down position. The back of the saddle is grasped in one hand. With the unicycle frame slightly off balance forward, the foot is stepped from the upper-positioned pedal forward to the riding surface. Then the other foot is brought from the lower-positioned pedal off forward to the riding surface so that

the unicyclist is standing with both feet on the ground. The unicycle is held up by the back of the saddle so that it does not fall to the ground.

This skill should be learned on both sides, even though one way will probably feel most natural.

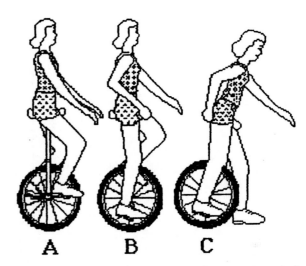

Fig. 6-7. Dismounting forward: (A) Forward riding; (B) Pedal action stops in vertical position with unicycle slightly off balance forward; (C) Foot is brought from upper pedal to ground.

Turning While Riding Forward

Turning while riding forward is an important riding skill (Fig. 6-8). The pedal action should be continuous and good riding posture should be maintained throughout the turn. For artistic riding, it is generally good technique to do the turning without noticeable twisting in one spot on the wheel. To accomplish this, the turning should be done primarily by leaning rather than by action-reaction twisting. Turning while riding forward should be mastered both to the right and to the left.

The radius of the turning can vary from large to quite small, the smallest being the point where the rider is still able to turn without twisting or spinning in one spot (these skills are detailed later in this chapter). Keep in mind, however, that there is a very fine line between turning without twisting and turning with twisting, and twisting is often combined with turning by leaning.

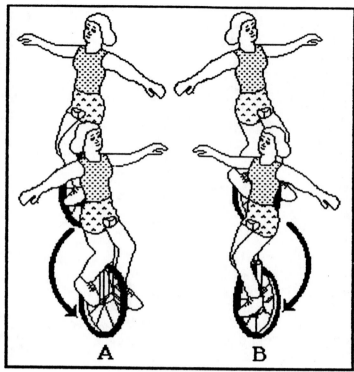

Fig. 6-8. Turning while riding forward: (A) Left turn; (B) right turn.

Methods for learning basic turning are covered in Chapter 4. The turning should now be refined for artistic riding so that it can be done smoothly and without action-reaction twisting. A good way to practice this is to try to make turns with the arms extended outward without using any twisting actions of the body.

Circles

Riding in a continuous circle (Fig. 6-9) is an extension of basic turning. Begin by making a large radius turn and continue in a circle pattern, following the same track each time around. The riding should be turning without noticeable twisting of the unicycle wheel in one spot.

Next, try riding in a continuous large radius circle in the opposite direction. Practice circles both directions, even though one direction will probably seem easier than the other. Many artistic riding skills require turning both directions.

Over a period of time, gradually shorten the radius of the circles until you can ride in the smallest possible circle without twisting actions. The pedal action should be smooth and continuous. Maintain good riding posture throughout. Learn both turning directions.

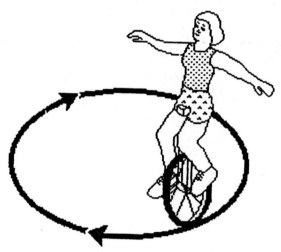

Fig. 6-9. Riding forward in circle pattern.

Half-Circle Pattern

Once continuous circles can be made in both turning directions, the half-circle pattern (Fig. 6-10) should be easy. From forward riding, a half circle is made in one direction, followed by another half circle in opposite direction. The pattern is continued.

The turns should be smooth and rhythmical. One turning direction should flow into the next. The unicycle should become an extension of the rider.

Fig. 6-10. Half-circle pattern.

Begin with large-radius half circles. Gradually work down to smaller radius half circles. A variation is to do half circles of diminishing size in sequence (Fig. 6-11).

Fig. 6-11. Pattern of half-circles of diminishing size.

Figure-Eight Pattern

The popular skating figure-eight (Fig. 6-12) comes next. Easiest is a fairly large figure-eight.

Then try smaller ones. To learn an even figure-eight pattern, mark a figure-eight on the riding surface. Then try to follow the lines. The turning should be done primarily by leaning. Use a rhythmical action.

Also, try riding the figure-eight pattern more than one time. A variation is to make each time through the pattern a smaller and smaller figure-eight. After the smallest possible leaning (without twisting) figure-eight, try increasing the size of the circles and work your way back out.

Serpentine Pattern

The serpentine pattern (Fig. 6-13) is another popular unicycle pattern. This pattern should not present any difficulty once figure-eights have been mastered.

Loops in Alternate Directions

Still another related pattern is loops in alternate directions (Fig. 6-14). Hundreds of other similar patterns are also possible. Let your imagination go to work here.

Riding Backwards

If you have continued to practice half-pedal revolutions backwards with the helpers, as detailed in Chapter 4, you should be well on your way to learning to ride backwards (Fig. 6-15) by this time. Begin with two helpers, as detailed in Chapter 4 for making half-pedal revolutions backwards. Try making a full pedal revolution before freezing the pedals in the horizontal position. After

Fig. 6-12. Figure-eight pattern.

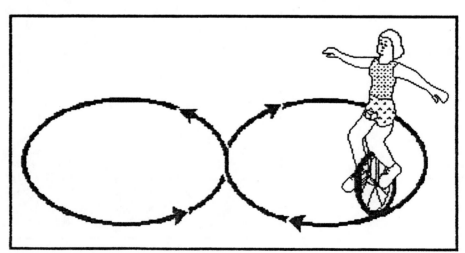

Fig. 6-13. Serpentine pattern.

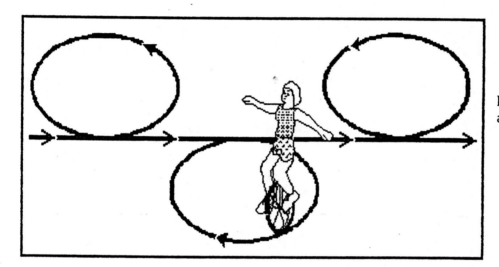

Fig. 6-14. Loops in alternate directions.

Fig. 6-15. Riding backwards.

you have learned full pedal revolutions, try one-and-a-half revolutions, then two. Continue practice until you can ride backwards with continuous pedaling action with the two helpers. Then gradually reduce the amount of hand pressure.

When you can ride backwards with good posture and control with light hand pressure with the two helpers, you are ready to try riding backwards with one helper. The helper should stand directly to your side but facing in the opposite direction to allow walking forward while you ride backwards. Maintain good riding posture. Ride backwards with a smooth pedaling action.

Gradually use less and less hand pressure until you can ride backwards solo. Maintain good riding posture and strive for smooth and continuous pedal action.

Riding backwards solo is shown in Figure 6-15. A variety of other arm positions can also be used, such as with the arms extended to the sides (Fig. 6-16).

Solo backward riding can begin in a number of ways. One method is to mount against a fixed support, such as a wall or post, and then go into backward riding. Another method is to first ride forward, come to a stop with the pedals in a horizontal position, and then reverse the pedal direction to backward riding. More difficult is to mount in the open and then immediately start backward riding. Use a helper for learning this skill. Continue practice until you can do it solo.

Fig. 6-16. Riding backwards with arms extended to sides.

Making Turns Riding Backwards

Turning while riding backwards is an important riding skill (Fig. 6-17). Begin by riding backwards and than make gradual turn. The turning should be done primarily by leaning. The pedaling should be continuous. Maintain good riding posture. Learn to make turns both to the right and to the left.

To learn to make turns riding backwards, you may first want to try this skill with two helpers. Then work down to one helper and finally to riding solo.

Fig. 6-17. Turning while riding backwards: (A) Left Turn; (B) Right turn.

Circles and Patterns Riding Backwards

Riding backwards in a continuous circle (Fig. 6-18) is an extension of basic turning while riding backwards. Begin by making a large radius turn while riding backwards and continue in a circle pattearn, following the same track each time around. The riding should be turning without noticeable twisting of the unicycle wheel in one spot.

Next, try riding backwards in a continuous large radius circle in the

55

Fig. 6-18. Riding backwards in circle pattern.

Fig. 6-19. Continuous half-circle pattern riding backwards.

Fig. 6-20. Pattern of half-circles of diminishing size riding backwards.

opposite turning direction. Practice circles both directions, even though one way will probably seem easier than the other. Many artistic riding skills require being able to turn in both directions.

Over a period of time, gradually shorten the radius of the circles until you can ride backwards in the smallest possible circles without twisting actions. The pedal action should be smooth and continuous. Maintain good riding posture throughout. Learn both turning directions.

A variety of patterns can be ridden backwards, including continuous half circles of the same size (Fig. 6-19), continuous half circles of diminishing size (Fig. 6-20), figure-eight (Fig. 6-21), serpentine (Fig. 6-22), and loops in alternate directions (Fig. 6-23).

Idling with Half-Pedal Revolutions

Idling is rocking back and forth in one place with pedal actions in alternating directions. Idling is usually done with half-pedal revolutions (Fig. 6-24). There are two different patterns that can be used. One has the right foot making the lower half of the pedal cycle

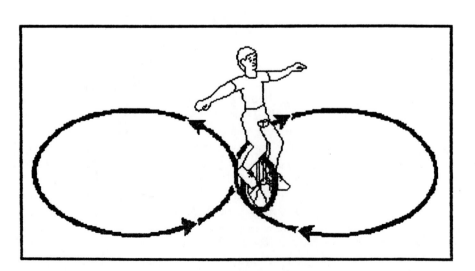

Fig. 6-21. Figure-eight riding backwards.

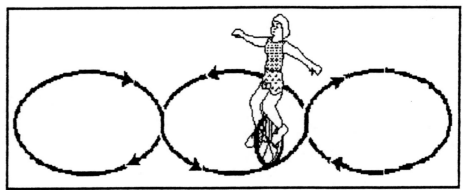

Fig. 6-22. Serpentine pattern with backward riding.

Fig. 6-23. Loops in alternate directions riding backwards.

and the left making the upper half, as shown in Figure 6-24. The other pattern is the reverse (Fig. 6-25).

Begin practice with one or two helpers or by using a wall or post as a hand support. The basic principle of idling is to lose balance forward, then pedal the wheel under the balance point until balance is lost backwards, then pedal the wheel back under the balance point until balance is lost forward. Practice with the helpers or support until you can do idling solo.

Learn idling with both foot patterns. This is important for learning more advanced skills.

When done correctly, the idling should be with complete half-pedal revolutions. The motion should be rhythmical. The basic idea is to be off balance backwards, then make half-pedal revolution backwards to bring the unicycle to an off balance forward position. Then make half-pedal revolution forward to bring the unicycle back into an off balance

Fig. 6-24. Idling with half-pedal revolutions with right foot making lower half of pedal cycle.

Fig. 6-25. Idling with half-pedal revolutions with right foot making upper half of pedal cycle.

Fig. 6-26. Idling with full-pedal revolutions with right foot forward at ends of cycles..

backward position. Continue with a half-pedal revolution backwards. And so on.

After you can do idling solo, try to increase the number of back-and-forth cycles you can make in sequence. Or try to see how long you can continue. Gradually work up to more cycles or longer time periods. Be sure to practice both side patterns. Try to keep good riding posture and work for control.

Idling can be started from a mount, from forward riding, or from backward riding. Learn all three of these methods. Also try combinations, such as ride forward, go into idling, then ride backwards from the idling.

Idling with Full-Pedal Revolutions

Idling with full-pedal revolutions (Fig. 6-26) should be fairly easy if you have mastered idling with half-pedal revolutions on both sides. For full-pedal revolutions, begin from horizontal pedal position. From off-balance position backwards, make one full pedal revolution backwards to bring the balance back over the saddle and then into forward off-balance position. From the horizontal pedal position, reverse the pedal direction

to forward to bring the balance over the saddle and into backward off-balance position. Continue with this idling pattern.

When done correctly, the idling pattern should be done with complete full-pedal revolutions from horizontal pedal positions around to the same horizontal positions. The right foot can be forward at the ends of the pedal cycles, as shown in Figure 6-26, or back, as shown in Figure 6-27. Learn both patterns.

On the first attempts, use two helpers. The helpers should stand directly to your sides. When this can be done with only light hand pressure, use one helper only. Continue practice until you can do idling with full-pedal revolutions solo.

After you can do idling with full-pedal revolutions solo, try to increase the number of back-and-forth full-pedal sequences or time you can do it without stopping. Maintain good riding posture and work for control and rhythm. Working in a half-revolution idle will change the pattern of the forward foot for idling with full-pedal revolutions.

Idling with full-pedal revolutions can be started from a mount, from forward

Fig. 6-27. Idling with full-pedal revolutions with left foot forward at ends of cycles.

riding, or from backward riding. Also try combinations, such as ride forward, go into idling with full-pedal revolutions, then ride forward or backwards.

Action-Reaction Twisting

Action-reaction twisting is done by twisting arms and upper body rapidly in one direction so that unicycle and lower body twist in the other direction, causing the unicycle wheel to turn to a new direction (Fig. 6-28). If the arms and upper body are brought back to original position slowly, the unicycle wheel will remain facing in the new direction. If the arms and upper body are returned to starting position in the same plane and at the same speed, the unicycle wheel will

return to the original position. In any case, no total angular momentum is developed. When you stop all upper body movement, the twisting also stops. You have turned, but you have not established a continuous spinning action.

By doing a series of action-reaction twisting movements in sequence with slow return motions, you can turn the unicycle all the way around, provided, of course, that you can maintain the upright balance of the unicycle at the same time.

Learn action-reaction twisting in both directions. This will be necessary for more advanced riding skills.

If you find that action-reaction or other types of twisting are causing wear in one spot on the unicycle tire, rotate the tire on the rim from time to time (see Chapter 3).

Zigzag Pattern

Action-reaction twisting allows riding a zigzag pattern (Fig. 6-29). To do this pattern, ride forward. Do action-reaction twisting so that unicycle makes quick turn to new direction. Ride forward for a short distance, then execute action-reaction turn in direction opposite the first one. Continue with this sequence to do zigzag pattern. Try to ride forward equal distances between twisting actions.

Action-reaction twisting can also be used for riding other patterns, such as squares, rectangles, and triangles. Two action-reaction movements in succession give greater twisting movement.

Fig. 6-28. Action-reaction twisting: (A) Ready for action; (B) Action movement; (C) New direction.

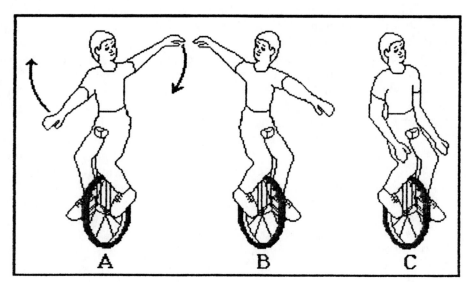

Fig. 6-29. Riding zigzag pattern.

Circling While Idling with Half-Pedal Revolutions

This skill combines idling with half-pedal revolutions and action-reaction twisting. Begin by starting idling with half-pedal revolutions. Then, with each idling action, do an action-reaction twisting movement so that the unicycle twists about an eighth of a turn. Return the arms and upper body to the starting position slowly so that the wheel stays in the new position. Do another action-reaction turn in the same direction on each idling action until you have turned all the way around and are back in the original direction again.

Learn this skill with the twisting in both directions. Also try making a full circle one direction and then go immediately to a full circle the other direction.

Circling While Idling with Full-Pedal Revolutions

This skill combines idling with full-pedal revolutions with action-reaction twisting. Begin with idling with full-pedal revolutions. Execute an action-reaction twisting movement at the center of the idling swing (when the unicycle passes the upright position) and slowly return arms and upper body to original position so that unicycle wheel remains in new direction. Repeat an action-reaction twisting action at the center of each idling swing. Continue until a full circle has been completed and you are facing the original direction.

Learn this skill with the twisting in both directions. Also try making a full circle one direction and then go immediately to a full circle the other direction.

Touching Riding Surface

Touching riding surface while mounted on a unicycle (Fig. 6-30) requires flexibility and control. This is one of those skills that is difficult to place in a progression, as some riders find it easy and others impossible. This skill is useful for picking up objects from the ground, as detailed in Chapter 7.

This skill is easier on a 20-inch unicycle than on one with a larger wheel. If possible, learn to touch ground with both right and left hands.

Fig. 6-30. Touching ground from unicycle.

Combining Elementary Skills

The elementary artistic unicycling skills described above can be done in combinations to form sequences and routines. Sequences and routines are used for demonstrations, parade riding, performing, and artistic competition. Once you have mastered the individual skills, you can start putting them together in combinations.

In order to begin riding, you first do a mount. From a regular mount, you can ride forward, go into idling, or ride backwards, giving three different combinations.

From forward riding, you can dismount backwards or forward, go into idling, or reverse directions to backward riding.

From idling, you can ride forward or backwards or dismount backwards or forward.

From backward riding, you can dismount backwards or forward, go into idling, or change to forward riding.

From forward and backward riding, you can turn right or left, ride patterns, do action-reaction twisting, or touch the riding surface.

From idling you can do action-reaction twisting to rotate unicycle in circle. You can change from half-pedal revolution idling to full-pedal revolution idling or vice versa.

The elementary skills detailed above can be put together in a phone-book number of combinations. Try to put skills together so that one stunt flows into the next. In some cases, a combination of two stunts can be much more difficult than the individual elements in the combination.

I recommend that unicyclists begin putting individual skills into combinations as soon as they have mastered individual skills.

INTERMEDIATE SKILLS

Once you have mastered the elementary skills detailed above, you will probably want to go on to intermediate skills. You've probably noticed by this time that as the skills become more difficult, it usually takes more practice time to learn them. As the skills become even more difficult, it will probably take even more practice time to learn them.

One-Foot Riding Forward

This skill can be done with the non-pedaling foot extended forward at a low angle (Fig. 6-31), the leg in a horizontal position (Fig. 6-32), or the foot resting on the unicycle frame above the wheel-well (Fig. 6-33). The skill is usually learned with the free foot extended forward at a low angle first.

One full pedal cycle of one-foot forward riding with the free leg at a low angle is shown in Figure 6-34. Begin by forward riding. Remove weight from one pedal and provide pedal power with other foot. The main difficulty is in providing enough power to get the pedal over the top of the cycle. Use other foot to assist when necessary, but gradually use other foot less and less until you can ride using one foot only. Use a powerful downward stroke on the pedal so that it will have the momentum to make it back around and

over the top of the pedal cycle again.

When you can do the pedal action with the other foot on the pedal, but with

Fig. 6-31. Free leg extended forward at low angle.

Fig. 6-32. Free leg extended horizontally forward.

Fig. 6-33. Non-pedaling foot resting on unicycle frame above wheel-well.

no power being provided to the pedal, try lifting the foot off the pedal briefly and then replacing it again while you ride forward with the other foot. Continue practice until you can ride with the foot forward of and free from the pedal. Gradually work up to the point where you have the leg straight and extended forward with the toe pointed (Fig. 6-35).

Once this skill is mastered, it usually isn't difficult to place the free foot on the unicycle frame above the wheel-well (Fig. 6-36).

These skills should be learned on both sides. Try riding forward with one foot, then switch feet and continue with one-foot riding forward with the other foot. This can be done both with the free foot forward and with the free foot on the unicycle frame.

One-Foot Idling with Half-Pedal Revolutions

Considerable power is required to do one-foot idling with half-pedal revolutions. This skill is usually first learned with the free leg extended forward at a low angle (Fig. 6-37). Begin with regular idling with half-pedal revolutions. Remove pedal pressure from one foot so that you are providing the power primarily with the other foot. Try to maintain a full half-pedal revolution with each downward foot action. Use other foot only when needed to maintain pedal power. Continue practice until you can do the idling with one foot.

The next step is to do the one-foot idling with the other foot completely off the pedal. Gradually extend the foot forward until you are able to do one-foot idling with the leg straight and extended

Fig. 6-34. One-foot riding forward with free leg forward at low angle.

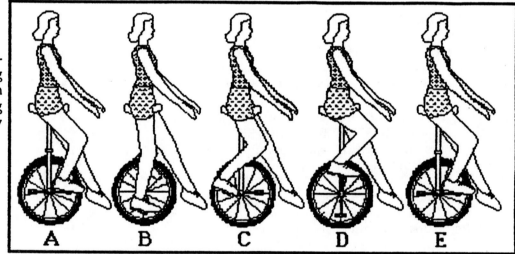

Fig. 6-35. One-foot riding forward with free leg extended horizontally forward.

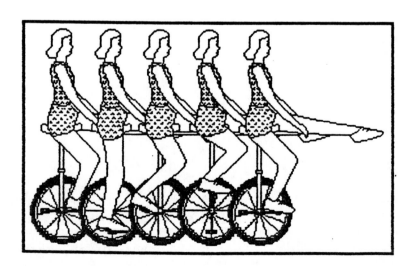

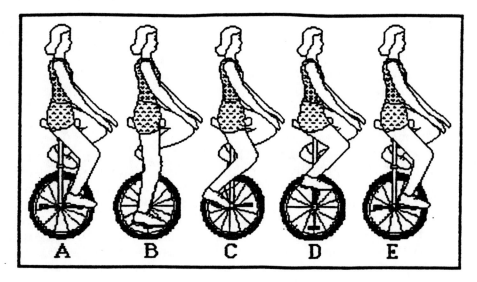

Fig. 6-36. One-foot riding forward with non-pedaling foot resting on fork above wheel-well.

Fig. 6-37. One-foot idling with half-pedal revolutions and free leg at low angle forward.

Fig. 6-38. One-foot idling with half-pedal revolutions and free leg horizontally forward.

forward at a low angle with the toe pointed (Fig. 6-37).

After you can do one-foot idling with rhythm and control with the free leg at a low angle forward, gradually increase the leg height until you can do the skill with the leg extended horizontally forward (Fig. 6-38).

When this can be done, try one-foot idling with the free foot resting on the unicycle frame above the wheel-well (Fig. 6-39).

Learn one-foot idling with each of the free leg positions on both sides, even though you will probably find one side more difficult. However, it is important to be able to do the skills with either foot for more advanced artistic riding.

Fig. 6-39. One-foot idling with half-pedal revolutions with non-pedaling foot resting on fork above wheel-well.

Turning and Patterns While One-Foot Riding Forward

Turning while riding forward with one foot (Fig. 6-40) is an important artistic riding skill. The techniques for turning are similar to regular forward riding, with the added difficulty of having to pedal with one foot. Learn to turn both to the left and to the right. Learn on both sides with free leg extended forward at low angle (Fig. 6-31), horizontally forward (Fig. 6-32), and with non-pedaling foot resting on unicycle frame above wheel-well (Fig. 6-33).

A variety of patterns can also be ridden forward pedaling with one foot, including circle, figure-eight, continuous half circles of the same size, continuous half circles of diminishing size, serpentine, loops in alternate directions, and zigzag. The patterns can be ridden pedaling with right or left foot with free leg in variety of positions.

Circling While One-Foot Idling

This skill combines one-foot idling with action-reaction twisting. Begin by starting one-foot idling with half-pedal revolutions. Then, with each idling action, do an action-reaction twisting movement so that the unicycle twists about an

eighth of a turn. Return the arms and upper body to the starting position. Do another action-reaction twist in the same direction on each idling action until you have turned all the way around and are facing in the original direction again.

Learn this skill with the twisting both to the left and to the right. Also try making a full circle one direction and then go immediately to a full circle the other direction. Learn with free leg extended forward at low angle (Fig. 6-31), with leg horizontally forward (Fig. 6-32), and with non-pedaling foot resting on unicycle frame (Fig. 6-33).

Bouncing

Bouncing up and down while mounted on a unicycle is essentially using the unicycle as a pogo stick (Fig. 6-41). This is a fun and challenging skill, but it can be somewhat damaging to the unicycle wheel and spokes, so you may not want to us your best unicycle for learning this skill.

To do bouncing, pause with the pedals in a horizontal position. Grasp the saddle with both hands at the front of the saddle or one hand at the front of the saddle and the other hand at the back of the saddle. Jump. Pull the unicycle to your

Fig. 6-40. Turning while riding forward with one foot: (A) Left turn; (B) Right turn.

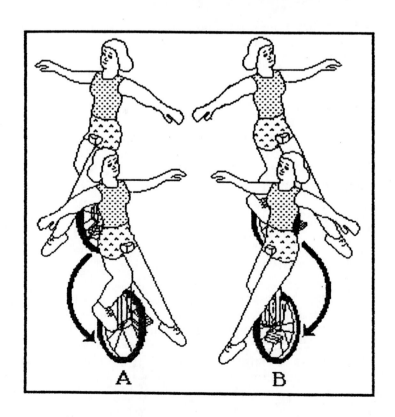

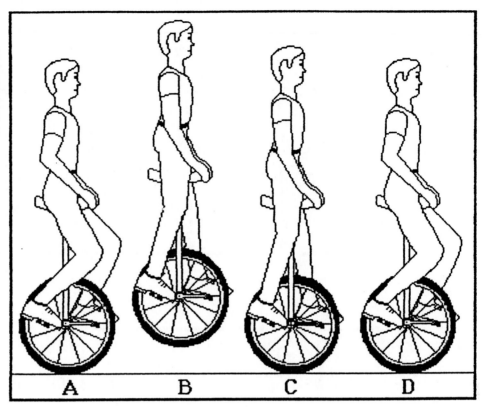

Fig. 6-41. Bouncing: (A) Pause, grasp saddle, and jump; (B) Pull unicycle to feet; (C) Landing; (D) Return to starting position.

feet by the saddle so that the unicycle goes up in the air with your jump.

A series of bounces can be done in series, bouncing in directions to maintain balance. Bouncing can also be done while riding, with one or more bounces to each half-pedal revolution. Even more difficult are bounce turns to change the direction of the unicycle. Half turns and more are possible.

Some riders are also able to do jumping by squeezing the saddle between their legs without grasping the saddle with their hands. The use of foot and waist straps to hold the rider to the unicycle are covered in Chapter 7.

One-Foot Riding Backwards

Once one-foot riding forward and one-foot idling have been mastered, one-foot riding backwards (Fig. 6-42) can be attempted. One-foot riding backwards is generally much more difficult to learn.

Begin by riding backwards. Remove one foot from pedal and continue to ride backwards with one foot. Use a powerful downward stroke on the pedal so that it will have the momentum to make it back

around and over the top of the pedal cycle again. Gradually work up to the point where the free foot can be placed forward at a low angle with the toe pointed (Fig. 6-42).

Continue practice, gradually working up to the point where you can ride backwards with one foot with the other leg extended horizontally forward with the toe pointed (Fig. 6-43). Once this skill is mastered, it usually isn't difficult to place the free foot on the unicycle frame above the wheel-well (Fig. 6-44).

These skills should be learned on both sides. Try riding backwards with one foot, then switch feet and continue with one-foot riding backwards with the other foot. This can be done with the free leg extended forward at a low angle, horizontally forward, and with the non-pedaling foot resting on the unicycle fork above the wheel-well.

Turning and Patterns While One-Foot Riding Backwards

Turning and patterns while one-foot riding backwards are advanced skills that usually require considerable practice to master. Basic turning while riding

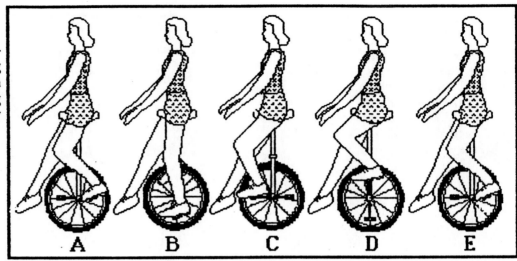

Fig. 6-42. One-foot riding backwards with free leg forward at low angle.

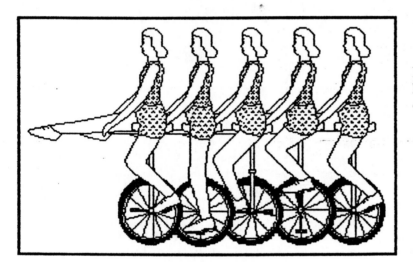

Fig. 6-43. One-foot riding backwards with free leg extended horizontally forward.

Fig. 6-44. One-foot riding backwards with non-pedaling foot resting on fork above wheel-well.

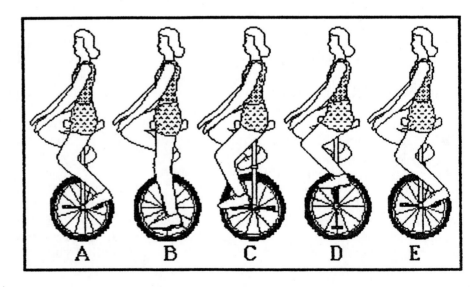

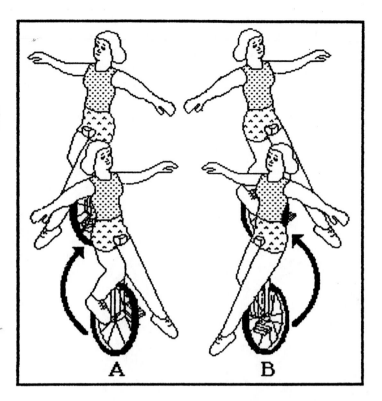

Fig. 6-45. Turning while riding backwards with one foot: (A) Left turn; (B) Right turn.

backwards with one foot is shown in Figure 6-45. The techniques for turning are similar to regular backward riding, with the added difficulty of having to pedal with one foot. Learn to turn both to the left and to the right. Learn on both sides with the free leg extended forward at low angle (Fig. 6-31), horizontally forward (Fig. 6-32), and with non-pedaling foot resting on unicycle frame above wheel-well (Fig. 6-33).

A variety of patterns can also be ridden backwards pedaling with one foot, including circle, figure-eight, continuous half circles of the same size, continuous half circles of diminishing size, serpentine, loops in alternate directions, and zigzag. The patterns can be ridden pedaling with right or left foot with free leg in variety of positions.

Mounting with Unicycle Behind You

Mounting with the unicycle behind you (Fig. 6-46) is a novelty method for getting "aboard." Begin with the unicycle positioned as shown. Place one foot on pedal that is positioned forward and down. Apply downward pressure on the pedal as you step other foot from ground to free pedal. The pedal action is used to draw the unicycle saddle up under you.

Continue pedal action until pedal that was forward is in horizontal position to rear. From this position, you can continue to ride forward or go into idling or backward riding.

Learn with both right and left feet as starting foot.

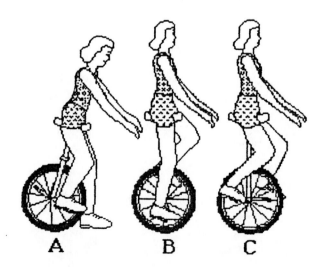

Fig. 6-46. Mounting with unicycle behind you: (A) Starting position; (B) Forward pedal action; (C) Horizontal pedal position.

One-Foot Mounting

One-foot mounting (Fig. 6-47) begins like regular mounting. However, when the last foot steps from the riding surface, it is moved over the upper pedal to a position forward of the pedal. After mounting, you can change to forward riding with one foot, or continue with backward riding with one foot.

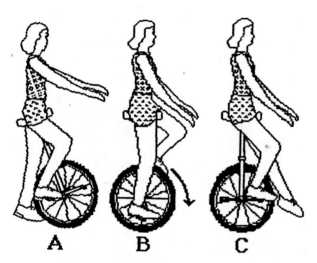

Fig. 6-47. One-foot mounting: (A) Starting position; (B) Last foot to leave riding surface steps over upper pedal; (C) Free leg is extended forward.

Jump Mount

The jump mount is shown in Figure 6-48. The rider grasps the front of the unicycle saddle and jumps from both feet to the horizontally positioned pedals. Feet land on pedals. Once mounted, hands are released from saddle and forward or backward riding or idling can begin.

More difficult is to begin in the same manner, but release hands from saddle before landing on pedals and saddle.

Riding Around Wheel

Riding in a small circle around wheel (Fig. 6-49) is an impressive skill. When done correctly, the turning is done by leaning and pedaling around the edge of the wheel rather than by action-reaction twisting.

Learn by riding in smaller and smaller circles until you are riding around edge of wheel in smallest possible circle without twisting actions.

Fig. 6-49. Riding small circle around wheel.

Fig. 6-48. Jump mount: (A) Starting position; (B) Jump to mount; (C) Mounted.

Spinning

Spinning or pirouetting with total angular momentum (Fig. 6-50) is a spectacular unicycling skill. The spinning is often started from either forward or backward riding with circling. The basic idea is to convert forward and/or turning momentum into angular spinning or pirouetting momentum. It usually takes considerable practice to learn to do this, however.

Once spinning with total angular momentum has been established, the speed of spinning can be increased by bringing

Fig. 6-50. Spinning or pirouetting with total angular momentum.

Fig. 6-52. Backward riding into 180-degree spin, followed by forward riding.

the arms in close to the body. In this manner, a number of unicyclists can do six or more complete spins. The difficult part is establishing sufficient initial total angular momentum.

Begin with half spins. This can be done by riding forward and turning sharply to initiate 180-degree spin, then riding backwards (Fig. 6-51). An alternate method is to ride backwards, turn sharply to initiate 180-degree spin, then ride forward (Fig. 6-52). Full 360-degree spins can be done from forward or backward riding.

Once 360-degree spins can be done,

gradually increase the number of spins that can be done. In order to do two or more spins, it is necessary to establish strong total angular momentum and then bring the arms in close to the body.

One-Foot Riding Around Wheel Pivoting on Other Foot

One-foot riding around wheel in small circle while pivoting on other foot on riding surface (Fig. 6-53) is a unique riding skill. Begin by riding around wheel in small circle, as detailed above in this chapter, then remove foot from inside pedal and place toe portion of sole of shoe on riding surface. One-foot ride with

Fig. 6-51. Forward riding into 180-degree spin, followed by backward riding.

Fig. 6-53. One-foot riding around wheel pivoting on other foot.

outside foot in small circle around the wheel, pivoting around foot on riding surface.

Also learn in opposite direction, pivoting and one-foot riding with opposite feet. Extremely difficult is to do one-foot riding around wheel pivoting on other foot, then switch feet and circling directions. This combination is close to the line of being in the advanced category of skills, as detailed below in this chapter.

Riding Off Saddle Holding Saddle Forward

Riding off the saddle is a difficult skill, but doing it holding the saddle in front of you (Fig. 6-54) is one of the easiest ways of doing this on a standard unicycle. Begin by riding the unicycle forward. Grasp the saddle in front of you in both hands. Slide your body back off the saddle and ride the unicycle "standing" while supporting yourself with your arms.

This skill can also be done with backward riding and idling, which add to the difficulty. One-foot riding and one-foot idling are even more difficult. Still another possibility is to do a regular mount while holding the saddle in front of you.

Fig. 6-54. Riding off saddle holding saddle forward.

Combining Intermediate Skills

The intermediate skills described above can be combined in hundreds of different ways to form sequences and routines. By combining elementary skills with intermediate skills, the possibilities are further increased.

Once you have mastered the individual skills, you can start putting them together in combinations. From one-foot mounting, you can go into one-foot forward riding, one-foot backward riding, or one-foot idling. From one-foot forward riding, you can switch to one-foot idling or one-foot backward riding. From one-foot backward riding, you can switch to one-foot idling or one-foot forward riding. While doing one-foot sequences, the positions of the free leg can be changed from extended forward at low angle to horizontally forward or with non-pedaling foot resting on unicycle frame above wheel-well.

Circling, one-foot riding around wheel pivoting on other foot, and spinning can be used with regular and one-foot riding skills to form hundreds of artistic combinations.

The jump mount can be followed by regular forward or backward riding or regular idling, or one-foot forward or backward riding or idling.

The elementary and intermediate skills detailed above can be put together in a phone-book number of combinations. Try putting skills together so that one stunt flows into the next.

ADVANCED SKILLS

Once you have mastered the intermediate skills detailed above, you are ready to go on to advanced skills. The advanced skills detailed below are some of the most difficult stunts that are presently being done on standard unicycles. The practice time required for learning a single advanced skill is often greater than what was used for learning a number of easier skills.

Walking Wheel from Saddle

This is a method of unicycling with the feet on the tire rather than the pedals (Fig. 6-55). The feet are used to rotate the wheel forward, and in some cases, backwards or with idling action.

Fig. 6-55. Wheel-walking from saddle.

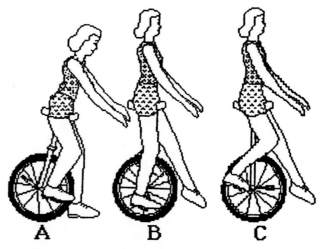

Fig. 6-56. One-foot mounting with unicycle rearward: (A) Starting position; (B) Forward one-foot pedal action at vertical position; (C) Forward pedal action at horizontal position.

The riding is easiest forward and usually learned first. From slow riding forward, remove one foot from pedal and place on tire. Turn toe inward and work foot forward and downward on tire to rotate wheel forward while one-foot riding with other foot. With continuing practice, gradually do more and more of wheel movement with foot on tire and less with pedaling foot. When this can be done with control, remove other foot from pedal and use both feet on tire. At least one foot should be on tire at all times so that wheel cannot free-wheel. The main technique to learn is to control the rotation of the wheel in relation to the unicycle saddle so that balance can be maintained.

Wheel-walking is usually first learned with forward motion, but idling and backward riding are also possible. It is also possible to mount directly to wheel-walking. Extremely difficult is wheel-walking with one foot. A few advanced riders have managed to do unicycling routines without placing feet on pedals, using wheel-walking only.

One-Foot Mounting with Unicycle Behind You

One-foot mounting with unicycle behind you (Fig. 6-56) is an advanced method for getting on a unicycle. Begin with the unicycle positioned as shown. Place one foot on pedal that is positioned forward and down. Apply downward pressure on the pedal as you step other foot from ground to position forward of pedal. Continue pedal cycle all the way around forward for forward one-foot riding or go into one-foot idling or backward one-foot riding at horizontal pedal position. The main difficulty is getting necessary force on pedal. This skill requires considerable leg strength.

Try to learn with both right and left feet as pedaling foot, even though the "weak" side will probably be much more difficult.

Riding Off Saddle Holding Saddle Behind You

Ride forward and grasp saddle in both hands behind you. Slide body forward off saddle and ride unicycle "standing" while supporting yourself with your arms (Fig. 6-57). This skill is generally much more difficult to master than riding off saddle holding saddle forward, as described above in this chapter.

Even more difficult, but possible, are riding backwards, idling, and one-foot riding and idling. It is also possible to mount off the saddle with the unicycle rearward. Extremely difficult is one-foot mounting off the saddle with the unicycle rearward.

Fig. 6-57. Riding off saddle holding saddle rearward.

Backward Riding Around Wheel

Riding a small circle backwards around wheel (Fig. 6-58) is an impressive advanced skill. When done correctly, the turning is done by leaning and pedaling around the edge of the wheel rather than by action-reaction twisting.

Learn by riding backwards in smaller and smaller circles until you are riding around edge of wheel in smallest possible circle without twisting actions.

Fig. 6-58. Backward riding in small circle around wheel.

One-Foot Riding Backwards Around Wheel Pivoting on Other Foot

One-foot riding backwards around wheel in small circle while pivoting on other foot on riding surface (Fig. 6-59) is a unique advanced riding skill. Begin by riding backwards around wheel in small circle, then remove foot from inside pedal and place toe portion of sole of shoe on riding surface. One-foot ride backwards in small circle around the wheel, pivoting around foot on riding surface.

Also learn in opposite direction, pivoting and one-foot riding backwards with opposite feet. Extremely difficult is to do one-foot riding backwards around wheel pivoting on other foot in one circling direction, then switch feet and circling directions.

Fig. 6-59. One-foot riding backwards around wheel pivoting on other foot.

Jump Mount with Unicycle Rearward

The jump mount with the unicycle rearward is shown in Figure 6-60. The rider positions the unicycle and grasps the saddle with one hand as shown. Jump is from both feet to horizontally positioned pedals. Hand is released from saddle and then both hands grasp saddle in front. Feet land on pedals. Once mounted, hands are released from saddle and forward or backward riding or idling can begin.

An alternate method is to do the mount without grasping saddle with hands after the jump. This adds to the difficulty of the skill.

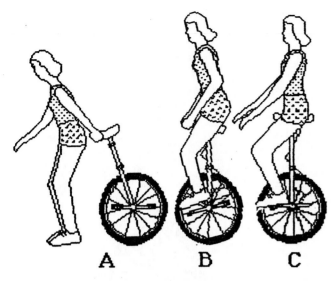

Fig. 6-60. Jump mount with unicycle rearward: (A) Starting position; (B) Landing on unicycle; (C) Completed mount.

Riding with Chest on Saddle

An advanced novelty skill is riding with chest on saddle with hands grasping saddle (Fig. 6-61) or with hands free of saddle (Fig. 6-62). The skill is usually learned first with hands grasping saddle. The skill can be started with feet on ground by placing chest on saddle and mounting unicycle or from riding off saddle holding saddle in front of you.

After you can ride forward with chest on saddle with hands grasping saddle, try riding backwards and idling. Even more difficult are one-foot riding skills. More advanced is to do the skills with chest on saddle with hands free of saddle (Fig. 6-62).

Fig. 6-61. Riding with chest on saddle and hands grasping saddle.

Fig. 6-62. Riding with chest on saddle with hands free of saddle.

Riding off Saddle to Side of Unicycle

This is another method for riding off the unicycle saddle (Fig. 6-63). The skill can be done with one foot placed on top of the other one on the pedal or with one foot only on the pedal. In either case, this is a difficult and challenging method for riding a unicycle.

The skill can start from regular riding. Then grasp saddle forward and swing one leg around to side and move body off unicycle. Another method is to mount directly into riding off saddle to side of unicycle from ground.

Riding off saddle to side can be done in either pedal direction. Try riding one direction, then switch to other direction. Turns and patterns are other possibilities.

Fig. 6-63. Riding off saddle to side of unicycle: (A) With one foot on top of other; (B) With one foot only on pedal.

Wheel-Walking Off Saddle with Saddle Forward.

Wheel-walking off saddle with saddle forward (Fig. 6-64) is an extremely difficult skill. The wheel-walking is usually done with backward riding, as this is the easiest direction to move and control the wheel from this off-saddle position.

Fig. 6-65. Wheel-walking off saddle with saddle rearward.

Fig. 6-64. Wheel-walking off saddle with saddle forward.

Wheel-Walking off Saddle with Saddle Rearward

Walking the wheel from off the saddle with saddle rearward (Fig. 6-65) is usually done with forward motion, but is extremely difficult because it is difficult to support body weight and make the foot actions on the wheel.

Wheel-Walking off saddle from side

Wheel-walking off saddle from side is shown in Figure 6-66. The rider's weight is supported on saddle by arms. One foot is used on each side of wheel, making it possible to ride to one side with one foot and to the other side with the other foot. This makes it possible to ride either direction or do idling. The wheel-walking can be started from the ground or from regular riding. It's also possible to change from wheel-walking off saddle from side to regular riding or switch sides.

Fig. 6-66. Wheel-walking off saddle from side.

Gliding

Gliding (Fig. 6-67) is basically coasting on a unicycle using the feet on the wheel with a braking action, but not to provide motion to the wheel. To learn, do wheel-walking from saddle forward, then try to continue forward motion with feet dragging on wheel. By applying the correct amount of pressure on the wheel, the forward motion of the wheel and the friction of the feet against the wheel are used to maintain balance.

Fig. 6-67. Gliding.

Fig. 6-68. Coasting.

Coasting

Coasting (Fig. 6-68) is an advanced skill that a few advanced riders have mastered. The basic idea is to ride forward and take the feet off the pedals and continue to coast with the feet free of the pedals and wheel, usually with one or both feet propped on unicycle frame above wheel-well. Gliding, as detailed above, can be used as an intermediate step for learning this skill. Learn first with one foot on frame and other on tire.

Coasting backwards is an even more difficult possibility.

Other Advanced Skills

The above skills are some of the primary advanced individual artistic skills that are being done on standard unicycles without props today. Other advanced stunts that are now being done include riding the unicycle wheel like an ultimate wheel with the saddle dragging the floor; riding forward and bouncing unicycle saddle off floor while riding wheel as ultimate wheel and then catching and remounting unicycle saddle again; various kick-up mounts where the unicycle is placed on side on floor and unicyclist kicks unicycle upright and jump-mounts all in one smooth action; riding from side with back facing unicycle; and one-foot

wheel walking from saddle and off-saddle positions. And new skills are still being invented.

Advanced Combinations

The advanced skills described above can be combined in hundreds of different ways to form sequences and routines. By also using elementary and intermediate skills, the possibilities are further increased. Combinations are often more difficult than the skills individually. Try putting skills together so that one stunt flows into the next.

Once you have mastered individual advanced artistic riding skills, you can start putting them together. From wheel walking from saddle, you can go into wheel walking off saddle with saddle rearward or switch to wheel walking from side. From riding off saddle holding saddle behind you, you can switch to riding off saddle to side of unicycle. From riding with chest on saddle with hands on saddle you can switch to riding off saddle with saddle forward. Wheel-walking with saddle in front to with saddle at side to saddle rearward and then to side and with saddle in front again (making complete circle around saddle) is an impressive combination.

75

Chapter 7

SOLO ARTISTIC RIDING ON STANDARD UNICYCLES WITH PROPS

This chapter covers solo artistic riding on standard unicycles with handlebar units and a variety of other props.

USING A HANDLEBAR UNIT

A handlebar unit and matching standard unicycle are shown in Figure 7-1. A handlebar unit is an exciting addition to unicycling that makes possible many different artistic riding skills. These units are not presently being manufactured. However, they are easy to assemble from standard bicycle parts and do not require welding, as detailed in my book, **How To Build Unicycles and Artistic Bicycles** (available from Solipaz Publishing Company, P.O. Box 366, Lodi, California 95241).

It may appear that a handlebar unit

Fig. 7-1. Handlebar unit and matching standard unicycle.

would make riding a unicycle easier, serving as a training aid. But in practice this usually isn't the case. While the handlebar unit may serve a beginner to help maintain balance, it occupies the hands and it is possible to fall onto the unit. I recommend that a person learn, as a minimum, the skills described in Chapter 4 before attempting to ride with a handlebar unit.

Basic Forward Riding with Unit

The first skill to learn is to use the handlebar unit in connection with the standard unicycle as though riding a bicycle (Fig. 7-2). To learn, place handlebar unit where it can be reached after mounting the unicycle, or have someone standing by to hand the handlebar unit to you. Mount unicycle. Holding onto support, hold handlebar unit in other hand, as shown in Figure 7-3. Ride the unicycle away from the support and immediately place the hand from the support to the handlebar grip. Ride forward with the handlebar unit as though

Fig. 7-2. Basic riding with handlebar unit.

Fig. 7-3. Holding onto support with one hand and handlebar unit with other hand.

riding a regular bicycle. Try to avoid letting the handlebar unit angle too far forward. Leverage can be applied to the grips to bring it into the correct position. Maintain good riding posture. Try to hold the handlebar unit in line with the unicycle (Fig. 7-4). From a view in front of the handlebar unit, it appears to be an ordinary bicycle.

Dismounting with Handlebar Unit

This is one of the few times that I feel that it is easier and looks better to dismount forward from the unicycle rather than behind it. To dismount, release one hand from the handlebar unit and grasp the back of the unicycle saddle as the dismount is made forward from the unicycle. When done properly, the rider will be standing between the unicycle and handlebar unit, holding the handlebar unit

in one hand by one grip and the unicycle by the back of the saddle in the other hand. A flashy finish is to dismount quickly and then hold both the unicycle and handlebar unit in the air.

It is also possible to dismount to the rear of the unicycle. To do this, release one hand from the handlebar unit and grasp front of saddle as dismount to rear is made.

Making Turns

The next skill to master is making turns while riding forward with the handlebar unit (Fig. 7-5). This should not present any problem if turning has been learned on the unicycle without the handlebar unit. With the handlebar unit, turn the handlebars as though making a turn on a bicycle. The unicycle should then follow the line of the front wheel. Leaning slightly into the turn adds to the effect.

At first, practice making turns on a large radius. Learn all turns both to the

Fig. 7-4. Handlebar unit in line with unicycle.

Fig. 7-5. Turning as though on a regular bicycle.

left and to the right. Gradually work down to turns of smaller radius.

Circles and Patterns

Next, practice riding circles and patterns. Begin with a complete circle, then try a series of circles. Gradually work down to smaller circles. Learn both turning directions. It's possible to make much tighter turns with the unicycle-handlebar combination than on a regular bicycle.

Zigzag, figure-eight, alternate half circle, serpentine, and other patterns can be ridden. These are usually easy once the patterns can be done on the unicycle alone.

Riding with One Hand

Begin by riding forward with handlebar unit. Then release one hand from the handlebar unit and ride forward holding the handlebar unit with the other hand (Fig. 7-6). Also learn the skill with the opposite hand holding the handlebar unit.

Try riding turns and patterns with one hand. This skill allows giving turn signals with one hand.

Fig. 7-6. Riding holding handlebar unit with one hand.

Maintaining Balance in One Spot

With the handle-bar unit, it is easy to come to a complete stop and maintain balance in one spot. This skill looks much more difficult than it actually is, perhaps because those watching often know how difficult it is to keep stationary balance while mounted on a bicycle. This skill is actually much easier on the unicycle with the handlebar unit, as the unicycle and handlebar unit are separate and can be placed slightly out of line. With a bicycle, the wheels remain in line. Also, with the unicycle you have direct control of the wheel on the unicycle and can make balance corrections by applying pressure on the handlebars, using the wheel as a balance prop.

Mounting in Open

Figure 7-7 shows the basic starting position for mounting in the open. The unicycle is then mounted as was done previously without the handlebar unit. After mounting, ride forward.

This skill is fairly easy, as the handlebar unit can be used to help maintain balance. It is also possible to mount and then immediately hold balance in a stationary position.

Riding with Handlebar Unit to Side with Wheels Parallel

While riding forward, move the handlbar unit back and to one side until the wheel is lined up with, and parallel to, the unicycle wheel. Also learn the skill to the other side.

Turning and Spinning Handlebar Unit

While riding forward, spin the handlebar unit one-half turn and reverse your hand grips. Continue riding forward with the handlebar unit held backwards. Then make another half turn of the handlebars to the regular position.

Slightly more difficult is a full spin of the handlebar unit. To do this, follow the handlebars around with one hand, maintaining loose contact with the grip. This is an imitation of a stunt that can be done on an artistic bicycle.

Still another possibility is two or more full spins of the handlebar unit. Learn to spin the handlebar unit both directions.

Fig. 7-7. Basic starting position for mounting in open.

Riding Forward with Handlebar Unit Behind You

Ride forward and switch the handlebar unit to a position behind you. To do this, first bring the handlebar unit to your side. Then spin it one-half turn while reversing hand grips. Release the grip closest to the unicycle. Reach around with this hand and bring the handlebar unit directly behind you. The handlebar unit is then following the unicycle in a reversed position. When desired, the switch can be made to the standard riding position again.

Riding with Handlebar Unit Overhead

An important skill is to ride the unicycle while holding the handlebar unit in the air overhead (Fig. 7-8). On the first attempts, ride forward and lift the handlebar unit off the ground. Immediately lower it to the ground again. Gradually increase the height that the handlebar unit is taken from the ground. Work up to the point where you can raise the unit over your head. On the first attempts at this, the unit can be immediately returned to the ground. Work

Fig. 7-8. Riding with handlebar unit overhead.

up to the point where you can hold the unit over your head and continue riding the unicycle.

Next, practice making turns with the handlebar unit in the air. Add to the effect by steering with the unit in the air.

Circles and patterns can also be done with the handlebar unit held in the air. Advanced riders can also do more difficult riding skills while holding the handlebar unit in the air, such as riding backwards, idling, and one-foot riding.

Riding Backwards

A popular advanced skill is to ride backwards with the handlebar unit in the normal riding position. This is generally easier than riding backwards with just the unicycle, and it isn't necessary that the rider know how to ride backwards solo without the handlebar unit. But it helps.

On the first attempts, ride forward, come to a stop, then start riding backwards. Pedal one-half turn backwards, pause, then start forward again. Repeat, adding an additional half turn of the pedals each time. Continue practice until you can ride backwards with control.

Turns and Patterns While Riding Backwards

Turns while riding backwards with the handlebar unit can be attempted next. Try gradual turns first. Learn both right and left turns. Gradually work down to tighter turns.

Circles while riding backwards with the handlebar unit can be attempted next. An interesting combination is to first ride a circle forward, then reverse directions and follow the same circle line backwards.

Figure-eights and other patterns can also be done while riding backwards. An interesting combination is to first do a pattern forward, then reverse directions and follow the same pattern line backwards.

Idling

Another possibility is to do idling with the handlebar unit held in normal position. A difficult combination is to begin idling with the handlebar unit held in normal position, then to lift and hold the handlebar unit overhead while continuing idling on the unicycle.

One-Foot Riding Forward

Ride forward and switch to one-foot riding with the handlebar unit held in the normal position. The free foot can be held forward or positioned resting on the unicycle frame above the wheel-well. A difficult combination is to do one-foot riding with the handlebar unit held in the normal position and then lift and hold the handlebar unit overhead while continuing one-foot riding forward.

One-Foot Idling

One-foot idling can be done with the handlebar unit held in the normal position. The free foot can be held forward or positioned resting on the unicycle frame above the wheel-well. A difficult combination is to do one-foot idling with the handlebar unit held in the normal position and then lift and hold the handlebar unit overhead while continuing one-foot idling.

One-Foot Riding Backwards

An advanced skill is one-foot riding backwards with the handlebar unit held in the normal position. The free foot can be held forward or positioned resting on the unicycle frame above the wheel-well. A difficult combination is to do one-foot riding backwards with the handlebar unit held in the normal position and then lift and hold the handlebar unit overhead while continuing one-foot riding backwards.

Turns and circles and patterns can be done while one-foot riding backwards with the handlebar unit held in the normal position. Even more difficult are turns and circles and patterns while one-foot riding backwards with the handlebar unit held overhead.

An Easy Novelty Stunt

An easy stunt that is effective for clowning and comedy is to loosen the nuts that hold the wheel of the handlebar unit to the fork. Insert the wheel in the fork with the nuts loose. Then ride forward. Lift the handlebar unit upwards so that the wheel comes off and rolls away.

Continue riding and steering as though the wheel were still in place. A variety of stunts can be done with an imaginary wheel in place.

Combinations and Routines

After learning some of the skills detailed above with a standard unicycle and handlebar unit, you can begin to put them together in combinations and routines. Routines imitating bicycle riding are popular.

OTHER SOLO SKILLS WITH PROPS

Many other props besides the handlebar unit can be used with solo riding on a standard unicycle. In some cases, these stunts require not only skill in riding a standard unicycle, but also skill in some other activity, such as jumping a rope, using a hula-hoop, or juggling.

Hula Hooping

All kinds of possibilities exist with hoops. Spinning them on the arms while riding or idling is a starter. While idling with one leg extended forward, one or more hoops can be added to the leg and spun. A large hula hoop (these can be purchased from toy and department stores) can be used around the waist (Fig. 7-9). Learn to work hula hoop around waist before attempting this stunt on a unicycle. The hula hooping about the waist can be done while riding forward, backwards, or idling.

Picking Up Objects from Floor

There are several ways to start. One way is to use an empty quart plastic bottle. This should be easy, since it stands well above the ground. Next place the bottle on its side. This makes it more difficult. A large ball is another way to begin. Then work down to smaller ones. A third way is to place a small object, such as a ball, on a box or other platform. Then gradually reduce the height until the small object can be picked up from the ground.

In order to reach the ground with your hand, it is necessary to lean well forward by bending at the waist without losing your balance. Also, it is generally easier to reach the ground from a unicycle with a small wheel than from one with a large wheel.

If the rider can reach down and touch the ground while riding the unicycle, there should be no problem in picking up small objects from the ground. Flexibility, of course, plays an important role in the ability to do this skill. Some people have a great deal of natural flexibility, others have a lesser amount. Flexibility exercises can be done to increase flexibility. It also helps to have both knees bent when reaching down from the unicycle.

Figure 7-10 shows picking up a ball and a juggling club. These skills are useful for juggling on a unicycle, as detailed below in this chapter.

Flying a Kite

A novelty idea is to fly a kite from a unicycle, as shown in Figure 7-11. This requires not only kite-flying skill, but also good control on the unicycle.

Fig. 7-9. Unicycling while working hula hoop about waist.

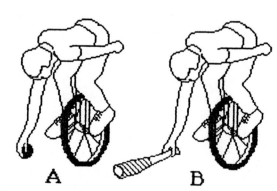

Fig. 7-10. Picking objects up from floor: (A) Ball; (B) Juggling club.

Fig. 7-11. Flying a kite from a unicycle.

Riding Around Plastic Bottles and Other Objects

Plastic bottles or other objects can be set up on the riding surface for riding around or through a course (Fig. 7-12). Plastic bottles and other objects can also be used for games and races, as detailed in Chapter 11.

Balancing, Spinning, and Juggling

An easy stunt to start with is to balance a broomstick or other suitable pole in the palm of the hand while riding a unicycle (Fig. 7-13). Next try balancing it on one finger. Slightly more difficult is to balance the broom while idling on the unicycle, rather than riding forward. Objects can also be balanced on the forehead or, while idling with one foot, on the foot or toe. A wood pole with rubber chair-leg caps on the ends is ideal for this.

Another possibility is spinning a disk or plate on the end of a pointed stick (Fig. 7-14). Ones that are easy to work can be purchased at toy and novelty stores.

A yo-yo can be used while riding the unicycle (Fig. 7-15). Various yo-yo skills, such as walking the dog or rocking the baby in the cradle, can be performed. In a similar manner, diabolo (a spinning top used on a string attached to two sticks)

Fig. 7-12. Riding around plastic bottle.

Fig. 7-13. Balancing pole in palm of hand.

Fig. 7-14. Spinning plate on end of stick.

skills can be performed while riding a unicycle (Fig. 7-16). Performing with devil sticks (Fig. 7-17) is another possibility. Still another idea is spinning an AstroWheel on a tether line (Fig. 7-18).

Balls (Fig. 7-19), rings (Fig. 7-20), clubs (Fig. 7-21), or other objects can be juggled while riding the unicycle. It is usually easiest to juggle while riding forward. Generally more difficult is to juggle while idling, riding backwards, one-foot riding, and so on. It makes things easier if you can pick up dropped objects from the floor without dismounting from

Fig. 7-15. Using a yo-yo.

Fig. 7-17. Performing with devil sticks.

Fig. 7-18. Oak View Unicyclist Mike Hinton spinning Astrowheel on a tether line (photo courtesy Jim Moyer).

Fig. 7-16. Using a diabolo.

Fig. 7-19. Juggling three balls.

Fig. 7-20. Juggling three rings.

the unicycle. Juggling three balls is generally easier than three clubs. Cascading (criss-crossing) is generally easier than showering (juggling in a circle). Incidentally, juggling clubs should be light in weight. Don't, for example, try to juggle wooden Indian clubs. Sources for obtaining juggling clubs and other related equipment are included in the Appendix.

Hundreds of juggling skills are possible while riding a unicycle.

Jumping Rope

Rope jumping (Fig. 7-22) while on a unicycle is easiest if pedal straps and/or waist straps are used, but it is also possible without these straps. Bicycle pedal straps will usually work. These should be adjusted to hold the feet to the pedals, but not so tight that you can't get your feet free for dismounting. Elastic cords can be used for waist straps. These can attach to the unicycle saddle and the rider's waist. Hooks can be used so that the straps can be released quickly. Use a jumping rope with swivel handles. The rope itself should be heavy enough to give the necessary weight for easy spinning.

The rope can be spun forward or backwards. This skill involves being able to bounce on the unicycle wheel like a pogo stick (see Chapter 6) and jump rope at the same time. It should be noted that this stunt can be somewhat destructive to unicycle wheels.

Fig. 7-21. Juggling three clubs.

Fig. 7-22. Jumping rope while bouncing on a unicycle.

Riding on Ramps

Unicycles can be ridden on a variety of ramps, such as shown in Figure 7-23. Ramps can be constructed to give various degrees of riding difficulty.

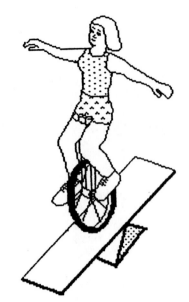

Fig. 7-24. Riding over teeter-board.

Fig. 7-23. Riding on ramp.

Riding Over Teeter-Board

Riding a unicycle over a specially constructed teeter-board (Fig. 7-24) is a popular skill. One end of the teeter-board can be weighted so that it stays down. The unicyclist then rides the unicycle onto that end of the teeter-board and continues to the center of the board until the board pivots to the other end. The unicyclist then rides the unicycle on off the other end. Other possibilities include riding over the teeter-board backwards and starting forward and then making 360 degree spin to backward riding.

Teeter-boards can be constructed of various heights, lengths, and widths to give various degrees of riding difficulty.

Riding Stairs

Riding down stairs (Fig. 7-25) is another popular skill. However, keep in mind that this can be somewhat destructive to the unicycle wheel. One method of going down stairs is to ride off the edge of the stairs straight forward.

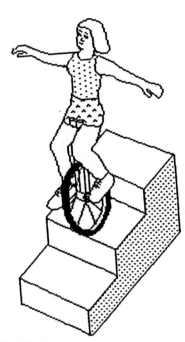

Fig. 7-25. Riding down stairs.

More difficult is to bounce off to the step below. Foot and/or waist straps can be helpful here.

More advanced is to ride or bounce down the stairs backwards. The bouncing can also be done at an angle to the edge of the stairs.

It is also possible to ride and bounce up stairs of limited height.

Riding on Tables and Platforms

Unicycles can be ridden on top of small tables and platforms (Fig. 7-26). The riding is usually idling. Easiest is with both feet, but it can also be with one foot. Use a sturdy table or platform. Begin by using a piece of plywood the same size as the top of the table or platform on the riding surface. Practice mounting and idling on the wood until you are certain that there is no danger of you going off the edges.

Riding on tables or platforms can be combined with juggling, balancing, and spinning skills to add to the difficulty and artistic effect.

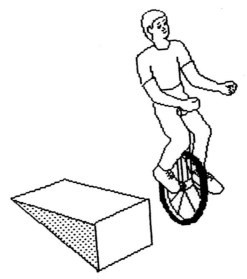

Fig. 7-27. Jumping from ramp.

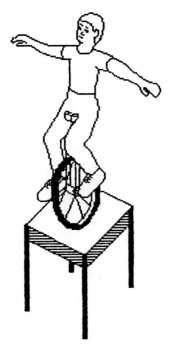

Fig. 7-26. Riding unicycle on top of table.

Ramp Jumping

Ramp jumping is a popular skill for shows and demonstrations. One possibility is to ride forward and over ramp to jump to riding surface (Fig. 7-27). Another method is to have a second ramp for landing. The jumping can also be over people or various objects, but be extremely careful here. Jumping even from low heights and short distances can be damaging to unicycle wheels. In any case, start with low ramps and slow speeds and work up gradually to higher ramps and faster approaches.

Riding Unicycle on Tightwire

Riding unicycles on tightwires is a subject in itself. Basically, the unicycle is ridden on the wire without a tire so that the rim fits over the wire (Fig. 7-28). The tightwire needs to be properly designed and set up. For learning, the wire should be low to the ground. A balancing pole makes this skill much easier. Extremely difficult is riding without a balance pole.

The riding can be forward, backward, or idling with both feet pedaling or one-foot pedaling. For even greater difficulty, try riding a unicycle on a tightwire while juggling or doing other related skills.

Other Skills

I have tried to include what I consider to be some of the main props that can be used with solo artistic riding, but there are actually hundreds of other possibilities. Unicyclists seem to be constantly coming up with new props that can be used for artistic unicycling. There are also a number of props that can be used for comedy and clowning (see Chapter 12).

A number of people have mentioned props that can be used for unicycling that I failed to include in the original **The Unicycle Book.** I have tried to include these here. One that several people singled out was one-foot idling on a unicycle while kicking up saucers, cups, and spoons and catching and balancing

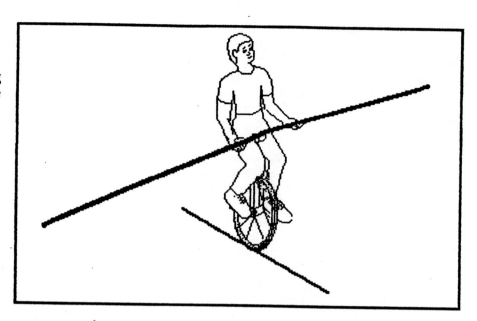

Fig. 7-28. Riding unicycle on tightwire with balancing pole.

them on top of the head. There are some amazing professionals who actually do this incredible skill. I include this now.

There are also a number of props that can be used for setting records or performing unusual feats (see Chapter 15).

Combinations and Routines

The solo artistic skills with props described above can be put together in hundreds of combinations and routines. In many cases, you will need to spend additional time learning juggling, balancing, spinning, tightwire, or other skills in addition to unicycling. Still more time is required to put these skills together. Many people do just this. For example, there are many unicyclists who also juggle, and there are many jugglers who also unicycle, and many of these people blend the two activities together.

Chapter 8

PARTNER AND GROUP ARTISTIC RIDING ON STANDARD UNICYCLES

Partner and group riding adds to the fun and challenge of unicycling. Partner or pairs unicycling requires two performers with at least one and most often both riding standard unicycles. Group riding involves three or more performers with at least one and often all riding standard unicycles. Partner and group riding can also be done on giraffe and other types of unicycles, including mixing of standard and giraffe models (see Chapter 9).

Some stunts are included where one or only part of the riders are riding the unicycles, with the other person or persons performing some other role, such as sitting on the shoulders of the person riding the unicycle. The use of various props is also included in this chapter. As a minimum starting level for learning partner and group riding skills, all riders should be able to do the basic unicycling skills described in Chapter 4. More advanced partner and group riding requires some of the solo artistic riding skills detailed in Chapter 6 and some stunts with props require techniques covered in Chapter 7.

Fig. 8-1. Riders facing same direction with locked arms.

PARTNER OR PAIRS RIDING

Performing with a partner on standard unicycles is also called "pairs." The riders can be of the same or different sex.

Basic Positions

A basic contact position for partner riding is with the riders facing the same direction with locked arms (Fig. 8-1). This skill was introduced in Chapter 4.

A second basic contact position is with the riders facing the same direction holding hands (Fig. 8-2). The contact arms

Fig. 8-2. Riders facing same direction holding hands.

are usually extended; the other arms can be extended outward or in any other desired positions. This skill was introduced in Chapter 4.

A third basic contact position is with the riders facing in opposite directions with locked arms (Fig. 8-3).

A fourth basic contact position is with the riders facing in opposite directions holding hands (Fig. 8-4).

These four basic contact positions make hundreds of riding patterns and combinations possible. They are used not only for partner or pairs riding, but also for group skills, as detailed later in this chapter.

Riding Forward Facing Same Direction

This skill can be done with locked arms (Fig. 8-5) and holding hands (Fig. 8-6). The basic techniques for doing these skills were introduced in Chapter 4. These should now be refined and thoroughly mastered before going on to more difficult skills.

The skill can be done with locked arms by riding forward side-by-side with partner and then locking arms (Fig. 8-5). Continue riding forward in a straight line with the unicycle wheels parallel to each other. Maintain good riding posture. The riders can separate on signal and ride solo away from each other.

The skill can be done holding hands by riding forward side-by-side with your partner and then joining hands (Fig. 8-6). Continue riding forward in a straight line with the unicycle wheels parallel to each other. Maintain good riding posture. The riders can separate on signal and ride solo away from each other.

When riding forward with partner, try to maintain the same riding speed. However, at this stage, it isn't necessary to have the pedal actions synchronized or in some planned phase to each other, although this is a possibility for more advanced work later.

Fig. 8-3. Riders facing opposite directions with locked arms.

Fig. 8-4. Riders facing opposite directions holding hands.

Fig. 8-5. Riding forward with locked arms.

90

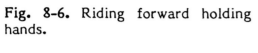

Fig. 8-6. Riding forward holding hands.

Making Turns While Riding Forward Facing Same Direction

Ride forward with locked arms and make turns. Try large radius turns first and work down to smaller ones. Learn to make turns both to the left and right. One rider can tell the other rider the direction of the turns. Later, for more advanced riding or competition, you will probably want to use pre-arranged sequences or "silent" signals.

Next, ride forward in same direction holding hands. Try large radius turns first and work down to smaller ones. Learn to make turns both to the left and right. One rider can tell the other rider the direction of the turn to be made.

Riding in Circle Facing Opposite Directions

The riders face in opposite directions and ride forward in a circle. To do this with locked arms (Fig. 8-7), the riders come together from opposite directions riding forward and join arms. They then circle, each rider riding forward and following the same circle route on the opposite side of the circle. Finish by releasing arms and each rider going forward in opposite directions.

To ride in circle facing opposite directions holding hands (Fig. 8-8), the riders come together from opposite

directions riding forward and join hands (Fig. 8-9). They then circle, each rider riding forward and following the same circle route on the opposite side of the circle. The riders should maintain outward pressure on the hand holding. Finish by releasing hands and each unicyclist riding forward in opposite directions. An impressive ending for advanced riders is to release hands while doing fast circles and then ride rapidly away as though spun apart.

Fig. 8-7. Riding in circle facing opposite directions with locked arms.

91

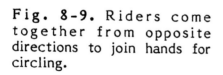

Fig. 8-8. Riding in circle facing opposite directions holding hands.

Circles and Patterns Riding Forward Facing Same Direction

A variety of circles and patterns can be made while riding forward facing the same direction with locked arms and holding hands, including continuous circles, zigzag patterns, and figure-eights. There are hundreds of other possible patterns. The outside rider on a turn must go faster than the inside rider.

Riding Backwards Facing Same Direction

This skill can be done with locked arms (Fig. 8-10) and holding hands (Fig. 8-11). To do this with locked arms, the riders ride forward with locked arms and come to a stop. They then reverse pedaling to backward riding. The riders often change again to forward riding before separating.

To do backward riding facing the same direction holding hands, the riders ride forward holding hands and come to a stop. They then reverse pedaling to backward riding. The riders often change again to forward riding before separating.

More difficult is to begin with both riders going backwards solo before joining hands.

Mounting Facing Same Direction

Once solo mounting can be done by both riders in the open, mounting with locked arms and holding hands should be easy. Position the unicycles the correct

Fig. 8-9. Riders come together from opposite directions to join hands for circling.

Fig. 8-10. Riding backwards facing same direction with locked arms.

distance apart for mounting with locked arms or holding hands. Riders position unicycles and themselves as for solo mounting. Riders then lock arms or join hands and mount simultaneously on signal.

Dismounting Facing Same Direction

Once solo dismounting to the rear can be done by the riders, this skill can be attempted simultaneously with a partner with locked arms and holding hands. First try it from forward riding with locked arms. Riders come to stop and each rider grasps front of unicycle saddle with free hand. Then dismount to rear maintaining locked arms.

Next try dismounting to rear holding hands, which should not be much more difficult.

Dismounting forward can be done from both locked arms and holding hands in a similar manner. More difficult mounts, such as one-foot, mounting with unicycle rearward, and jump mounts, can be attempted by advanced riders.

Circles and Patterns Holding Hands Facing Same Direction Riding Backwards

A variety of circles and patterns can be made while riding backwards facing the same direction with locked arms and holding hands, including continuous circles, zigzag patterns, and figure-eights. There are hundreds of other possible patterns.

Riding Backwards in Circle Facing Opposite Directions

The riders face in opposite directions and ride backwards in a circle. To do this with locked arms (Fig. 8-12), the riders can begin riding circle forward facing opposite directions with locked arms. On

Fig. 8-11. Riding backwards facing same direction holding hands.

signal, come to stop and reverse pedaling to backward riding. Switch can be made again to forward riding on signal.

To ride backwards in circle facing opposite directions holding hands (Fig. 8-13), the riders can begin riding circle forward facing opposite directions holding hands. On signal, come to stop and reverse pedaling to backward riding. Switch can be made again to forward riding on signal.

Fig. 8-12. Riding backwards in circle facing opposite directions with locked arms.

Fig. 8-13. Riding backwards in circle facing opposite directions holding hands.

Other Skills Facing Same Direction

A variety of other stunts can be performed with riders facing same direction both with locked arms and holding hands, including one-foot riding forward, one-foot riding backwards, and regular and one-foot idling. An advanced skill is wheel-walking from saddle.

Other Skills Facing Opposite Directions

A variety of other stunts can be performed with riders facing opposite directions both with locked arms and holding hands, including one rider going forward and the other backward in a straight path (Fig. 8-14 and Fig. 8-15), one rider going forward and the other backwards in circles and patterns, idling, one-foot riding forward in circle, one-foot riding backwards in circle, and various mounts and dismonts.

Fig. 8-14. Facing opposite directions with locked arms with one person riding forward and the other backwards.

Combinations and Switching Patterns

A variety of combination and switching patterns with locked arms and/or holding hands with and without releases can be performed.

One possibility is for both riders to begin holding hands riding forward in the same direction. One rider then makes a pivoting half turn as hands are released

Fig. 8-15. Facing opposite directions holding hands with one person riding forward and the other backwards.

and then regrasped with riders facing opposite directions. One rider can then ride backwards and the other forward or both riders can move forward in a circle pattern. By pivoting hands overhead, half turns can be made without releasing hands, similar to square dancing. Going into and out of partner skills from solo movements adds to the possibilities.

Partner Acrobatics on One Unicycle

A variety of acrobatic stunts can be performed on one unicycle, such as riding unicycle with person sitting on shoulders (Fig. 8-16), standing on shoulders (Fig. 8-17), or in some other balancing position. These skills are actually a combination of unicycling and acrobatics (a reference source is my **Acrobatics Book**, published by Anderson World Publications).

Partner Skills with Props

Many props can be used for partner or pairs artistic riding. Passing juggling clubs from person to person while mounted on unicycles is an example. By using an exercise wheel, one person can be pushed like a wheelbarrow by a person on a unicycle (Fig. 8-18). Partners can also ride patterns on unicycles over ramps and teeterboards. Or have one person on

a unicycle and partner on stilts or a pogo stick or some other device.

Fig. 8-16. Riding unicycle with partner sitting on shoulders.

Fig. 8-17. Riding unicycle with partner standing on shoulders.

stunts can be performed with more people than there are unicycles. Group riding can also be done with some riders on standard unicycles and others on giraffe unicycles, as detailed in Chapter 9.

All Riders on Standard Unicycles

By having three or more riders on standard unicycles, artistic riding can be done in a manner similar to partner or pairs riding, except with added possibilities by having additional riders. For example, a group of riders can perform skills with locked arms (Fig. 8-19) or holding hands (Fig. 8-20). The possibilities for doing drills and patterns are almost unlimited. Group riding is ideal for parades and demonstrations, as detailed in later chapters. Spectacular patterns, like a square dance on wheels, are possible.

Fig. 8-18. Scott Dineen, Oak View Unicyclist, pushes Jason Dempsey on an exercise wheel (photo courtesy Jim Moyer).

Group Acrobatics

A variety of acrobatics can be done with three or more performers, at least one of whom is on a standard unicycle. A three-high sitting on shoulders with the bottom person riding a unicycle is shown in Figure 8-21. A formation with two riders holding hands with partners on shoulders also holding hands is shown in Figure 8-22.

GROUP RIDING

For our purposes here, group riding will be considered three or more performers, with at least one person on a standard unicycle. Acrobatic balancing

Fig. 8-19. Four riders with locked arms.

Fig. 8-20. Four riders holding hands.

Fig. 8-21. Joel Dempsey rides standard unicycle with Karin and Alicia Gildea on his shoulders (photo courtesy Jim Moyer).

Fig. 8-22. Formation with Glen Granberry and Cathy Fox on unicycles and Dale Granberry and Rachel Ojala on shoulders (photo courtesy Seth Granberry, Jr., Mobile Unicycle Club).

Group Skills with Props

Many different props can be used effectively for group artistic riding. Possibilities include juggling, poles and platforms carried by riders on unicycles, ramps (Fig. 8-23), stilts (Fig. 8-24), and parachutes (Fig. 8-25).

Fig. 8-24. Oak View Unicyclists demonstrate the use of stilts with standard unicycles (photo courtesy Jim Moyer).

Fig. 8-23. Unicyclists of the Oak View Elementary School Exhibitional Activities Club perform on four-way ramp (photo courtesy Jim Moyer).

Fig. 8-25. Oak View Unicyclists demonstrate use of parachute for riding formations (photo courtesy Jim Moyer).

Chapter 9

GIRAFFE UNICYCLING

Giraffe unicycling (Fig. 9-1) is an exciting step upward from standard unicycles. This chapter covers learning to ride and doing artistic skills on giraffe unicycles that are from about five to six feet tall (measured from ground to top of saddle when unicycle is upright). Most of the presently manufactured giraffe unicycles are in this size range (see Chapter 3). You can also learn on a giraffe unicycle that is shorter than this, but a taller model is not recommended until you have mastered at least the basic riding skills on a giraffe unicycle under six feet tall. I recommend a 20-inch wheel, but other wheel sizes from 16-inches to 26 inches can also be used.

It is important that the giraffe unicycle be well constructed. A strong chain should be used and the chain should be in good condition. A problem area on some manufactured giraffe unicycles is sprockets that are fastened with threaded-on nuts, which tend to slip. If your unicycle has this arrangement, it generally works best to ride the unicycle with the sprocket on the left side (opposite to that of a bicycle). In this way the greatest stress, which usually occurs during mounting, will tighten rather than loosen the sprocket. While riding forward the strain is generally not enough to loosen the sprocket. A sprocket that fits in grooves on the hub and is held in place with a snap-ring will not have this slipping problem.

Before attempting to ride a giraffe unicycle, you should first master, as a minimum, the elementary riding skills on a standard unicycle, as detailed in Chapter 6. At the very least, you should be to the point where falling is no longer a problem

Fig. 9-1. The author riding a giraffe unicycle.

on the standard unicycle.

Many skills are essentially the same on a giraffe unicycle as on a standard unicycle, except that you are further from the ground and there will probably be a greater fear factor. Some skills that can be done on a standard unicycle are not possible on the giraffe unicycle, such as reaching down and touching the ground or putting a foot on the ground to do foot-pivoting circles. Other stunts, such as mounting, are performed in a different manner. There are also skills that are unique to giraffe unicycling.

BASIC RIDING TECHNIQUES

This section covers the basic techniques for learning to ride a giraffe unicycle. If you have mastered at least the elementary skills on a standard unicycle covered in Chapter 6, you should be able to learn basic riding on a giraffe unicycle in a short period of time.

Adjusting the Unicycle

Before actually starting, it's important to have the unicycle properly adjusted. The saddle height is correct when, mounted on the unicycle, your leg is almost extended to reach the pedal in the down position (lowest point in relation to the ground). This should be possible, however, without having to lean the body to that side in order to keep the ball of the foot flat on the pedal. This is the same as for a standard unicycle unicycle, except it's more difficult to try out the fit. An easy way to adjust the giraffe is to use the adjustment on your standard unicycle as a pattern.

The saddle height adjustment on most giraffe unicycles is made by loosening the saddle-post clamp, sliding the post up or down in the fork stem until the saddle is the desired height, and then retightening the clamp. The saddle angle should be adjusted to the same angle as you use on your standard unicycle. Many advanced riders prefer to have the front of the saddle about three inches higher than the rear of the saddle.

Training Aids

The basic training aids that you will need are a 4 x 4 inch block of wood a couple of feet long to use as a stop-block or a curb about six to eight inches high that is located adjacent to a suitable riding surface, two partners to assist you in learning (it is not necessary that they know how to ride unicycles), and a ladder that is securely fixed in place to a wall or other suitable support. The ladder should be at least eight feet tall to allow mounting the giraffe unicycle and give you something to hold onto while mounting.

A Place to Learn

Learn on a hard smooth surface, such as asphalt, concrete, or a wooden floor. This can be indoors or outdoors. In either case, you will need a large open space.

After learning to ride, it will no longer be necessary to be so selective as to where the unicycle is ridden.

Safety and Protection of Unicycle

Learn one step at a time. Master each step before going on to the next one. It is extremely important to learn the correct techniques right from the start.

Don't forget about the "safety" of the unicycle. If you have learned to catch a standard unicycle by the saddle when dismounting, it shouldn't be much of a problem to do the same thing with the giraffe unicycle. Remember, the giraffe unicycle has further to fall, so dropping it can be even more damaging than is the case with a standard unicycle.

Learning to Solo

Perhaps the greatest problem that the rider faces in moving up from a standard unicycle to a giraffe unicycle is "getting aboard." This is often much more of a challenge than riding the giraffe unicycle, assuming of course that the person can already ride a standard unicycle.

Opinions vary as to what method to use for mounting the giraffe unicycle on the first attempts. One method is to use a stop-block or curb and two helpers (Fig. 9-2). Another method is to use a ladder, along with a stop-block and at least one helper. A third method is to use the ladder alone, without stop-block or helper, but I don't recommend this until riding proficiency is attained. The first method with a stop-block or curb and two

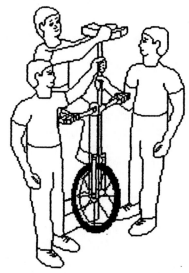

Fig. 9-2. Mounting with stop-block and two helpers.

helpers has the advantage of teaching the basics for later mounting solo in the open. To mount with the assistance of the two helpers, position the unicycle with the wheel against the stop-block or curb with one pedal down and back (Fig. 9-3). The helpers continue to hold the unicycle as shown in Figure 9-2 while the rider mounts the unicycle following the steps shown in Figure 9-3.

In any case, the first step is to mount

the giraffe unicycle. Once mounted, you can use the assistance of the two helpers with hand holding on the first attempts at riding forward. Practice riding forward with light hand holding. Use good riding posture, which should be automatic if you have mastered this on the standard unicycle.

Next, practice riding forward with one helper with light hand pressure. When you can do this with control and confidence, you are ready to solo (Fig. 9-4).

Figure 9-5 shows the basic dismount to the rear of the giraffe unicycle. On the first attempts, you can use two helpers to assist you. When you are ready to dismount, release one hand from a helper and grasp end of the saddle in front of you. Dismount to the rear by stepping the foot from the upper-positioned pedal down to the ground to the rear of the unicycle. Continue practice until you can dismount solo, as shown in Figure 9-5).

Next, practice riding forward longer distances until you can ride for at least 100 yards. Whenever you want to dismount, dismount to the rear of the unicycle and be sure to catch the unicycle.

The next step is to try turning, which

Fig. 9-3. Mounting giraffe unicycle with stop-block or curb: (A) Starting position; (B) Step from tire to pedal; (C) Mount over saddle; (D) Ready to ride forward.

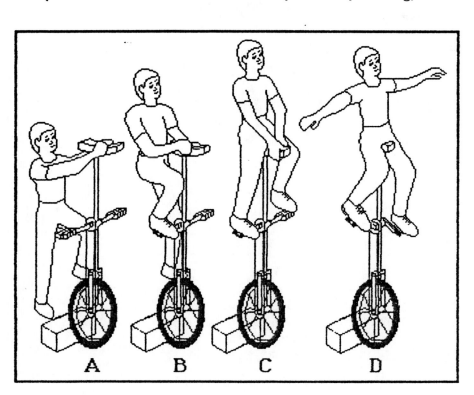

A   B   C   D

Fig. 9-4. Basic forward riding.

A B C

Fig. 9-5. Dismounting rearward: (A) Stop with one pedal in down position and grasp front of saddle; (B) Step foot off upper pedal; (C) Place foot on riding surface.

should not present any problems. However, you may want to use one helper on the first attempts. Have the helper walk along beside you with light hand pressure. Learn to make turns both to the right and to the left.

Once you have mastered the above skills, you will probably want to go on to artistic riding, as detailed below.

SOLO ARTISTIC RIDING WITHOUT PROPS

Some of the solo artistic riding skills on a giraffe unicycle are the same as on a standard unicycle; others must be done in a different manner or are unique to giraffe unicycles.

Standard Unicycle Skills on Giraffe Unicycle

It is extremely important to learn the skills on a standard unicycle before attempting them on a giraffe unicycle. Many of the skills detailed in Chapter 6 for standard unicycles can also be done on giraffe unicycles, including circles and patterns while riding forward, riding backwards (Fig. 9-6), circles and patterns riding backwards, idling, action-reaction twisting, one-foot riding forward, backwards, and idling (Fig. 9-7), bouncing, riding small circles around wheel forward and backwards, spinning, riding off saddle with saddle forward, rearward, and to one side, riding with chest on saddle, and possibly coasting. The techniques for these stunts are basically the same as on a standard unicycle, except that you are

Fig. 9-6. Riding backwards.

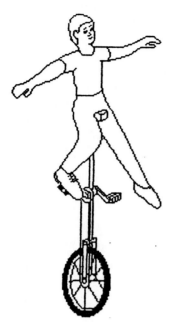

Fig. 9-7. Riding with one foot.

further from the ground and they may seem more difficult.

Strive to do all the skills on the giraffe unicycle with control and good riding posture. The same basic progression that was used for learning on the standard unicycle can be followed on the giraffe unicycle.

Dismounting

The most important dismount is rearward, as detailed above in this chapter and shown in Figure 9-5. The dismounting should be done with control. When done properly from a five- or six-foot giraffe unicycle, the distance to step down to the ground is not great, and many riders can reach the first foot to the ground with the other foot still on the down-positioned pedal.

Dismounting is a method for getting off the unicycle in graceful style. Practice until you can make it look like a skill rather than "falling off the unicycle." There's a big difference.

A second main method for dismounting from a giraffe unicycle is forward, similar to dismounting forward from a standard unicycle except that it is much further down and difficult to do gracefully.

Mounting in Open

Mounting solo in the open is shown in Figure 9-8. Before attempting this skill,

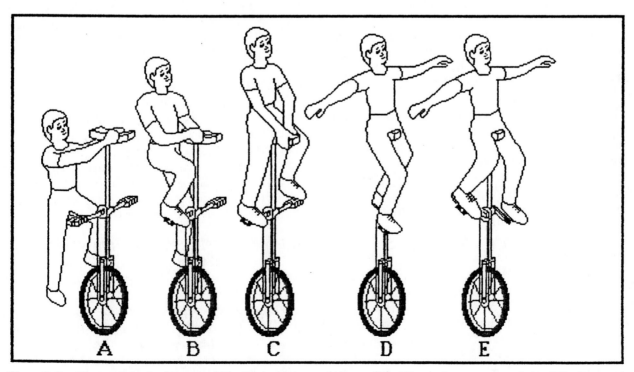

Fig. 9-8. Mounting in open: (A) Starting position; (B) First foot to pedal; (C) Second foot to pedal; (D) Backward pedal to horizontal position; (E) Forward pedal action.

however, it is important to first learn to mount with the aid of a stop-block or curb, as shown in Figure 9-3.

Begin by mounting with the stop-block or curb and two helpers, as detailed above in this chapter. The stop-block or curb is used to prevent the wheel from rolling backwards. To mount, position the unicycle and hold the saddle as shown in Figure 9-3. Place one foot on the tire at the wheel-well. Lean the unicycle slightly forward. Bring the foot from the ground and step up to the pedal that is down and back. At the same time, quickly straddle over the saddle and bring the foot from the tire to the pedal that is upward and forward. Ride forward away from stop-block.

This, of course, is quite difficult. For most riders, it will take many trials to learn this skill. Consistency requires even more practice. Continue practice until you can do this skill with one helper and finally solo.

The next step is to mount in the open without a stop-block or curb (Fig. 9-8). One method is to begin with one or two helpers. Another method is to try the skill alone on soft grass. While it is generally more difficult to ride a unicycle on grass than on a hard riding surface, the grass works well for learning this particular skill.

In any case, the foot that is placed on the wheel-well stops the wheel from rolling at first. When the foot is brought from the ground to the pedal that is down and back, this pedal is used to control the wheel. I like to continue the backward pedal rotation until the pedals are in a horizontal position, but some riders prefer to immediately start a forward pedal action when the foot that moves from the wheel to the upper pedal contacts the pedal. It is perhaps best to learn both actions so that you can do whatever is required to bring the unicycle into balance.

It generally takes many trials before this skill can be done. It is usually a happy day in the life of a unicyclist when he or she first successfully mounts a giraffe unicycle in the open solo without the use of a stop-block or curb. It then usually takes many more practice attempts before the skill can be done

consistently. Advanced riders can often do this skill many times in a row without a miss (see Chapter 15 for records on this and other skills).

Extremely important to success in mounting in the open is to learn to control the pedal action, and thus the unicycle wheel, as soon as the first foot reaches the pedal. Advanced riders frequently have good control of the pedal action well before they have mounted the saddle.

While the usual procedure for mounting a five- to six-foot giraffe unicycle is to use the tire at the wheel-well as a step, some riders with long legs have managed to mount giraffe unicycles this tall by placing first foot directly from ground to pedal, eliminating the tire step entirely. On shorter giraffe unicycles, this becomes practical for more riders, as detailed later in this chapter.

Wheel-Walking Skills

A number of wheel-walking skills are possible on a giraffe unicycle. This is usually not possible from the saddle like on a standard unicycle, but can be done off the saddle with arm support on the saddle and/or frame bar below the saddle from the side or with the saddle forward or rearward. These skills tend to be somewhat awkward on the giraffe unicycle, however, as the chain and turning pedals get in the way.

Combinations and Routines

Solo riding skills on giraffe unicycles can be combined to form sequences and routines for demonstrations, acts, competition, and so on (Fig. 9-9). Once you have learned a few skills, you can start putting them together in combinations in the same manner as was done on a standard unicycle.

SOLO ARTISTIC SKILLS WITH PROPS

Many different props, including handlebar units, juggling, balancing and spinning equipment, ramps, teeter-boards, and jumping ropes, can be used with giraffe unicycles. The techniques for using these are essentially the same as on standard unicycles, with the added difficulty of being further from the ground.

artistic riding skills can be done on giraffe unicycles, including partner riding with locked arms (Fig. 9-10) and holding hands (Fig. 9-11) with both riders on

Fig. 9-9. Dale Granberry of the Mobile Unicycle Club performing routine on giraffe unicycle (photo cortesy Seth Granberry, Jr.).

In some cases you will also have the added difficulty of not being able to pick up things from the ground, such as when you drop a juggling ball or club. To get around this problem, you can have a partner on foot or a standard unicycle pick these up for you.

Using a handlebar unit can present special problems on the giraffe unicycle, since the handlebar unit is much taller. To use the handlebar unit, you can position the handlebar unit against something so that you can get it after you have mounted the giraffe unicycle or have someone ready to hand it to you. Mount the unicycle and then take the handlebar unit in your hands by the handlebar grips. Ride forward. One way to finish is to have a helper on the ground take the handlebar unit from you before you dismount. Another method is to return the unicycle to a support where you can leave it without the unit falling. You can also dismount from the unicycle and catch the handlebar unit. Still another method, not recommended, is to drop the handlebar unit before dismounting from the unicycle.

PARTNER AND GROUP ARTISTIC RIDING

A variety of partner and group

Fig. 9-10. Riding with partner with locked arms.

Fig. 9-11. Riding with partner holding hands.

105

giraffe unicycles, similar stunts with one rider on a giraffe unicycle and the other on a standard unicycle, group stunts with locked arms and holding hands, and partner and group juggling, balancing, spinning, acrobatics, and ramp and teeter-board riding.

Partner and group artistic riding skills can be combined to form many interesting routines.

SHORTER AND TALLER GIRAFFE UNICYCLES

Many of the skills detailed above in this chapter can also be done on shorter and taller giraffe unicycles. In most cases, the skills are easier on shorter giraffe unicycles and more difficult on taller models. The juggling of three fire batons atop a 10-foot giraffe unicycle is shown in Figure 9-12.

If you want to ride giraffe unicycles taller than about six feet, work up in small steps. Ladders or stands are usually used for mounting these cycles.

Fig. 9-12. Joel Dempsey juggles three fire batons on a 10-foot giraffe unicycle (photo courtesy Jim Moyer).

Chapter 10

RIDING NOVELTY UNICYCLES

Riding novelty unicycles is a fun part of unicycling. Some of these cycles allow artistic stunts; for others it's enough just to be able to ride them for a short distance. For our purposes here, we will consider any unicycles that do not fit into the classifications of basic standard unicycles or basic giraffe unicycles as being novelty unicycles. A variety of novelty unicycles are described in Chapter 1. Some novelty unicycles are not much more difficult to ride than an ordinary standard unicycle. Others are a little more difficult to ride, and a few are extremely difficult to master.

PONY-SADDLE UNICYCLES

Riding a pony-saddle (Fig. 10-1) or other animal unicycle is not much more difficult than riding an ordinary standard unicycle. A pony-saddle unicycle is a real attention-getter for parade riding.

MIDGET STANDARD UNICYCLES

The basic idea is to ride a standard type unicycle that is very small in comparison to the size of the rider (Fig. 10-2). Main difficulties are in keeping the saddle under you and pedaling with bent knees. Stunts can also be performed, such as riding locked arms with a person on a regular standard unicycle (Fig. 10-3) and riding midget unicycle with partner sitting on shoulders (Fig. 10-4).

BIG-WHEEL UNICYCLES

Riding a big-wheel unicycle (Fig. 10-5) is more difficult than riding a regular-size standard unicycle, at least until you get the knack of it. While you get a lot of track distance for each turn of the wheel, you don't have much leverage for braking. When you try to stop rapidly from riding, the pedals have the leverage to carry your feet around with them. However, once you get the knack of a big-wheel unicycle, they are ideal for riding long distances. They are also attention-getters for parade riding.

Mounting and dismounting from a big-wheel unicycle is similar to a regular standard unicycle, except that the hub is much further from the ground and you have less leverage on the pedals.

Fig. 10-1. Riding a pony-saddle unicycle is not much more difficult than riding an ordinary standard unicycle.

Fig. 10-2. Riding a midget unicycle.

Fig. 10-3. Riding midget unicycle locked arms with person on standard unicycle.

Fig. 10-4. Joel Dempsey carries Elizabeth Baumstark on his shoulders while he rides a midget unicycle (photo courtesy Jim Moyer).

hub to mount the unicycle. Dismounting is generally best done to the rear of the cycle in a manner similar to dismounting from a regular standard unicycle, except that it is further down to the ground.

FEET-WHEEL STANDARD UNICYCLES

A standard unicycle with a feet-wheel (Fig. 10-6) is not much more difficult to ride than a regular standard unicycle, provided that the feet form a wheel that rolls easily without flat spots. This type of unicycle is ideal for parade riding and clowning on one wheel.

Figure 10-7 shows a large diameter feet-wheel unicycle.

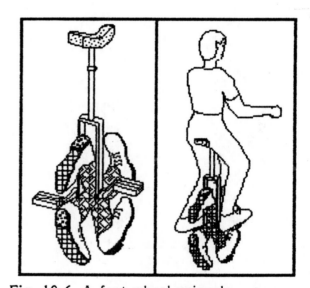

Fig. 10-6. A feet-wheel unicycle.

Fig. 10-5. Sem Abrahams riding a big-wheel unicycle (photo courtesy Unicycling Society of America, Inc.).

For mounting the big-wheel, it is helpful to grasp the tire forward of the wheel-well. Then pull yourself up over the

Fig. 10-7. Debbie Jones rides feet-wheel unicycle built by Tom Miller (photo courtesy Unicycling Society of America, Inc.).

STANDARD UNICYCLE WITH SADDLE AND HANDLEBARS

A standard unicycle constructed with both saddle and handlebars (Fig. 10-8) is only slightly more difficult to ride than a standard unicycle. Since it is somewhat risky to fall forward with the handlebars, the rider should be at a skill level where this will not happen before attempting to ride this cycle. This cycle gives the impression of a "one-wheel bicycle," making it ideal for parade riding.

STANDARD UNICYCLES WITH OFF-CENTERED, OUT-OF-ROUND, AND SQUARE WHEELS

The difficulty in riding these cycles (Fig. 10-9, Fig. 10-10, and Fig. 10-11) depends to a large extent on the amount that the wheels vary from centered and/or round. These unicycles are interesting novelties that are challenging to ride.

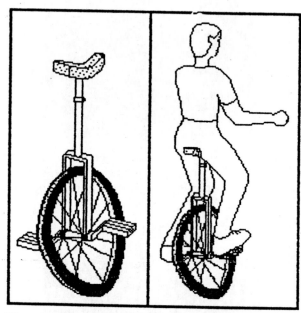

Fig. 10-10. Riding standard unicycle with out-of-round wheel.

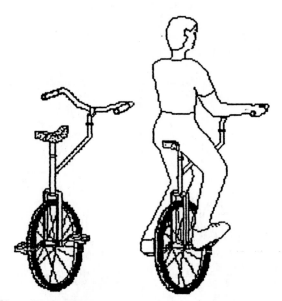

Fig. 10-8. Riding a standard unicycle with saddle and handlebars.

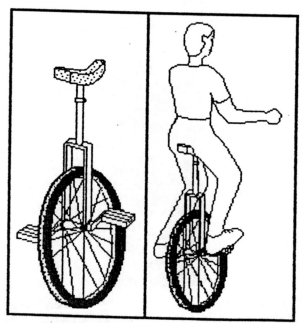

Fig. 10-9. Riding standard unicycle with off-centered wheel.

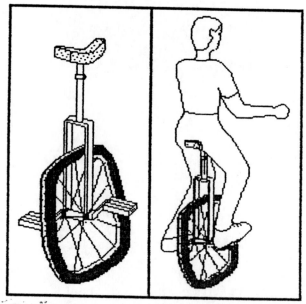

Fig. 10-11. Riding standard unicycle with square wheel.

STANDARD UNICYCLE WITH HANDLE-BARS INSTEAD OF SADDLE

A standard unicycle with handlebars instead of saddle can be ridden "standing" and sitting on the handlebars two different ways (Fig. 10-12).

All three ways are more difficult than riding an ordinary standard unicycle. Standing is similar to, but much easier than, riding an "ultimate" wheel, as detailed later in this chapter.

KANGAROO STANDARD UNICYCLE

A kangaroo unicycle has the crank arms adjacent to each other in the same direction from the axle (Fig. 10-13). The main difficulty is in getting the pedals over the top. A rhythmical action is used to accomplish this. The required action is difficult to learn, but once you get the knack of it, you will have a skill that not many others can duplicate, at least not on the first attempts.

This skill can be learned by first learning to ride a regular standard unicycle with one foot. Then ride the kangaroo unicycle with one foot and gradually work the other foot into the action.

Riding forward is easiest, but it is also possible to ride backwards and do idling action. Turns and patterns can also be ridden.

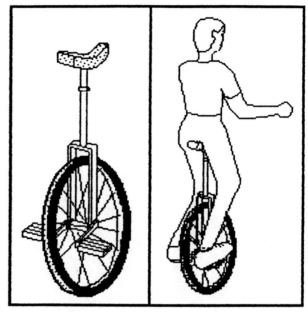

Fig. 10-13. Riding kangaroo standard unicycle.

STANDARD UNICYCLE POST INSTEAD OF SADDLE

A novelty variation of the standard unicycle is with a post instead of a saddle (Fig. 10-14). The cycle is ridden by holding the post in front of you or rearward. A variety of skills can be done, including riding forward and backwards, idling, and riding patterns.

Fig. 10-12. Riding standard unicycle that has handlebars instead of saddle: (A) The cycle; (B) Standing; (C) Sitting forward; (D) Sitting backward.

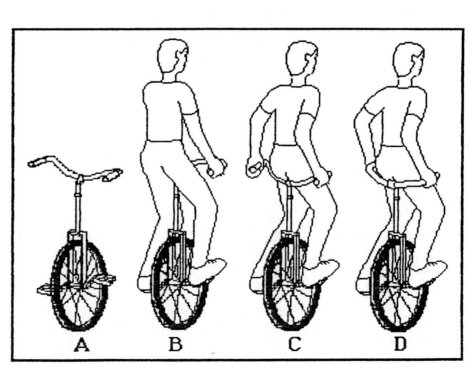

A   B   C   D

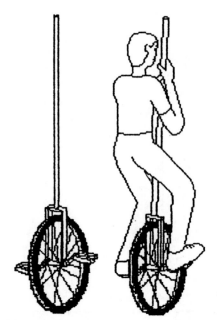

Fig. 10-14. Riding standard unicycle that has post instead of saddle.

STANDARD UNICYCLE WITH PARALLEL WHEELS

An interesting variation of the standard unicycle is a model with parallel wheels (Fig. 10-15). These are fairly easy to ride when the two wheels are connected together with a fixed axle.

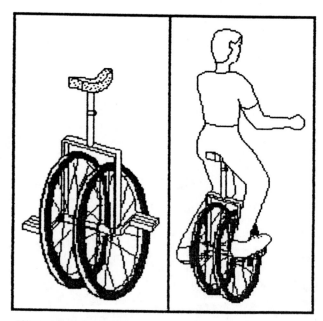

Fig. 10-15. Riding standard unicycle that has parallel wheels.

Making turns, however, is more difficult and limited than on a standard unicycle. Figure 10-16 shows one of these cycles being ridden.

More difficult to ride is a similar cycle with the wheels arranged so that they can turn independent of each other.

Fig. 10-16. Al Hemminger on a uni-bike (photo by John Foss and courtesy Unicycling Society of America, Inc.).

STANDARD UNICYCLE WITH CONNECTED HANDLEBAR UNIT AND BREAK-APART UNITS

A standard unicycle with connected handlebar unit (Fig. 10-17) and similar break-apart units can be ridden as bicycles with both wheels on the ground and as unicycles with the front wheel off the ground (Fig. 10-18).

Another type of break-apart bicycle is used by two riders (Fig. 10-19). The cycle breaks into two sections (various mechanisms are used to disconnect the sections) and the two performers ride off separately (Fig. 10-20). The cycle shown has a saddle mounted on the front section, but it is also possible to eliminate this and have the forward rider sitting on the handlebars.

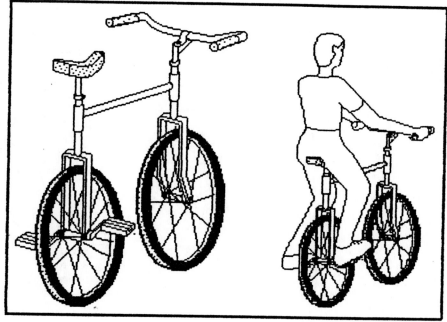

Fig. 10-17. Standard unicycle with connected handlebar unit.

Fig. 10-18. Standard unicycle with connected handlebar unit being ridden with front wheel off the riding surface.

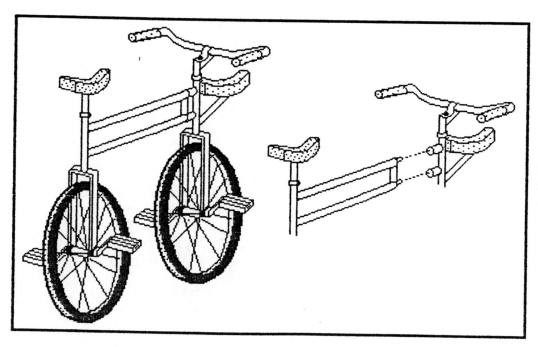

Fig. 10-19. Break-apart bicycle forms two unicycles.

Fig. 10-20. Cycle breaks into two parts that are ridden away separately.

TANDEM STANDARD UNICYCLE

This type of cycle is usually considered to be a "standard" unicycle built for two riders (Fig. 10-21), even though it also has characteristics of a giraffe unicycle. This type of cycle has been ridden in a straight line, but turns are extremely difficult, although perhaps possible.

ULTIMATE WHEELS

An ultimate wheel (Fig. 10-22) is very difficult to ride. A double-wheel ultimate cycle (Fig. 10-23) is somewhat easier and may provide a learning step toward mastering the regular ultimate wheel. Typical learning methods include practicing in a narrow hallway using the walls for hand supports and using two

Fig. 10-21. Tandem standard unicycle.

helpers, who walk along directly to your sides with hand holding.

Ultimate wheels with the pedals attached close to the centerline of the wheel are generally easiest to ride. More difficult is a wheel from a standard unicycle with the frame removed (Fig. 10-24).

Fig. 10-24. Beth Boswell successfully rides a regular unicycle wheel with the frame and seat removed (photo courtesy Jim Moyer).

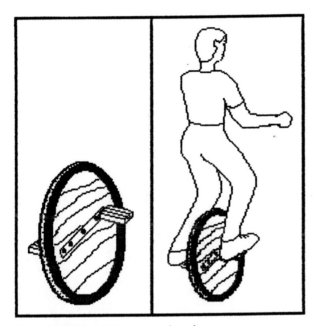

Fig. 10-22. Ultimate wheel.

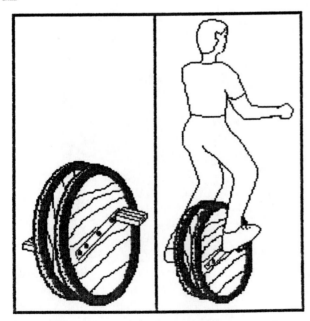

Fig. 10-23. Double-wheel ultimate cycle.

SMALL-WHEEL GIRAFFE UNICYCLES

Small-wheel giraffe unicycles (Fig. 10-25 and Fig. 10-26) are an interesting novelty variation of the basic giraffe unicycle. These unicycles often have a gear ratio (larger sprocket at crank than at wheel hub) to make the pedal action similar to unicycles with larger wheels. These cycles often become more difficult to ride as the wheels get smaller. Cycles with wheels four inches and less in diameter have been constructed and ridden.

MULTI-WHEEL GIRAFFE UNICYCLES WITH REGULAR PEDAL DIRECTIONS

Multi-wheel giraffe unicycles with or without supporting chain drives with three (Fig. 10-27), five (Fig. 10-28), or some other odd number of wheels (Fig. 10-29), or with an even number of wheels and a reversing gear at the cranks are

Fig. 10-25. Riding small-wheel giraffe unicycle.

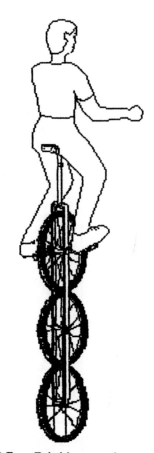

Fig. 10-27. Riding three-wheel multi-wheel unicycle.

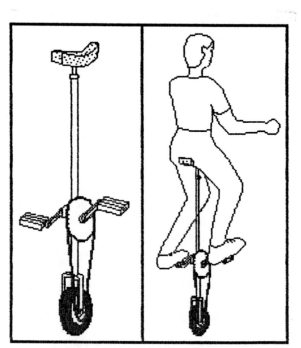

Fig. 10-26. Riding a tiny-wheel giraffe unicycle.

Fig. 10-28. John Foss riding a five-wheel multi-wheel giraffe unicycle (photo courtesy John Foss and the Unicycling Society of America, Inc.).

116

Fig. 10-29. Riding a variety of multi-wheels (photo courtesy Unicycling Society of America, Inc.).

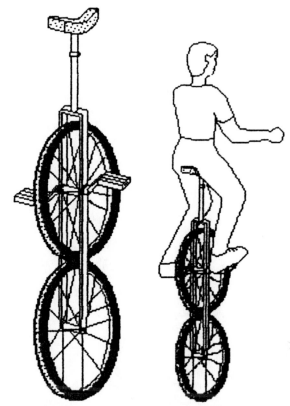

Fig. 10-31. Riding a multi-wheel giraffe unicycle with reversing pedal directions is difficult.

essentially the same as regular giraffe unicycles in the sense of the wheel with the cranks turning the same direction as the ground wheel. These cycles are generally similar to riding regular giraffe unicycles.

MULTI-WHEEL GIRAFFE UNICYCLES WITH REVERSING PEDAL DIRECTIONS

Multi-wheel giraffe unicycles with wheel drives with an even number of wheels (usually two, as shown in Figure 10-30 and Figure 10-31, but sometimes four or more) have a unique feature that makes them extremely difficult to ride--the ground wheel turns the opposite

direction from the pedal cranks. To ride such a cycle, you have to do everything in reverse of what your natural instincts tell you to do. Nevertheless, a number of advanced unicyclists have mastered these cycles. Those who can ride these cycles often say that it helps to concentrate the weight on the saddle rather than the pedals.

ZIGZAG GIRAFFE UNICYCLES

Zigzag giraffe unicycles are popular novelty cycles (Fig. 10-32). They are constructed in a variety of configurations. Riding a zigzag model is similar to riding a regular giraffe unicycle of the same ground to top of the saddle measurement, except that the unicycle frame on the zigzag model can be in the way and perhaps present an additional safety hazard for dismonting and falling. For this reason, only people who have thoroughly mastered regular giraffe unicycles should attempt zigzag models.

Fig. 10-30. Teresa Hemminger displays a two-wheeler (photo courtesy Unicycling Society of America, Inc.)

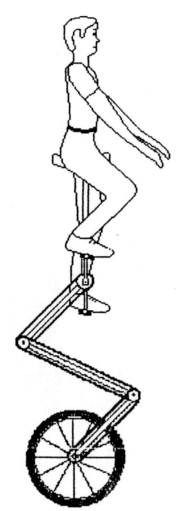

Fig. 10-32. Riding a zigzag giraffe unicycle.

TANDEM GIRAFFE UNICYCLES

Tandem giraffe unicycles, such as the design shown in Figure 10-33, have been successfully ridden. I've had no actual experience with these, but have been told that riding is easiest if the top person does the actual pedaling and keeping balance while the bottom person follows the pedal action with light pressure on the pedals.

Specially designed tandem artistic bicycles have also been ridden with the riders pedaling from the saddle on one wheel like a tandem giraffe unicycle.

ARTISTIC BICYCLES

Artistic bicycles can be ridden on one wheel like giraffe unicycles from the saddle (Fig. 10-34), fork-head tube, and from unicycle saddle mounted to fork

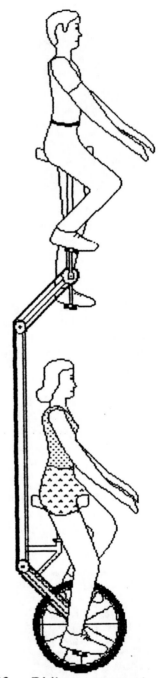

Fig. 10-33. Riding a tandem giraffe unicycle.

head tube (Fig. 10-35). I plan to cover artistic bicycling in a separate book that I'm presently researching and writing.

OTHER NOVELTY UNICYCLES

Other novelty unicycles, such as walking cycles, motor-driven one-wheel cycles, giraffe models that off-set to one side and giraffe unicycles that are ridden

Fig. 10-34. Riding an artistic bicycle on one wheel from saddle.

on tightwires, are detailed in later chapters. Two ideas for giraffe unicycles that I often hear proposed, but have not seen any working models actually constructed, are with gear ratios that can be changed while riding and with mechanisms that allow changing the height while riding. I have also seen unicycles "hidden" inside things, such as a golf bag, that are interesting novelty cycles.

Fig. 10-35. Mike Hinton rides his home-made artistic bicycle (photo courtesy Jim Moyer).

Chapter 11

GAMES AND RACES FOR FUN AND COMPETITION

Games and races are the logical outcome of more than one unicycle rider getting together. These activities are ideal for clubs and some of them are used for higher level competition, including national and international events.

GAMES

Unicycles give new dimensions to old games. Here are some popular choices.

Tag

Many variations of tag can be played while riding unicycles. The simplest is the "touch your're it" version. The person who is it must be on the unicycle before he or she can tag another player. A confined area marked with a boundary line, such as a basketball court, will help the game move faster.

Many versions of team tag played on foot can be adapted to unicycles.

Basketball

Here's a fun way to play basketball. With slight modifications, the game can be played on unicycles, either half or full court. Typical rules include allowing only three wheel revolutions without dribbling the ball and that if a player touches one or both feet to the ground while in possession of the ball, the ball goes to the other team.

Skills needed by all players to make the game fun and exciting are mounting in the open and being able to pick the basketball up from the floor. Each player should learn to dribble the ball while riding. Drills can be set up to learn passing and shooting. It also helps if all players can mount a unicycle while holding a basketball. This way, play can

start out of bounds with the player on a unicycle before throwing the ball in.

Basketball is an ideal activity for competition between unicycle clubs and has been played at some of the National Unicycle Meets, which are sponsored by the Unicycling Society of America, Inc. (see Chapter 13 and Appendix for more information about this organization).

Hockey and Polo

Hockey and polo can be adapted to unicycles. Sticks can be cut from plywood. For hockey, a flat round puck can be used; for polo, a ball. A rubber ball about four to six inches in diameter works well. Large cardboard boxes can be used for goals, or goals can be constructed from wooden frames and netting material. Rules for putting the puck or ball in play can be devised. For hockey, a penalty box can be used. No standard rules for unicycle hockey or polo have been established, but it should be possible to modify the rules for bicycle polo or indoor cycle ball (where the ball is moved by the cycle wheels rather than a stick) for playing on unicycles.

Follow-the-Leader

The old game of follow-the-leader becomes a real challenge when played on unicycles. This game can also be used for exhibitions and demonstrations. A rehearsed version is sometimes used. A clown, who does everything wrong, can add to the novelty.

Add-On

This is a game of both skill and memory. The first rider does a unicycle stunt. The second rider has to do that and then add one. The third rider does those two and adds another. A rider is out if he or she misses a stunt or does the wrong one. Last one in the game is the winner.

Dodge Ball

Many versions can be played on unicycles. For example, all but one player can start inside a marked circle mounted on unicycles. A soft inflated rubber ball can be used. The person outside the circle must be mounted on unicycle before throwing the ball. A player inside the circle is out if he or she touches one or both feet to the ground or gets hit by the ball. The last player in the circle is the winner.

Another version is to have a set number of players inside the circle. When hit, the player who put him out goes in the circle and the other comes out. In this version, the inside players must remount immediately without taking any steps if they fall from the unicycles. The outside players must be mounted on their unicycles before they can put a player out.

A variation is to use two balls to make the games go faster.

RACES

Racing can add to the fun of unicycling. These can be informal to highly organized. A number of races are used as events at the National Unicycle Meet and International Unicycling Federation Meet.

Sprints

These races test speed. To give each unicycle rider an equal opportunity, all unicycles used should have the same wheel size and length of crank arms. For informal races, differences in unicycles can be overlooked. Sprints can be over any desired distance. Twenty-five yards is good for a start. Riders can race against each other or one at a time against a stopwatch. Racers can start behind a line in the mounting position with one foot on the ground. On the "go" signal, mount unicycle and ride as rapidly as possible to the finish line. First over, or fastest time, is the winner.

Events, rules, and age-groupings for the National Unicycle Meet and

International Unicycle Federation Meet are detailed later in this chapter.

Distance

Longer distances test both speed and endurance. These can be in a straight line, around a track course, or cross-country. For long distances, large groups can participate at the same time. If a rider's foot touches the ground, he or she can remount the unicycle and continue, but is not allowed to move forward with the unicycle.

A cross-country course adds to the fun. The course can have both smooth and rough terrain and, if practical, up and down hill areas. Make certain that the course is safe from automobile traffic and other such hazards. The course can be any desired length. Races have been held for distances of one mile and even longer.

Track

Both sprinting and distance racing can be held on a track. The track can be marked off on a flat area with old tires or similar markers. For one-lap sprint racing, a staggered start can be used so that the inside riders will not be at an advantage. If enough riders are entered, time trials and heats can be held. On short races, a spill generally eliminates a rider from the race.

Distance races start the same way. Generally after the start any rider can take the inside lane. A rider who touches a foot to the ground is allowed to mount again and continue, but is not allowed to walk.

An interesting variation is to start two riders on opposite sides of a small track. The first to pass the other is the winner. This, of course, is a real test of endurance.

A larger track can be used for more riders. At the start, the racers are spaced equal distance around the track. On the "go" signal, the riders mount and start around the track. Any rider passed is out of the race and must leave the track. The last rider on the track is the winner.

Relays

The possibilities here run into the hundreds. A simple starter is for two teams to line up with their unicycles as shown in Figure 11-1. Plastic bottles can be used as markers. These can be placed at a distance from the starting line. At the start of the race, on the "go" signal, the first two riders mount, then race down and around the markers, and return. The next rider on each team must wait until the rider on the same team has crossed the starting line before mounting. The first team to finish is the winner. Three or more teams can also be used.

Many variations are possible. For example, each rider must circle the marker one complete revolution before returning to the starting line. Baton relays can also be held. These can be as above, except that a baton is passed from rider to rider.

Relay races between teams can be held on a track. A baton can be used. A ten-foot area can be marked off for passing the baton. This allows a moving start for passing the baton. If the pass is not made within the marked off area, the team is disqualified.

Obstacle Courses and Slaloms

The quick turning of unicycles make them ideal for riding obstacle courses and slaloms. Figure 11-2 shows a couple of

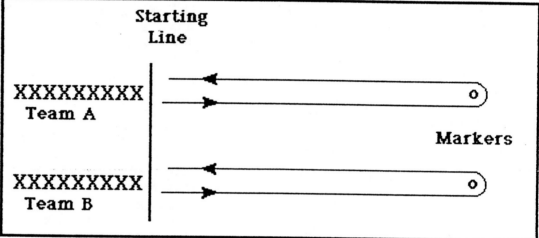

Fig. 11-1. Relay race.

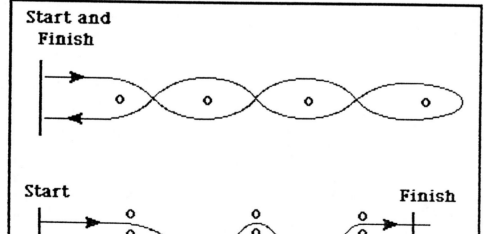

Fig. 11-2. Obstacle and slalom courses.

possibilities. There are, of course, hundreds of others. Plastic bottles can be used to mark the courses (Fig. 11-3). Two riders can race through a course, or each can go alone for time, as is generally done in skiing. If a rider hits a marker, he or she is disqualified. Generally, each rider gets three trials. His or her best time counts. It is also possible to add to the rider's time for hitting a marker rather than disqualifying him or her. The amount of time added will depend on the course. The scoring should, however, penalize a person hitting a marker.

RACING COMPETITIONS

The Unicycling Society of America, Inc., has sponsored a National Unicycle Meet every year since 1973. Racing events have been an important part of each of these national competitions.

Over the years, the rules have been modified to make the racing as fair and safe as possible and more closely carry out the aims of the Unicycling Society of America, Inc. The following is a summary of the most recent rules proposal for racing events at the Unicycling Society of America, Inc., National Unicycle Meets,

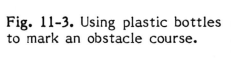

Fig. 11-3. Using plastic bottles to mark an obstacle course.

which are included here with permission of the Unicycling Society of America, Inc. The rules are subject to changes and revisions, so if you plan to compete, write to the Unicycling Society of America, Inc., P.O. Box 40534, Redford, Michigan 48240, and request a copy of the latest rules. Enclose a stamped, self-addressed envelope with your request.

Races will be run in accordance with standard high school track rules, with the following exceptions:

All races will be started with rider mounted, holding to support, except second, third, and fourth relay riders, who will have a starting distance to receive the baton.

All races will be started with words "ON YOUR MARK, GET SET," and then firing of starting gun. If any rider jumps the gun, starter will stop the race quickly and start it over. If any rider jumps the gun more than two times, he or she may be disqualified in that race.

Any rider fouling (interfering with other riders) shall be disqualified from that race.

Any rider intentionally fouling shall be disqualified for that race and may be barred from further competition and forfeit any and all awards.

Disqualification decisions will be made by the "Head Racing Official."

Riders must ride across the finish line, not fall across. Final decisions of this nature will be made by the "Head Racing Official."

All riders starting in a race, whether they finish, disqualify or not, must report to the official or timer at the end of the track so their identification and time (if any) can be recorded.

If rider falls or dismounts, that rider is disqualified, except in relay, 880-yard or mile races, where rider may remount without running.

Riders must be in race starting area 10 minutes before each race they wish to compete in.

All riders must stay in their lanes. If rider gets out of his or her lane and immediately gets back without interfering with other riders, that rider will not be disqualified. In certain races, such as 880-yard or mile races, specific rules may apply on lane usage.

For relay races, the age group of each team is determined by oldest rider in that team. No rider can be in the same relay twice.

For slow races, rider must ride in a straight forward continuous motion. Rider may not rock, bounce, twist, go backward or stop. If wheel goes any more than 45 degrees out of line, or if any backward motion of the wheel is observed, that rider is disqualified.

In the obstacle course, each rider shall be allowed two rides with the best time being official. Pylons may be hit but not knocked over. If any pylon falls, the rider will be disqualified in that attempt.

All races are timed finals, at the discretion of the "Head Race Official."

The Age Groups are as follows: 7 years old and younger; 8 to 10; 11 and 12; 13 and 14; 15 and 16; 17 and 18; and 19 and older. Age group jumping is allowed.

The unicycles must meet certain specifications. Riders in the first two age groups will ride unicycles with wheels no larger than 20-inches, with crank arms no shorter than 5-inches. Riders of these ages with 24-inch wheels must ride with the 11 and 12 year old age group.

Riders 11 years old and older will ride unicycles with wheels no larger than 24 inches and crank arms no shorter than 5-1/2 inches. This accommodates almost every standard unicycle on the market, and allows the maximum number of unicyclists to participate with their own unicycles without making modifications to the cycles. A common modification to a standard unicycle is to change from standard pedals to rattrap pedals. This is allowed. Any other modification or addition to a unicycle that would, in the opinion of the "Head Racing Official," be an unfair advantage, may be disqualified. However, experimentation is encouraged, and some modifications, such as making a unicycle lighter, counterbalancing the cranks, or adding built-on handles to the unicycle, may be allowed.

There will be separate events for boys and girls. At the time of this writing the races are still in yards, but plans are underway to change this to meters sometime in the future.

The regular forward riding events are 100-yard sprint; 220-yard sprint; 880-yard race (for those 11 years old and under); 1-mile race (for those 12 years old and over); and a special one-mile race for riders over 30 years of age. Other racing events are 50 yards riding backwards; 50 yards riding with one foot (riders start with both feet pedaling, but must be using only one foot when they cross the line 5 yards from the start line, other foot may be braced against the fork or extended forward, whichever the rider prefers); 10-yard slow race; 10-yard walk-the-wheel race (riders start with feet on wheel and push tire only, not including pedals or spokes, with feet and must be in a fairly balanced position all the way across the finish line); obstacle course (see Figure 11-4; rider starts in a mounted position, holding onto support at the line with no running starts being allowed); and relay races (first rider will start mounted, in the usual way, and second, third, and fourth riders will have a 10 yard starting distance in which to receive the baton; baton must stay with riders to the finish).

At the time of this writing, the rules for the racing events for the first International Unicycling Federation Meet (scheduled for 1984) are still tentative, but will basically be the same as for the National Unicycle Meet. The Age Groups planned are 10 years old and under; 11 to 13; 14 to 16; and 17 and older. There will be separate events for boys and girls. The events, except for one mile, will be in meters. For latest information and rules, write to International Unicycling Federation, 67 Lion Lane, Westbury, NY 11590. Enclose a stamped, self-addressed envelope with your request.

TIPS FOR COMPETITIVE RACING

Racing differs considerably from artistic riding, just as racing in swimming differs considerably from springboard and platform diving. In racing, it is not how you look but how fast you can get from one point to another on a unicycle that counts.

Most champion racers adjust their unicycles so that their legs will have only a slight bend at the bottoms of the pedal

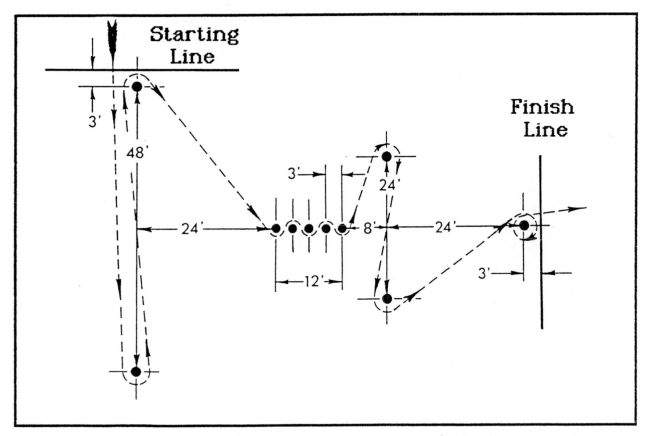

Fig. 11-4. Official Unicycling Society of America, Inc., obstacle course (courtesy Unicycling Society of America, Inc.).

cycles when their feet are properly positioned on the pedals. Champion racers typically hold the front of the saddles throughout sprint and distance races.

The secret to winning races is to go fast, at least faster than your competitors. High speeds require extreme forward lean. This, however, must be carefully controlled to keep from falling. Remember, when you are pedaling as fast as you possibly can, there is no way to recover from too much forward lean. To avoid falling, you must make certain that you do not get into this situation.

Safety equipment is an absolute necessity for anyone who is a serious unicycle racer. As a minimum, I recommend a pair of heavy gloves, knee and elbow pads, and a lightweight bicycle racing helmet. It is my feeling that at least the above safety equipment should be required for competitive racing, especially for events where high speeds are obtained.

Very controversial is the use of pedal straps and toe clips. These serve to hold the feet to the pedals and allow lifting the pedals upward as well as applying downward force. However, they are also a trap for holding your feet to the pedals in case of a fall.

Riding the obstacle course requires not only speed, but also turning ability.

Fig. 11-5. Champion unicycle racer Floyd Crandall demonstrates extreme lean required to make fast time around obstacle course (photo courtesy Unicycling Society of America, Inc.).

The extreme lean required to round a pylon is shown in Figure 11-5 by champion obstacle course racer Floyd Crandall.

NATIONAL UNICYCLE MEET RECORDS

The following are the fastest times recorded at the National Unicycle Meets from 1973 through 1983 and are reprinted here with permission of the Unicycling Society of America, Inc.

Records for girls riding unicycles with 20-inch wheels: 100-yard sprint, 17.6 seconds, Carol Haines, 1976; 220-yard sprint, 41.5 seconds, Carol Haines, 1976; 440-yard race, 1:28.2, Carol Haines, 1975; 880-yard race, 3:08.5, Carol Haines, 1975; one-mile, 8:24.9, Carol Bahorich, 1979. For boys: 100-yard sprint, 17.6 seconds, Clyde Crandall, 1974; 220-yard sprint, 39.4 seconds, Davey Upham, 1975; 440-yard race, 1:20.6, Davey Upham, 1975; 880-yard race, 2:25.2, Davey Upham, 1975; one-mile race, 6:39.9, Jeff Layne, 1979.

Records for girls riding unicycles with 24-inch wheels: 100-yard sprint, 14.8 seconds, Penny Elliott, 1976; 220-yard sprint, 41.5 seconds, Penny Elliott, 1975; 440-yard race, 1:11.4, Penny Elliott, 1974; 880-yard race, 2:34.6, Sue Donovan, 1974; indoor one-mile race, 5:39, Cathy Fox, 1983; outdoor one-mile race, 5:24.5, Carol Haines, 1975. For boys: 100-yard sprint, 13.5 seconds, Floyd Crandall, 1973 and 1979; 220-yard sprint, 30.4 seconds, Floyd Crandall, 1975; 440-yard race, 1:02.0, Floyd Crandall, 1975; 880-yard race, 2:12.8, Floyd Crandall, 1975; indoor one-mile race, 4:40, Mark Schaefer, 1983; outdoor one-mile race, 4:33.02, Mark Schaefer, 1982.

Records for other events for girls: 50-yard backward, 11.5 seconds, Kathy Skinner, 1976; 50-yard one foot, 10.2 seconds, Sue Donovan, 1975; 10-yard wheel walk, 4.74 seconds, Julie Marquart, 1982; 10-yard slow, 31.1, Cathy Fox, 1983; obstacle course, 23.6 seconds, Kathy Skinner, 1975. For boys: 50-yard backward, 9.3 seconds, Mark Schaefer, 1983; 50-yard one foot, 8.42 seconds, Floyd Crandall, 1975; 10-yard wheel walk, 3.77 seconds, John Foss, 1982; 10-yard slow, 42.0 seconds, Sem Abrahams, 1983; obstacle course, 18.95 seconds, Floyd Crandall, 1981.

Chapter 12

PERFORMING AND ARTISTIC COMPETITION

Most unicycle riders enjoy showing their artistic skills to others. There are a number of ways to do this, including working up a stage act, comedy and clowning, giving demonstrations, parade riding, and artistic unicycling competition.

UNICYCLE ACTS

The line between an act and a demonstration team is not clearly defined. Here an act will be considered a routine done in typical stage or circus fashion, whereas a demonstration team will be considered a large group of unicyclists that perform primarily to show what unicycling is all about. Demonstration teams are covered in a separate section below in this chapter.

Acts generally start out as amateur acts, but they are of the type that could, and sometimes do, become professional acts. Regardless of whether you want to remain amateur or go on to the professional ranks, a good way to start is to work up a unicycle act either solo or with one or more other riders and then perform wherever possible. This may be in YMCA circuses, at P.T.A. meetings, in school shows, or at charity benefits. After the first appearance, the second should be easier to find, and so on.

Always try to improve your act. Find out what goes over and what doesn't. Study and learn from professional acts.

Most amateur acts that become professional pass through an intermediate "semi-professional" stage. This is where the act will have to prove itself. There will be some money made here, but often this barely covers expenses.

To move to the professional rank, a professional act is needed. In fact, it almost needs to be better than any of the present professional acts. A musical arrangement to fit the act will be a necessity. Costumes and professional appearance are other requirements. Most professional acts have agents. Without an agent, booking is difficult.

Some amateur unicycle acts are of professional caliber, but want to stay amateur. In the future, when unicycling becomes more established as a competitive sport, it seems likely that some of the best unicyclists will remain amateurs for competitive purposes. Thus, unicycle acts can be whatever the performers wish to make of them. Running away with a circus is definitely not a requirement, but it is still a possibility.

Single Acts

The purpose here is to give a skeleton for a basic one-person unicycle act. The quality of the act will depend to a great extent on the rider's skill in performing the artistic unicycling skills described in preceding chapters. Any special stunts that can be done well can be added to the act.

1. Ride a standard unicycle. Start by mounting on stage, or ride on from off stage. Do routine of best stunts on standard unicycle, such as circles, patterns, spins, riding backwards, idling, one-foot riding and idling, and so on. Try to combine the stunts so that one flows into the next. Try to make the act build. Each stunt should appear more spectacular than the last. In fact, this is the real key to a successful act. It should have a beginning, a middle, and an end. This point is often overlooked. Without this

suspense, the audience will quickly lose interest and become bored.

2. Ride unicycle with handlebar unit. Do turns and circles as though riding a regular bicycle. Ride backwards. Come to a standstill and hold balance. Ride slowly and spin handlebar unit. Then lift the handlebar unit into the air and ride circles and do other stunts such as riding backwards and idling with the handlebar unit overhead. The skills for this part of the act are covered in Chapter 7. Again, arrange the skills so that suspense builds. End this part of act with the stunt that looks the most difficult.

3. Ride a basic giraffe unicycle. Mounting can be from a ladder off stage or at the side of stage or on stage in the open if you have mastered this skill. Combine your giraffe unicycling skills so that the act builds.

4. Now for a little comedy before the finale. This might be riding a midget unicycle, the smaller the better, or performing with a break-apart bicycle that separates into a standard unicycle and a handlebar unit, or some other novelty unicycle.

5. Now for the conclusion. This should top everything. The audience will be disappointed if it doesn't. A taller unicycle would do it. The finale, which may or may not be announced, should bring the greatest applause.

Other points to keep in mind: Each part of the act should move into the next. Breaks must be kept to a minimum. The act must move. There should be a minimum of time when nothing is happening.

The act should not be too long. There is a limit to how long interest (and suspense) can be maintained. Don't pass this point. It's best to finish with the audience still wanting more. Experience will tell how long the act can, or should be.

This basic one-person act can be used by those at all levels of skill. For some, this will mean only a standard unicycle. For the more advanced, other stunts should be added to the skeleton. Regardless, try to include only stunts that have been perfected and can be done without a miss or only rarely missed. This is something different than the deliberate missing that is sometimes used. A stunt is announced. The performer tries it but misses it. He or she tries it again. Another miss. The third time, the performer makes it. This is all part of the act.

What else? Music helps to build up the act. Lighting helps. Costumes help. But most important, in the end, are the skills on the unicycles and showmanship.

Another possibility is a one-person comedy or clown act (comedy and clowning is covered later in this chapter).

Acts with Two or More Riders

The same basic principles apply, only in this case continuity is easier because at least one rider can always be doing something while the others are mounting, resting, and so on.

1. All riders begin on standard unicycles. Individual maneuvers are combined with group stunts. Learn to work in a small area. Keep the act moving, and don't forget to keep increasing the difficulty. If possible, this part of the act should end with a stunt involving all riders.

2. Bring one or more handlebar units into the act. Go rapidly from one stunt to the next. End with the audience still wanting more.

3. Next, have one or more of the riders on basic giraffe unicycles. Combine individual maneuvers and group stunts.

4. For comedy, have a rider come on stage with a midget unicycle while at least one giraffe unicycle is still being ridden.

5. The last part of the act should top everything. For two riders, it can be taller giraffe unicycles. For three riders, it can be a midget unicycle, a basic giraffe unicycle, and a taller giraffe model. Regardless, build to the finale, which should be the most spectacular part of the act.

Some points to keep in mind: if giraffe unicycles are mounted with a ladder, mount tall unicycles while one or more other riders are performing. However, try to keep all performers on stage as much as possible. Have mounting platform, if used, in convenient location

Fig. 12-1. Practice session for a unicycle act in the Great Y Circus (photo courtesy Warren C. Wood).

just off stage or at side of stage. Have all unicycles and other equipment arranged and ready to go. Some acts use a special rack to hold unicycles and equipment. This can be on wheels (with locks). In this way, the equipment can be rolled from the stage entrance to the edge of the stage. A mounting platform can be attached to the rack.

Group acts require organization and many practice sessions (Fig. 12-1) to put together an effective show.

Specialty Acts

Many specialized unicycle acts are possible. These can be with one or more performers. Often, other skills are combined with unicycling. Here are some possibilities:

1. An act based on juggling on a unicycle. There are many possibilities here. Skill in juggling as well as unicycling is required.

2. A balancing act where one performer rides unicycle and carries other person on shoulders (Fig. 12-2) and/or does other acrobatic stunts. This type of act, in addition to unicycling skills, require advanced acrobatic techniques.

3. Riding unicycles on tightwire (Fig. 12-3).

4. Going up and down stairs on a unicycle. Sturdy unicycle spokes are required for this one.

5. Riding over teeter-boards (Fig.

Fig. 12-2. In Great Y Circus performance Chuck Craw carries Lisa Floyd on shoulders while riding a unicycle (photo courtesy Warren C. Wood).

12-4) and/or up and down ramps, spiral platforms, and so on.

6. Riding a unicycle on a table or platform. This type of act often includes juggling and/or balancing a partner on shoulders and other acrobatic stunts.

7. Acrobatics done on or around pole (Fig. 12-5) or platform (Fig. 12-6) carried by two or more riders. There are many variations to this.

Fig. 12-3. Danny Haynes riding a unicycle across tightwire (photo by Bob Lynn and courtesy Hamilton Mini Circus).

Fig. 12-4. Riding over a teeter-board on giraffe unicycles (photo by Garretson and courtesy Hamilton Mini Circus).

130

Fig. 12-5. Members of the Hamilton Mini Circus perform a pole act on giraffe unicycles (photo by Bob Lynn and courtesy Hamilton Mini Circus).

Fig. 12-6. Practicing a platform act (photo courtesy Hamilton Mini Circus).

8. Comedy and clowning (see section below in this chapter).

9. Combination bicycle-unicycle acts. In these, both artistic bicycles and unicycles are used.

10. Animal acts. Monkeys, chimpanzees, and even bears have been trained to ride unicycles.

COMEDY AND CLOWNING

The ability to gain laughter from clowning seems to be largely inherited. One person tells a joke and leaves everyone in stitches. Another person tells the same joke. No one laughs. The same is true in comedy and clowning on unicycles. Of course, technique, equipment, and costume make a difference, but for any real success the natural gift must be there.

Clowning can add laughter and joy to unicycle acts and demonstrations. However, make sure it's funny before adding it to a show. A clown who draws no laughter can distract rather than add to the performance.

Three phases of clowning are considered: skill on the unicycle; special cycles and props; and costumes and make-up. While these are treated separately, they should be combined for greater effect.

Skill

Successful clowning on a unicycle requires consideraable riding skill. It's definitely not for a beginner. Much of clowning is deliberate violation of the "proper" method of performing unicycle skills. In order to do this, the rider must first know how to perform the skills correctly. A basic unicycling skill, for example, is to ride smoothly in a straight line. For clowning, a wobbly motion can be used with greater effect. An artistic unicycle stunt is done with control and precision. The clown will do the same stunt with what looks like complete loss of control, but not actual loss of control.

A basic clowning move is to ride forward and allow the unicycle to wobble with the pedal action. Try to exaggerate the action. Try to make it appear that all control has been lost. Add twist and leaning actions to the ride. To add to the effect, look in the direction opposite to the turning action. This creates the effect that the unicycle is always going the wrong way.

Next, try turning in one direction with an exaggerated lean while looking in the opposite direction. Try to be off balance to what looks like the point of no return, then recover at the last possible instant. Also make it appear that the you are not working together with the unicycle.

While learning unicycling skills, the importance of good posture was stressed. For clowning, ride bent forward so that the unicycle fork and your body form a curve. In this way, your upper body will form an angle to the unicycle frame. Also effective is to arch backwards while riding the unicycle. Also try leaning to one side so that the unicycle fork is angled in the opposite direction. The arms can be moved in an awkward manner, as though you are grabbing air to pull yourself back into balance.

A good sequence is to ride forward, lose balance sideways, then spin around quickly to recover balance and then ride on. Or ride forward, half spin, ride backwards, half spin, ride forward, and so on. The movement should be done so that it appears that the half spins are falls. Recovery should be at the last possible instant. By looking away from the falling direction, it's possible to add to the effect. Much of clowning is acting with the whole body, including facial expressions and use of eyes.

Next, try an uncontrolled-looking loop-the-loop ride. To do this, ride forward. Start to fall sideways. Make quick complete circle to recover. Ride forward and repeat the loop motion.

Even better are comedy actions and maneuvers while riding backwards. An uncontrolled-looking wobble will serve as a starter. Use the same principles to achieve effect as was done in forward riding.

Many clowning stunts involve fake falling. A problem here is that the unicycle can be damaged. For this reason, if these stunts are used, an old beat-up unicycle is often used. A typical movement of this type is to ride in an uncontrolled manner, then fall forward. Land on the feet with as much lean forward as possible. Immediately go into a forward or side tumbling roll. In the meantime, the unicycle crashes to the ground--a good clown stunt, but hard on unicycles.

Clowning can be added to many group stunts. For example, two clowns can start by doing various double stunts. Then they can "fake" trying to throw each other off balance. Of course, this should all be well rehearsed. For example, the two riders come toward each other at a rapid pace. They start to clasp hands and go into circles, only instead one rider spins the other and goes on forward.

Follow-the-leader type stunts also work well in clowning routines. Another possibility is for a clown to mimic stunts done by a serious rider.

A plant in the audience always seems to work well. Ask if there are any volunteers in the audience who would like to try to ride a unicycle. The plant in the audience puts his hands into the air and yells and runs up to the stage, tripping on the stairs on the way up. The unicycle clowning stunts described above can follow.

A clown drill team on unicycles can be a real show stopper. A good entry is to follow a regular drill team demonstration. The clown team trys similar patterns, only they get mixed up and bump into each other, cross the wrong way, end up without a partner, and so on.

A clown band on unicycles works well in parades. Bread-box drums and other improvised music instruments can be used.

Special Cycles and Props

A number of simple props can be used for clowning. The old water bucket routine always seems to work. Start by having two clowns riding unicycles, one chasing the other. The one doing the chasing carries a bucket of water. He or she catches up with the lead rider and throws water on him or her. The wet clown then rides off and returns with a bucket filled with paper confetti. He or she chases the clown who threw the bucket of water. The lead rider falls off unicycle near the audience and the chasing clown throws the bucket of confetti so that the confetti goes out over the audience.

Another good clown stunt requiring only a simple prop is the pole balancing sequence. A tray is securely fastened to the end of a pole. A number of light plastic items, such as cups and a pitcher, are connected to the tray by short lengths of string. The containers are placed on the tray and filled with confetti.

The clown then rides the unicycle and balances the pole on his hand. He rides toward the audience, lets the pole fall toward the audience and, at the last instant, catches the pole. The containers end up hanging by the pieces of string and the confetti falls over the audience. This works well, but be careful. Only a skilled performer should do the stunt, and even then it's best to do it over a part of the audience that has been planted, perhaps friends or members of the same unicycle club, that know what is going on.

Midget unicycles are ideal for clowning. A big fat clown contrasts with a tiny unicycle.

Another good possibility is to construct a junk unicycle. The unicycle should be functional, but everything else is done to make it look like a piece of junk. The builder can really let his or her imagination go here. For example, a bent fork can be used. Then weld it at an angle to the bearing housings. Smash in places as necessary so that the crank arms will clear the fork prongs. The wheel can be out of alignment or even off-centered. One pedal arm can be longer than the other. The saddle can be a torn piece of junk. A bulb-type horn can be attached to the fork. The tire can be taped in several spots. A junkyard is a good place to look for parts and also to get ideas.

The unicycle should look as hopeless as possible. Then ride it. The unicycle can really look hopelessly out of balance and still be ridden. This, incidentally, quickly dispels the idea that a unicycle must be perfectly balanced before it can be ridden.

This idea can be carried further. For example, weld a pipe to the frame and attach handlebars. Or a piece of bent tubing with an umbrella. Or attach pieces of junk for no reason at all. These, of course, are only a few of the possibilities, and you will probably want to add your original ideas.

A handlebar unit with loose front-wheel nuts (see Chapter 7) can be effectively combined with a fall-apart unicycle. The wheel will fall off, yet can be set in place and used again. Lift the handlebar unit upward while it is being used with forward riding on the unicycle and the wheel will come off and continue rolling.

Break-apart bicycles that form a unicycle and handlebar unit are also popular for clowning.

Junk unicycle concepts can also be applied to giraffe unicycles. Another possibility is to make the frame for a giraffe unicycle from or shaped like a ladder. One clown can perform on the ladder while another rider handles the unicycle from the saddle. The rider can pretend to be trying to get the clown off the ladder as though the clown is spoiling the act. This, of course, needs to be rehearsed.

Other ideas include unicycles constructed so that they fall apart and can be slipped together again and ridden and matching a midget unicycle with a midget handlebar unit and a tall giraffe unicycle with a tall handlebar unit.

Costumes and Make-Up

Costumes and make-up can add greatly to the success, or failure, of clowning. For a plant in the audience, ordinary street clothes can be worn. For riding in parades, a clown or tramp uniform can be used. The same applies to stage acts. In some routines, an ordinary costume (non-clown) is most effective. In this case, the clowning is done by skill and/or special cycles and props rather than by looking like a clown. In other cases, a clown costume is more suitable.

The same applies to make-up. For some acts, none is needed. For others it can add a great deal. Some clowns are happy clowns; sometimes more effective are sad ones. This can be achieved by make-up. Use the kind that's easy to remove. For the happy clown, use upward curved lines around the mouth. For the sad one, curve them downward. Practice the lines on paper first to see that the desired effect is achieved. Much can be done with lines painted around the eyes.

Special noses and ears can be purchased at novelty shops. Again, the suitability will depend on the type of clowning.

Another possibility is to use a mask. Some of these are held in place with an elastic strap; others slip over the head. With these, make sure that vision is not restricted and that circulation of air to the skin is not shut off.

Special hats are often used. These can be small ones or very large. Pointed, cone-shaped hats are an old standard for clowns.

Another clown item is big shoes. But make sure these won't get in the way when riding the unicycle. Or paint an old pair of tennis shoes. Or use two different kinds of shoes.

Some clowns are thin, but more often than not they are fat. Pillows can be used to make a thin clown fat. Place the padding so that it doesn't get in the way of the intended riding.

And suspenders. Clowns have traditionally used these as part of their costumes. On unicycles, they're good for pulling on. For example, one clown can grab the suspenders of another clown. When the clown falls from the unicycle, the baggy pants can fall down, leaving the clown in bright colored long underwear or other laugh provoking attire.

Other Ideas

The basic ingredients of clowning have been covered. But this is only the start. There are hundreds of ways to put them together. And original ideas to add to that. For example, why not include one of those paddles with a ball attached with rubber and string? Or a juggling clown? The possibilities go on and on.

DEMONSTRATION TEAMS

Demonstration teams have done much to promote unicycling as a recreational activity and sport. Many unicycle clubs have put on demonstrations as regular club activies. Essentially, everything covered in this book can be used here. Here are some additional suggestions:

Try to cover a number of unicycling activities in each demonstration. For example, include a drill team, unicycle races, artistic unicycling, and specialty acts.

Include all levels of skill, including some riders who have just learned basic riding.

Give each team member the time and place of the demonstration in writing. This is especially important when children are involved.

Rather than using special costumes, it's often easier to decorate the unicycles. Strips of crepe paper are ideal for this. Slip-on wheel discs and spoke covers, both available from bicycle stores, can also be used.

Adjust the demonstration to fit the performance area. If a large area is available such as a gym floor or section of a parking lot, take advantage of the large area. Also have routines that can be performed on small stages.

Take advantage of the performance area. For example, if a basketball court is used, play a short demonstration game of basketball as part of the show.

Prepare an announcer's sheet for the demonstration team. This helps to make things go more smoothly.

For the parts of the demonstration involving large groups, keep the routines simple. Always anticipate that at the last minute some won't show up.

If possible, provide your own announcer. This can make a big difference. Someone is needed who knows what unicycling is all about. If children are in the show, they like to hear their names announced.

In outdoor areas with large audiences and no loud-speakers, forget about trying to announce. Start the show and keep it moving.

An extremely important consideration, besides getting the performers there, is transporting unicycles and other equipment. One way to do this, if the unicycles are owned by the individual riders, is to have each person responsible for bringing his or her own cycle. For transporting club cycles or a number of cycles, special problems exist. A station wagon or truck will generally handle all but the extremely tall unicycles. For these, a car-top rack can be used (see Chapter 3).

Let's look at a basic structure for a unicycle demonstration. This, of course, is intended only as a guide.

1. Start with a unicycle parade with all riders on standard-size unicycles. Follow in line behind the leader. On signal, riders begin turning when a set point is reached, each rider breaking away in the direction opposite to the rider ahead. After a large circle, the line is reformed. Other similar maneuvers can also be included.

2. A unicycle game such as hockey or basketaball or whatever can be performed next. Don't continue this very long; make it short and snappy. Relay races are also effective.

3. Next, have a unicycle drill team performance. Start with all standard-size unicycles. End with all sizes. Various props, such as a long pole, are effective here.

4. Have some of the people who have just learned to ride demonstrate. Also, if possible, have someone very young (Fig. 12-7), then someone very old, ride unicycles to show that it is truly a sport for (almost) all ages. This part of a demonstration always seems to generate a lot of enthusiasm. The riders enjoy it; the audience likes it. It is from watching this that many people decide they want to learn too.

Fig. 12-7. Shalice Byrd of the Mobile Unicycle Club riding unicycle at age 6 (photo courtesy Seth Granberry, Jr.).

5. One or more advanced unicycles acts and/or performances of competition-type artistic routines are next. Specialty acts can be included here.

6. End with a finale parade, similar to the beginning only with all types of cycles represented. A good way to do this is to arrange them by size, from a midget unicycle to the tallest giraffe model. With this, the demonstration is brought to an effective climax.

PARADE RIDING

Indvidual and group unicycle riding is a popular attraction in parades (Fig. 12-8 and Fig. 12-9). Many parade committees will be happy to have unicyclists in the parades. Parades are often held on holidays, such as the Fourth of July, Veterans' Day, and Memorial Day. To participate, contact the chairman of the parade committee about a month before the parade is to take place. With approval, the details of the parade route and where and when to start will be given. Plan all details for group riding ahead of time. For larger groups, it is best to give in writing the time and place for meeting and exactly what equipment to bring. For clubs or other riding groups, a banner with the name of the club or group can be carried on a pole by two riders (Fig. 12-8). Costumes and decorated

Fig. 12-9. Oak View unicyclists riding in holiday parade (photo courtesy Jim Moyer).

unicycles will add to the effect.

Some parades judge the entries and recognition and awards are given in various categories, such as floats, marching bands, and so on. Once a person or group appears in a parade, there will probably be invitations to appear in future parades.

Some points to be taken into consideration when planning and working up routines are: 1) parades generally move slowly and at an erratic pace, 2) be prepared for some complete stops, and 3) find out where the reviewing stand is so that the best routines can be done at that point.

ARTISTIC COMPETITION

The Unicycling Society of America, Inc., has sponsored a National Unicycle Meet every year since 1973. Artistic riding events have been an important part of each of these national competitions. The following is a summary of the most recent rules proposal for the artistic riding events at the Unicycling Society of America, Inc., National Unicycle Meets, which are included here with permission of the Unicycling Society of America, Inc. The rules are subject to changes and revisions, so if you plan to compete, write to the Unicycling Society of America, Inc., P.O. Box 40534, Redford, Michigan 48240, and request a copy of the latest rules. Enclose a stamped, self-addressed envelope with your request.

Fig. 12-8. Redford Unicycle Club riding in parade with club banner (photo by John Foss and courtesy Unicycling Society of America, Inc.).

For Individual Artistic Riding, there are two categories, with riders being allowed to enter only one because of time limitations for the competition. The Standard Class is one standard unicycle, no props of any kind, no special costumes, and no music. For artistic riding, a standard unicycle is any unicycle with the crank arms connected directly to the wheel axle, regardless of wheel size or crank-arm length. Riders should be judged primarily on their unicycling skills with one-third on smoothness and choreography and two-thirds on skills presented. Dismounts will reduce rider's score more in this category than in others. The time limit for 12 and under riders is 2 minutes and for 13 and over is 3 minutes.

Open Class is any unicycle or unicycles with any props. Music and costuming are requirements. Riders will be judged on unicycle performing ability. Judging should be half on unicycle skill and originality and half on presentation, showmanship, and performing ability. The time limit for 12 and under riders is 2 minutes and for 13 and over is 3 minutes.

In both Standard Class and Open Class there are separate events for boys and girls.

Couples Artistic Riding is two riders performing on any types of unicycles with any props, music and/or costumes. Judging will be similar to Open Class for individuals, with an emphasis on rider teamwork, unity, and coordination. Many couples performances are styled after those of dancers and ice skaters. The time limit for 12 and under riders is 2 minutes and for 13 and over is 3 minutes. Age group is determined by older rider. Shorter time limit for younger riders is because it is assumed that the average rider of that age has less skills to offer than an older rider. Unsatisfied riders can jump age groups.

Group Artistic Riding is three or more unicyclists doing a performance which is judged in a way similar to the Couples and Open Class categories. The time limit is 10 minutes. Music and costumes should be used, but are not a requirement.

The Age Groups for artistic riding are as follows: 7 years old and younger; 8 to 10; 11 and 12; 13 and 14; 15 and 16; 17

and 18; and 19 and older. Professional riders who perform for personal gain on a regular basis are usually moved up one or more age groups, depending on age of rider and conditions of specific situations. "Head Artistic Events Official" will make these determinations. Any rider who wishes may move up as many age groups as he or she desires. Age grouping of rider is determined by rider's age on the first day of the meet, usually Saturday. The specifices are listed on the National Unicycle Meet registration form.

The artistic riding rules are:

1. Riders may compete in couples competition only once.

2. Usually, no more than 3 minutes is allowed for set-up. Use less if possible. Going over the time alloted can result in a reduction in score.

3. Music for acts should be on cassette, or live, unless other provisions are made.

4. Riders must nod or bow to the judges to indicate the start of their performance, or the timer will start with the start of their music, and the same for the end of the performance. A thirty-second warning whistle may be used by timers to cue the riders.

5. Going overtime will result in a reduction of score.

At the time of this writing, the rules for artistic riding events for the first International Unicycling Federation Meet (scheduled for 1984) are still tentative, but will basically be the same as for the National Unicycle Meet. For latest information and rules, write to the International Unicycling Federation, c/o Jenack Circus Corporation, 67 Lion Lane, Westbury, NY 11590. Enclose a stamped, self-addressed envelope with your request. The following is a summary of the proposed rules and skill levels for the 1984 competition, which are included here with permission of the International Unicycling Federation.

The Age Groups planned are 10 years old and under; 11 to 13; 14 to 16; and 17 and older. There will be separate events for boys and girls.

Couples Artistic Riding and Group Artistic Riding are scored 0.0 to 10.0 points for difficulty and 0.0 to 10.0 points for presentation for a maximum possible score of 20 points.

To compete for "World Individual Unicycle Champion," rider must enter both the Freestyle and Compulsory events in Individual Artistic Riding.

The Compulsory is the rider and one standard unicycle, no props, no music or special costumes. The time limit is 3 minutes. Skills demonstrated must be found in the International Unicycling Federation Skill Levels, as detailed later in this chapter. The idea is for the rider to demonstrate his or her riding skills on the unicycle with the most difficult figures they can do well. Falls will count more heavily against the score here than in the Freestyle category. Scoring is 0.0 to 15.0 points for difficulty and 0.0 to 5.0 points for execution for a maximum possible score of 20 points.

The Freestyle is the same as for the National Unicycle Meet Open Class event. Riders are judged on their ability to perform and create art as well as their pure riding skill. Scoring is 0.0 to 10.0 points for difficulty and 0.0 to 10.0 points for presentation for a maximum possible score of 20 points.

Compulsory and Freestyle scores are averaged to find the top scoring riders.

INTERNATIONAL UNICYCLING FEDERATION SKILL LEVELS

These are objective criteria for evaluating unicycle skills, and are performed by one rider on a standard unicycle with no props. Other than mounts, all skills listed below, unless otherwise indicated, start with the unicyclist riding forward or backward, sitting on saddle with both arms free, and end the same way; riding forward or backward, sitting on saddle with both arms free. All skills should be performed with control and mastery.

Measured distances in which the unicyclist must ride involve linear distances of 10, 25, and 50 meters, and circles of 50-centimeters, 1- and 3-meter diameters. There is also a figure-eight which consists of two tangent 3-meter circles.

One foot riding skills can be performed with the rider's free foot extended, or resting on the unicycle fork.

Riding with the saddle held to the front or rear of rider must be performed as follows: saddle is held by one hand only, and other hand and arm are extended to the side. There must be no contact between the unicycle saddle and any part of the body other than the hand, meaning that the saddle cannot rest against the body while riding.

International Unicycling Federation Definitions

Standard Unicycle: Any direct-drive unicycle where pedals turn the wheel that is on the riding surface.

Competition Standard Unicycle: Same as above but with restrictions on maximum wheel diameter and minimum crank length, and possibly others.

Dismount: Rider gets off unicycle, feet returning to floor; must be with intention.

Fall: Dismounting without intention, regardless of control.

Control: Ability to make unicycle do what rider wants it to do; ability to control unicycle and body in relation to unicycle.

Mastery: Ability to duplicate a skill at will and with control.

Foot in Control Position: This is the foot that is pedaling, or otherwise driving the unicycle.

Level 1

a. Mount unicycle without assistance (any type of mount).

b. Ride unicycle 50 meters.

c. Dismount gracefully with unicycle to front of rider.

Level 2

a. Mount unicycle with left foot in control position.

b. Mount unicycle with right foot in control position.

c. Ride 10 meters between two parallel lines 30 centimeters apart.

d. Ride in the figure-eight staying within 3-meter circles.

Level 3

a. Rolling mount. Mount unicycle while rolling it forward. Wheel may stop while rider steps on, but may not move backward.

b. Ride backward 50 meters.

c. Idle or rock in place for 50 back-and-forth half-revolution cycles with left foot in control position. Same skill also with right foot in control position.

d. Make sharp 90 and 180 degree turns to the left and right (maximum one-meter diameter).

e. Ride in a 3-meter circle with arms crossed and held tightly to body (no arm movement).

Level 4

a. Sidesaddle mount. Standing with unicycle to side of rider, step onto pedal with proper foot (left foot on left pedal or right foot on right pedal), swing other leg up and around front of saddle. Sit on saddle, place other foot on pedal and ride away.

b. Hop or bounce with pedals level, left foot back, so that tire lifts above riding surface five consecutive times. Same skill also with right foot back.

c. Ride unicycle 50 meters with saddle held to front of rider as described above.

d. Idle or rock one-footed for 25 back-and-forth half-revolution cycles with left foot in control position. Same skill also with right foot in control position.

e. Ride in two full circles within a one-meter circle.

Level 5

a. Free jump mount. Using hands, balance unicycle with pedals level. Before jumping, let go of unicycle so it is balancing free. Jump up and land on both pedals simultaneously. Sit down and ride away.

b. Ride one-footed 50 meters with left foot in control position. Same skill with right foot in control position.

c. Ride 50 meters in chest to saddle prone position, both arms extended straight out to sides.

d. Ride 50 meters with saddle held to rear of rider.

e. Ride backward in figure-eight.

f. Touch fingertip to riding surface while riding. Turning is permissible. Saddle must be at proper height for rider.

g. Idle or rock with saddle held to front of rider for 25 back-and-forth half-revolution cycles.

Level 6

a. Kick-up mount. Lay unicycle on riding surface with pedals level, standing on left pedal (left side of unicycle is up). Use right foot to kick saddle up so that it hits left leg. Sit on saddle, place right foot on right pedal and ride away. Same skill with right foot starting on right pedal.

b. Walk the wheel 25 meters.

c. Spin five full revolutions of body and unicycle within a one-meter circle.

d. Ride one-footed with left foot in control position within a 3-meter circle. Same skill with right foot in control position.

e. Maintain a stationary balance for 5 seconds; no twisting, rocking, or bouncing.

f. Jump with unicycle so that tire leaves the riding surface. Jump can be forward or to the side.

Level 7

a. Pick-up mount. Unicycle wheel upright, but with saddle on riding surface in front of wheel. Jump onto pedals, then lift up saddle (only after on pedals), sit on saddle and ride away. Mount must start with pedals level.

b. Ride in figure-eight with saddle held to front of rider.

c. Ride backward with saddle held to rear of rider for 25 meters.

d. Ride one-footed in figure-eight with left foot in control position. Same skill with right foot in control position.

e. Ride backward one-footed for 25 meters.

f. Walk the wheel one-footed with left foot pushing wheel for 25 meters. Same skill with right foot in control position.

g. Walk the wheel with hands, seated or with chest on saddle, for 10 meters.

h. Pirouette. Spin into circles of decreasing size until unicycle and rider are rotating on one spot (50-centimeter circle limit) for two full revolutions with no turning of pedals.

Level 8

a. Perfect spin mount. Swing leg onto pedal, spin at least 720 degrees (twice around) before pedaling and come to a complete standstill before riding away.

b. Ride backward into a spin of at

least five revolutions within one-meter circle; ride away forward.

c. Ride backward with saddle held to front of rider in figure-eight.

d. Walk the wheel in figure-eight.

e. Walk the wheel backward for 25 meters.

f. Ride with saddle held to front of rider one-footed for 25 meters.

g. Walk the wheel sideways. Stand on wheel with feet on either side of seat post holding saddle with hands, complete a circle within 3-meter diameter limit.

h. Ride one-footed backward for 25 meters with left foot in control position. Same skill with right foot in control position.

i. Glide for 10 meters. This is riding with foot sliding on top of tire for control, usually initiated from riding one-footed and lifting pedaling foot up to wheel.

Level 9

a. Free jump mount to one-footed wheel walk. Balance unicycle with hands until it is standing free, then jump up and land on saddle with one foot on wheel, walk the wheel one-footed away, continuing for 2 meters before returning feet to pedals.

b. Side ride. Ride unicycle with left foot on right pedal or right foot on left pedal, standing next to unicycle, for 10 meters, with non-pedaling leg extended. The skill only need be performed, without starting from, or returning to, standard riding position.

c. Ride with saddle held to front, hop up and spin unicycle 180 degrees in relation to body, landing on pedals with unicycle facing backward, continue riding with saddle held to front, hop up and spin unicycle again, landing with unicycle facing forward.

d. Ride backward one-footed in figure-eight.

e. Walk the wheel one-footed in figure-eight.

f. Walk the wheel backward in figure-eight.

g. Backward pirouette. Ride backward into circles of decreasing size until unicycle and rider are rotating on one spot (50-centimeter circle limit) for two full revolutions of body and unicycle with no turning of pedals.

Level 10

a. Seat behind rolling jump mount from the side, backward. With wheel rolling backward, jump onto pedals from side of unicycle while holding saddle behind rider. Continue riding backward at least two meters with saddle held to rear of rider.

b. Ride into a pirouette with saddle held to front of rider. Complete two revolutions of unicycle and body within 50 centimeter circle and ride away with saddle held to front of rider.

c. Balance on unicycle (no twisting, rocking or bouncing) for 30 seconds.

d. Walk the wheel with one hand backward in 3-meter circle.

e. Walk the wheel one-footed backward in figure-eight.

f. Extended pirouette. Complete five full revolutions of unicycle and body within 50 centimeter circle.

g. Coast in a circle (any size). No contact whatsoever with any part of pedal or crank or wheel unit of unicycle.

FUTURE OF ARTISTIC UNICYCLING COMPETITION

It is my belief that artistic unicycling competition is here to stay. This is a challenging sport that is growing in popularity. In the future I believe there will be many more local, regional, and sectional competitions. At the national level, there will be a need for both a national age-group championships and a national open championships. The national open championships could be used for selection of a team to represent the United States in international competition and world championships.

Chapter 13

CLUBS AND ORGANIZATIONS

Most unicycle riders enjoy sharing their interests with others. A unicycle club is a good way to do this. There's also an established national organization and, more recently, an international organization has been formed.

CLUBS

Clubs are now in operation in a number of areas (see Chapter 14). If no club has been formed in your area that will meet your needs, you can form one. An excellent source of information about unicycling clubs is the Unicycling Society of America, Inc., P.O. Box 40534, Redford, Michigan 48240 (send a stamped, self-addressed envelope with requests for information).

An easy way to start a unicycling club is to get together with other unicycle riders in your area. If no other riders can be located, start by teaching others to ride. Once a nucleus is formed, the rest is usually easy.

First, set up an informal meeting. Be sure to have everyone bring their unicycles along. The first meeting can be at someone's house. Later, as the club grows, other meeting places, such as a community center, school, or "Y" should be considered.

The small initial group can serve as a steering committee. The purpose and objectives of the proposed club can be formulated. Plans for the first regular meeting can also be made.

Clubs range from informal to highly organized. Typical activities include meetings, unicycling instruction, outings, competitions, and performing in demonstrations and shows. Members share experiences. In many cases, group pur-chasing of unicycles for members can result in substantial savings.

Many clubs have found it advantageous to organize their clubs within an established organization, such as a recreation department, school, "Y", or community center. Often, this adds prestige to the group. Other possible advantages include the use of facilities, organizational help, liability insurance coverage, advertising, and promotion.

If the membership is to be selective, word of mouth and invitations are means for gathering prospective members for the first regular meeting. For larger clubs, other means of promotion, such as posters, newspapers, radio, and television, can be used.

At the first regular meeting the organizational structure can be decided and officers can be elected. The purpose, objectives, and organizational structure should be written out. Often this is done in the form of a constitution.

Things that will help to make the first regular meeting a success are refreshments, name tags, a movie or demonstration, and having everyone bring their unicycles. After the business meeting, an informal unicycle riding session can be held.

The matter of dues should be considered at the first meeting. The amount will depend on the planned activities, whether or not a newsletter is to be published, and whether or not the club will own unicycles and other equipment. One unicycle club at a university, for example, charges a $5 lifetime membership fee. This club presently owns ten unicycles, which the members are entitled to borrow.

In most cases, regularly scheduled meetings work best. At each meeting, in addition to the business session, unicycling practice or other activity should be included.

As is the case with most clubs, the members will join for various reasons. As far as possible, it is best to take everyone's interests into consideration. The key to success of any club will depend to a large extent on the spirit of the members and the satisfaction they derive from the club experience.

After the purposes and goals have been established, provision made for election of officers, and regular meetings scheduled, committees can be formed to plan activities. The club will probably want to exchange information with other similar clubs and, if distance warrents, plan joint activities such as get-togethers and competitions.

Some clubs have found it advantageous to incorporate as non-profit organizations.

Group buying power is an important advantage of belonging to a club. Arrangements can often be made through local bicycle dealers for discounts on unicycles for club members. It's also possible that some members will have skills, talents and equipment for building unicycles.

Many clubs participate in civic events. This is perhaps the best advertisement your club can get. For example, riding in a parade will show the club to hundreds of prospective members.

Many clubs have designed club emblems. This helps to add distinction to the group. A banner carried by unicyclists (Fig. 13-1) at demonstrations and parades will help to advertise a club and promote unicycling.

Unicycling is such an attractive activity that many clubs, once started, have little difficulty in recruiting new members. However, for this recruitment to be effective, the club should offer instruction to beginners. This and other club activities are discussed below.

Instruction

Many people who learn to ride a unicycle enjoy teaching others how to ride. Many clubs hold teaching sessions

Fig. 13-1. A banner is carried by two unicyclists (photo courtesy Peter Hangach).

for beginners. In this way, the fun and enjoyment of unicycling is spread to others. Many of those who come for instruction will want to join the club.

Teaching unicycling, like swimming, almost always involves success, provided that the instructor has the patience to stay with the student long enough. However, wide variations in learning ability should be recognized.

Intermediate and advanced instruction should also be available. Advanced riders can help those at the intermediate level. And for advanced riders, the friendly competition involved in trying to learn a new skill before someone else is a good motivating factor.

Group Rides and Outings

Going on a unicycle "hike" provides an interesting diversion. This can be a club activity or just getting a group of unicycle riders together and taking off. Parks and areas without automobile traffic are best. The rides can be as short or long as desired.

The unicycle "hike" can be combined with a picnic and other activities, such as games and races.

In some cases, it may be desirable to have an automobile accompany the unicycle riders to carry picnic lunches and pick up riders who can't make it "all the way."

An outing can be set up by reserving a suitable spot at a park. Set the time and place and have everyone bring their unicycles. Committees can be formed to take care of the various phases of the outing, such as food, planning activities, and promoting the event.

Riding in Parades

Riding in parades is another popular club activity. Work up a parade riding routine (see Chapter 12). A banner with the club name can be carried on a pole by two riders. Costumes and decorated unicycles add to the effect.

Demonstrations

Once a unicycle club's performances are known in the community, the problem will most likely be to select which ones the club wishes to participate in. However, the club may have to seek out its first appearance. Before doing this, work up a demonstration routine (see Chapter 12). Then contact various organizations such as P.T.A.s and civic clubs and tell them about your demonstration team. This is almost like asking for an invitation, but after the first time it probably won't be necessary again.

In some communities, schools, YMCAs, and other organizations sponsor shows and circuses. Unicycle acts are generally a welcome addition. Another possibility is a charity show. Sometimes talent shows are held. A unicycle club performance stands a good chance of winning these.

Besides working up the demonstration, there are a number of details that should be considered. Club committees can be responsible for these. Not only must the performers be at the show site on time, but also all unicycles and other equipment and props. Before accepting an invitation, always go to the location and check to make sure there is enough room and that a hard riding surface is available. Otherwise, the club may arrive to find that they are expected to perform on a 4-foot by 4-foot stage or on soft grass or some other unsuitable surface. In some cases, the club can help with the promotion by providing details about the demonstration to newspapers, radio, and television.

Other Activities

Ideas for other activities will be found throughout the book. For example, some clubs sponsor unicycle competition. Or the club can play games, such as basketball and hockey, on unicycles. If another unicycle club is in the area, competition can be held between the clubs.

NATIONAL AND INTERNATIONAL ORGANIZATIONS

There is presently both a national and an international organization devoted to unicycling.

Unicycling Society of America, Inc.

The Unicycling Society of America, Inc., was founded in 1973 as a non-profit organization (see Chapter 14 for history of this organization). The aims of this organization are to foster social and athletic interest in and promote the healthy, wholesome sport of unicycling among youth and adults of the country by establishing voluntary standards of performance and sponsoring and over-seeing local and national meets and to disseminate knowledge and information on all phases of the sport to all interested parties throughout the country via a newsletter and information service.

The annual dues (at the time of this writing $6.00 for United States members and $8.00 for foreign members) includes a subscription to the quarterly newsletter, membership card, and voting privilege.

Most of the members are in the United States, but there are also members in many other parts of the world, including Canada, Japan, Puerto Rico, Germany, Sweden, Netherlands, England, Switzerland, Hong Kong, Denmark, and Australia.

Annual meeting of the membership is currently at the time of the National Unicycle Meet, which is sanctioned by the Society and held in a different part of the country every year. Membership offices include President, Vice-President, Secretary, Treasurer, Newsletter Editor, and three Directors. Any member of the society can vote at the annual meeting and all are encouraged to attend it, and the National Unicycle Meet, which is a weekend of fun and excitement.

At the National Unicycle Meets, there are competitions in group and parade formations, racing, and artistic skill riding for individuals, couples, and groups. There are age groups for 10 and under, 19 and over, and four groups inbetween, so there is competition for all ages and many awards to be won. There are unicyclists from all over the country and world with whom to meet and become friends. Ideas are exchanged and communicated to other people. Many riders come away able to ride better than they ever thought they could!

For information and applications, write to the Unicycling Society of America, Inc., P.O. Box 40534, Redford, Michigan 48240. Include a stamped, self-addressed envelope with your request.

International Unicycling Federation

The International Unicycling Federation declared itself officially alive on June 1, 1982, although the concept goes back much further than this (see Chapter 14). The organization is devoted to promoting unicycling on an international level. The first International Unicycle Convention sponsored by this organization was held at Syracuse University in Syracuse, New York, July 27-29, 1984, with plans to make this an annual event.

Information about this organization can be obtained from the International Unicycling Federation, c/o Jenack Circus Corporation, 67 Lion Lane, Westbury, New York 11590. Enclose a stamped, self-addressed envelope with your request.

Chapter 14

HISTORY AND DEVELOPMENT

This chapter covers the history and development of unicycles and unicycling at the professional and amateur levels. Feats and records are covered separately in Chapter 15.

HISTORY AND DEVELOPMENT OF ONE-WHEEL CYCLES

Over the years, I have tried to piece together the story of how monocycling and unicycling got started. This has been no easy task. While there are scattered references to monocycling and unicycling in writings of the late 1800s, it is often difficult to determine the authenticity and there are many conflicting claims.

There were two basic types of early one-wheel cycles: with the rider inside the wheel and with the rider above the wheel. For our purposes here, we will call a one-wheel cycle with the rider inside the wheel a "monocycle" and those with the rider above the wheel a "unicycle."

Monocycles

Drawings of people riding one-wheel cycles with the riders mounted inside the wheels appeared in the 1860s and perhaps even earlier.

In the 1860s there is reported to have been a controversy among inventers as to whether to put the rider on the inside or on top of the wheel. Apparently the "inside" won out at the time. The decision seems to have been based on which would lead to the best form of transportation.

A patent was made on a monocycle in 1869 by Richard C. Hemmings (Fig. 14-1). I have been unable to find out if this or other early monocycles were actually constructed.

A number of other monocycle patents followed. I have been unable to determine when the first working monocycle was actually constructed, but judging from the number of early patents relating to the monocycle, it seems likely that some of these cycles were actually constructed, perhaps in the 1870s or even earlier.

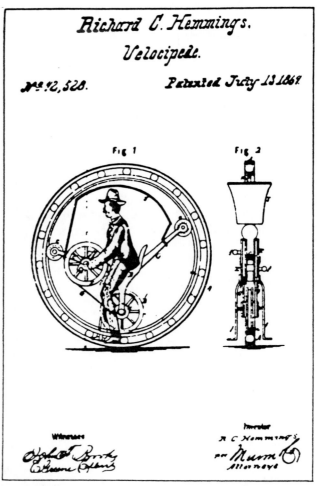

Fig. 14-1. A patent was made by Richard C. Hemmings on a monocycle in 1869.

Drawings of monocycles frequently appeared in early magazines and books. Similiar in principle to a monocycle but with greater transverse equilibrium is a "dicycle" with two wheels mounted on a common axis. White's cycle (Fig. 14-2) is an example of an early cycle of this type that was shown in an 1869 issue of **Scientific American**. A drawing of Gauthier's monocycle (Fig. 14-3) was in an 1877 issue of **La Nature**. An 1882 issue of **De Natuur** featured the monocycle shown in Figure 14-4. The novel monocycle with the rider inside the spokes shown in Figure 14-5 appeared in an 1884 issue of **Scientific American**. Harper's monocycle (Fig. 14-6), which appears to be a workable design, was in an 1894 issue of **Scientific American**. Archibald Sharp's famous 1896 treatise **Bicycles & Tricycles** showed a novel monocycle for two riders (Fig. 14-7).

James M. Pound of Long Beach, California, designed, built, and patented the monocycle shown in Figure 14-8 and Figure 14-9 in the late 1960s. A freewheeling bicycle hub turns the outside wheel. The hub braking system is also used. A small wheel is placed forward outside the large wheel in an attempt to prevent somersaulting if braking is too rapid.

From riding monocycles today, we can surmise what might have happened when (and if) early monocycles were actually constructed. Maintaining balance on a monocycle while moving is relatively easy since the rider's center of gravity is positioned (on most monocycles) below the center of the wheel. Braking can be a problem, since the rider tends to circle with the wheel if the riding platform inside the wheel is locked to the rim of the wheel for braking. This problem can be taken care of to a certain extent by using a stop wheel, such as shown on the cycle in Figure 14-8 and Figure 14-9.

A more difficult problem is steering. Turning a monocycle can be extremely difficult.

Except as a novelty device, the monocycle never became popular. Even though a monocycle can be freewheeling (i.e., it will coast when the pedals are

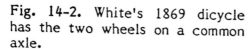

Fig. 14-2. White's 1869 dicycle has the two wheels on a common axle.

Fig. 14-3.
Gauthier's 1877
monocycle.

Fig. 14-4. An
1882 drawing
of a mono-
cycle.

Fig. 14-5. An 1884 drawing of novel monocycle with rider inside cage of spokes.

Fig. 14-7. Novel monocycle for two riders.

Fig. 14-6. Harper's 1894 monocycle.

Fig. 14-8. James M. Pound of Long Beach, California, designed and built this monocycle in the late 1960s (**Popular Mechanics** Magazine, by permission).

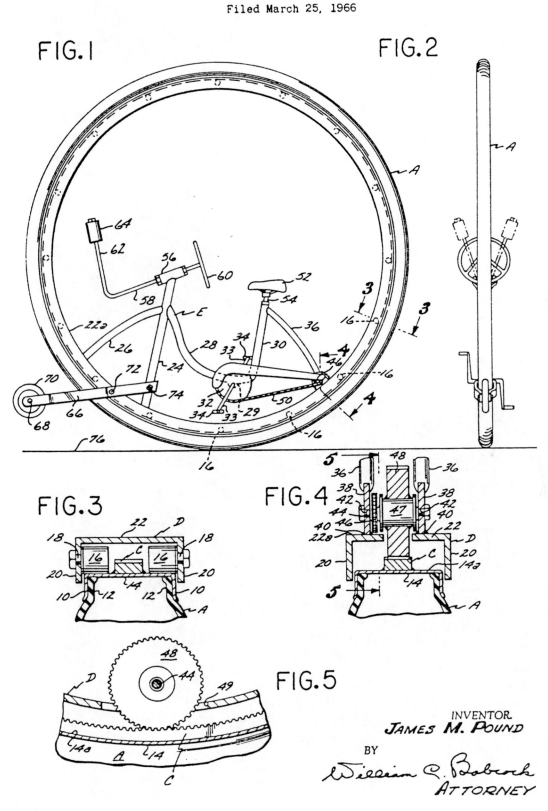

April 30, 1968   J. M. POUND   3,380,755

HOOP-TYPE CYCLE

Filed March 25, 1966

FIG.1   FIG.2

FIG.3   FIG.4

FIG.5

INVENTOR.
JAMES M. POUND
BY
William C. Babcock
ATTORNEY

Fig. 14-9. Patent drawings of James M. Pound's hoop-type cycle.

held stationary), it never developed as a form of transportation. This was probably because of the control limitations and because of the advantages inherent in the bicycle.

The monocycle will attract much attention today when ridden in a parade, but it apparently never became popular as a stage or show cycle.

A number of motor-driven monocycles have been built and ridden. Signor Lilio Negroni of Milan, Italy, built a monocycle powered by a gasoline motor and rode it at an automobile show in 1904.

Walter Nilsson, who made his fame as a unicyclist in the 1930s and 1940s (detailed later in this chapter and in Chapter 15), constructed and rode a monocycle that was powered by a single-cylinder 12-horsepower gasoline motor and had a 5-foot pneumatic tire. He called the cycle the "UNO-WHEEL."

Rudy Yung, now deceased, designed, built, and rode one in parades on the West Coast (Fig. 14-10 and Fig. 14-11).

LaFrance Bressen of Galesburg, Michigan, built a motor-driven monocycle with a 36-inch wheel (Fig. 14-12).

Fig. 14-10. Rudy Yung, now deceased, is shown riding motor-driven monocycle that he built (photo courtesy Herman Yung).

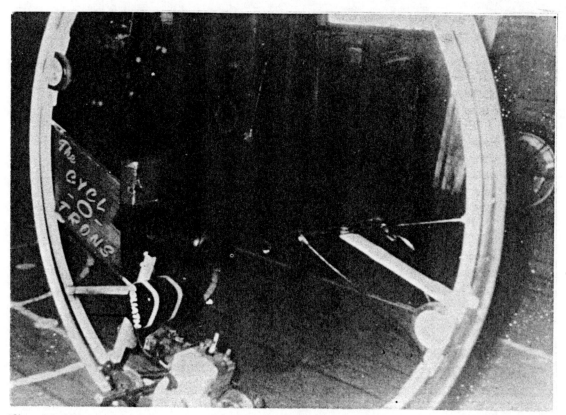

Fig. 14-11. Rudy Yung's motor-driven monocycle (photo courtesy Herman Yung).

Fig. 14-12. LaFrance Bressen of Galesburg, Michigan, built this motor-driven monocycle (**Popular Mechanics** Magazine, by permission).

Unicycles

With the rider above the wheel, and thus the center of gravity higher than the center of the wheel, the additional problem of keeping the rider over the wheel in a forward-backward direction enters the picture. The possibility of doing this would have seemed far fetched indeed in 1791 when, according to one account, Conte de Sivrac demonstrated a hobbyhorse (two wheels in line with a frame that the rider straddled) in a Parisian park and those watching thought that the only reason it could be ridden was because the feet were making contact with the ground. However, Conte de Sivrac must have realized that once in motion, balance was no major problem. Coasting downhill without the feet touching the ground would easily demonstrate this.

It should be pointed out that some historians now believe that Conte de Sivrac did not actually construct a hobbyhorse, and perhaps this device was not invented until 1817, when Baron Karl von Drais of Germany constructed and patented a hobbyhorse with the front wheel steerable by means of handlebars.

The first true bicycle, a two-wheeled

velocipede that could be ridden with the feet entirely off the ground, did not appear until 1839, when Kirkpatrick Macmillan of Scotland, a blacksmith, constructed a treadle-operated two-wheel machine, which was similar to Drais's steerable hobbyhorse except that it had treadle devices operated by the feet, supplying power to the rear wheel.

Pedal arms and pedals were added to the front wheel of a hobbyhorse by Ernest Michaux of France in 1861. He used a heavy iron frame, wooden wheels, and iron tires.

These early cycles were called "velocipedes." The front wheel assembly and hub had the pedal arms connected to an axle that was fixed to the hub and turned in blocks that were connected to the ends of the fork prongs, similar to those on modern standard unicycles.

From a bicycling point of view, these cycles had the problem of not being freewheeling unless the feet were taken off the pedals. One complete revolution of the pedals resulted in only one revolution of the front wheel. To give a longer tracking distance to the wheel, James Starley, an Englishman, constructed a variation of Michaux's design that had a larger front wheel and a smaller rear wheel. This was the beginning of the cycles that came to be known as the "ordinary" or "penny farthing."

These cycles soon spread to the United States. The Cunningham Company began importing them from Endland in 1876, and soon after that the Pope Manufacturing Company of Hartford, Connecticut, started making Columbia penny farthings in this country (Fig. 14-13). Thomas Stevens of the United States pedaled one of these cycles around the world in 1884.

The "safety" bicycle with a chain-driven rear wheel and a diamond-shaped frame and solid rubber tires was developed by John K. Starley of England in 1884. These early bicycles had a fixed rear hub that was not freewheeling, but freewheeling bicycles with coaster brakes were in use by 1900. By the mid-1890s, the penny farthing had largely been replaced by the safety bicycle, which developed into the modern bicycle as we know it today.

Fig. 14-13. An 1881 catalog illustration of the Standard Columbia penny farthing.

The origin of the unicycle is controversial. Unicyling probably did not evolve directly from monocycles (with the riders inside the wheels). The most accepted theory is that unicycling was discovered by accident while riding a penny farthing. With a small trailing wheel, the large front wheel was constructed on the lines of a modern-day unicycle. One of the hazards of riding a penny farthing was pitching over forward when decelerating (braking by slowing the direct drive pedal action) too rapidly. Some riders who started this pitching action must have remained balanced on the front wheel for a time before the rear wheel returned to the ground or the cycle pitched on over forward. Perhaps early riders had "contests" to see who could ride the longest distance on the front wheel alone, like children do today with wheelies on the rear wheels of high-rise bikes.

Sebastian Merrill Neuhausen, who died in 1972 at the age of 99 and was one of the first to make his fame and fortune as a professional cycle rider in vaudeville, stated in an interview shortly before his death that he had ridden a penny farthing on the front wheel in 1892.

A unicycle rider can easily demonstrate that a penny farthing can be ridden on one wheel.

Early drawings of unicycles, such as the sketch made in the 1870s that is in the Deutsches Museum, Munich, Germany, and is purported to be of John Hobby's unicycle (Fig. 14-14), the unicycle shown in Archibald Sharp's 1896 treatise **Bicycles & Tricycles** (Fig. 14-15), and the 1896 sketch showing cycles ridden in the Festival of Cyclists in London's Crystal Palace (Fig. 14-16), support this concept of the development of the unicycle. Note especially the unicycle in Figure 14-16 that is being ridden down the stairs. It is essentially a penny farthing with the frame cut off behind the saddle and the saddle mounted solid to the fork so that it does not turn. It is also interesting to note the number of different types and designs of cycles, including the so-called "ultimate wheel" (a wheel with pedal arms and pedals but no frame or saddle or handlebars) that were already in use by 1896.

John Hobby's unicycle (Fig. 14-14), if it was actually constructed and ridden, may have been the first unicycle with the rider above the wheel. It is interesting to note the extension rods on the pedals, which would allow the use of a larger wheel than could be used without the extensions. Some early penny farthings also had this feature. To date, this is the earliest reference to a unicycle with the rider above the wheel that I have found.

A number of people have made the claim of inventing the unicycle. One of these was Ahrens. His unicycle was on display at the Gift Shop in the Cliff House in San Francisco with the caption: "The First Unicycle, invented by Ahrens of California." Unfortunately, the Gift Shop was completely destroyed, together with the unicycle and a number of early bicycles, by a fire in November of 1963. To date I have not been able to locate any additional information on Ahrens or the unicycle.

Lou Lacher, who died at the age of 82 in 1965, also laid claim to the invention of the unicycle. His obituary said that he was also the first person to ride a unicycle on a tightwire and that he did this in New York City before the "turn of the century."

According to a 1902 editor of **Illustrated Arena**, the father of Albert H. Minting was the "world's first unicyclist."

George N. Hendee, a well-known trick rider in the 1880s, was reported to have

Fig. 14-14. John Hobby's unicycle.

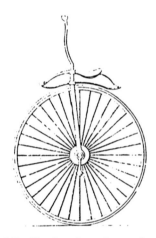

Fig. 14-15. Early drawing of a unicycle.

removed the rear wheel from a penny farthing and to have learned to ride the front wheel alone. A recent article stated, "It is a matter of record that Hendee is probably the first man to master the unicycle."

Sebastian Merrill Neuhausen, who rode a penny farthing on the front wheel in 1892, believed that he was the first unicyclist.

Others making the claim of having been the first to unicycle include Nick R. Kauffman, William Dinwindle, and Howard Seely.

Who was actually first remains controversial. It is possible that several people discovered the unicycle independently at different times.

Unicycling speed records were published in the **League of American**

Fig. 14-16. A sketch showing cycles that were ridden in the Festival of Cyclists in London's Crystal Palace in 1896 (from Clarence P. Hornung, **Wheels Across America**, Julien Yoseloff, A. S. Barnes & Company, by permission).

Wheelmen Bulletin in 1888. W. H. Barber is reported to have ridden a mile on his unicycle in 3 minutes and 27 seconds, 10 seconds faster than the world's record at that time. A later issue reported that Bert Myers rode the front wheel of a "Light Champion" penny farthing at Lake View Park in Peoria, Illinois, and broke all unicycle records from 2 to 14 miles. He rode 13 miles and 5,098 feet in one hour and 14 miles in one hour and 7 seconds. The article stated that this was the greatest distance ever ridden on one wheel without a dismount.

This indicates that unicycling was well-established by 1888 and that the riders were converting penny farthings to unicycles. There is an old photograph of a

rider on a unicycle of this type in the Technical Museum in Stockholm, Sweden. The unicycle has both a saddle and penny farthing style handlebars.

Chain-driven unicycles (also called "giraffe" unicycles) probably started with early direct-drive (non-freewheeling) bicycles. Sebastian Merrill Neuhasen reportedly purchased a safety bicycle in 1892. In an interview shortly before his death, he said that he quickly learned to ride it with the front wheel in the air.

In 1899, Nick R. Kaufmann of Rochester, New York, rode a direct-drive bicycle on the rear wheel as part of his trick riding act.

The giraffe unicycle as we know it today, along with many variations,

154

probably developed from riding direct-drive bicycles on one wheel.

Frank Kauffman, nephew of Nick R. Kauffman, claimed to have been co-inventor of the giraffe unicycle "well before the turn of the century." This could well have been the case, since Nick was riding a direct-drive bicycle on one wheel at least as early as 1899, and this could well have suggested the idea for a giraffe unicycle to Frank.

It is likely that the first standard-type unicycles had big wheels. The first giraffe unicycles, if patterned after the direct-drive safety bicycles of the day, probably had smaller wheels. This trend toward smaller wheels was also passed on to standard-type unicycles. A number of the cycles in 1896 Festival of Cyclists sketch (Fig. 14-16) employed wheels smaller than those used on the early penny farthings.

A successful motor-driven unicycle (Fig. 14-17 and Fig. 14-18) was not built until 1966. It all started when Frank Malick, an engineer at the Astronuclear Lab, bought a unicycle for his 14-year-old son Johnny. As he watched his son, who learned to ride the unicycle, pedal about, he began to think about the possibilities of attaching a motor to the wheel. After researching the idea, he became convinced that it could be done. He started development in February of 1965. The first stable ride took place in his basement on January 1, 1966. A one-horsepower gasoline engine was used.

To date, a number of operating models have been built and sold. One, for example, has a 16-inch rim motorcycle wheel, an 8-horsepower engine, and a top speed of about 25 miles per hour.

Malick holds patent number 3,399,742 on his invention (Fig. 14-19), which he calls the "Weelie." The vehicles are available from the Franklin Control Company, 518 Greenleaf Drive, Monroeville, Pennsylvania 15146.

A motor-driven unicycle with the rider above the wheel and no weights below the center of the wheel to offset the weight of the rider requires much more sophistication than connecting the engine to the wheel with a chain. The engine speed is kept constant by an electronic governor. The engine power is applied to the wheel by an electro-magnetic clutch. Braking torque is applied to the wheel by an electromagnetic brake.

Fig. 14-17. Frank Malick gets set to ride his invention--a motor-driven unicycle (photo courtesy Franklin Control Co.).

Fig. 14-18. Frank Malick goes for a ride on the "Wheelie" (photo courtesy Franklin Control Co.).

155

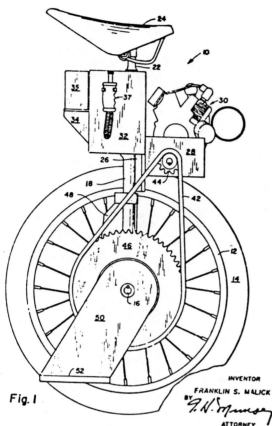

Fig. 1

INVENTOR
FRANKLIN S. MALICK
BY
ATTORNEY

Fig. 14-19. A patent drawing of Malick's powered unicycle.

A miniature transistorized computer causes the clutch and brake to work together so that the wheel runs at the speed demanded by the rider with his hand control.

According to the inventor, it's much easier to learn to ride than a pedaled unicycle. Balance is maintained by a delicate touch on the hand-held speed control, speeding up to counter a fall forward and slowing down to counter a fall backward. Starts are made from a stable position with the toes on the ground. The beginning rider slides his toes along until he gains skill and confidence. He is always in control of the speed of the vehicle; it can never run away.

The "Weelie" was demonstrated on the Carson Show and received considerable attention. Johnny Carson even took a turn on it.

A motor-driven unicycle with 400 pounds of weight added below the axle to counterbalance the weight of the rider was built and demonstrated in Japan at an inventor's show. This cycle is, in principle, a sort of monocycle with the rider above the wheel.

While it may not be a unicycle, the "Walking Thing" (Fig. 14-20 and Fig. 14-21) certainly is unique. This particular one was designed and built by Alvin Drysdale of Bradley Beach, New Jersey. A similar machine was used on stage by the Chick and Chicklets, a vaudeville act in the 1920s. Goran Lundstrom of Sweden recently designed and built another walking machine. Drysdale's "Walking Thing" is presently owned by David Metz of Freehold, New Jersey.

The "Walking Thing" is six feet high. The ankles have springs built in to give it heel and toe walking motion. Hip action is accomplished by two offset cams that raise each leg off the ground as it moves forward to walk. To use it, the rider mounts and pedals. The "Walking Thing" does the walking.

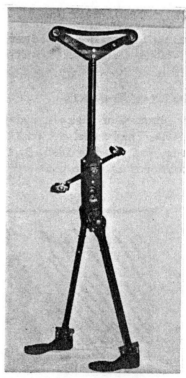

Fig. 14-20. The "Walking Thing" shown was built by Alvin Drysdale of Bradley Beach, New Jersey, and is now owned by David Metz of Freehold, New Jersey.

Fig. 14-21. When pedaled like a unicycle, the "Walking Thing" does the walking.

PROFESSIONAL UNICYCLING

Professional unicycle and bicycle acts were popular before the turn of the century. The Festival of Cyclist sketch shows the range of stunts that were being performed in 1896 (Fig. 14-16). By then, unicycling was already a highly developed art.

One of the leading early professional performers was Arnold Buchner (Fig. 14-22, Fig. 14-23, and 14-24). The photos were provided by and reprinted here with the kind permission of Arnold Buchner's grandson, John W. Buchner of San Bruno, California. About his grandfather, he said:

"Arnold Buchner was born in a small dairy town in Minnesota in 1884. He and his brother, Albert, put on shows for local people. In 1892, he moved to San Francisco.

"My grandfather ran away with the circus as a unicyclist in 1898. He went under the name of 'The Amazing Buchner' or 'The Amazing Arnold,' I'm not sure which; I've heard of both names.

"The act consisted of a ladder seventy feet long with the rungs spaced six inches apart, set at a forty-five degree angle secured to a platform fastened to the center pole of the tent; I believe it was a side-show tent. He would start a decent down the ladder on the unicycle removing the various hats and costumes that he was wearing. He was known to have five costumes and hats on at the start of his act.

"He traveled with the circus from 1898 to 1902 when he finally settled down. I do not know which circus he traveled with but he traveled mainly in the western states.

"I'm like my grandfather in that I have sawdust in my blood. I drive a team of horses to an air calliope and the running gear is approximately one hundred years old. My son also follows the circus by collecting and building circus wagon models."

Fig. 14-22. Arnold Buchner performing what appears to be switch from one unicycle to another (photo courtesy John W. Buchner).

157

Fig. 14-23. Arnold Buchner making his famous descent down seventy-foot ladder mounted at forty-five degree angle with rungs six inches apart (photo courtesy John W. Buchner).

Fig. 14-24. Arnold Buchner removing various hats and jackets during a descent down ladder (photo courtesy John W. Buchner).

Another early spectacular act was performed by Albert H. Minting, who was born in London about 1870. In 1902, his act included riding a unicycle on a 20-inch wide spiral track to a summit sixty feet above, then descending (Fig. 14-25). He was billed as the "Only Unicycle Ascensionist in the World."

Throughout the years, performing unicycle artists have continued to dazzle audiences. Some of the early acts have already been mentioned in connection with the invention of the unicycle, including Sebastian Merrill Neuhausen, Lou Lacher, George N. Hendee, Nick R. Kauffman, and Frank Kauffman. Others followed, including Joe Jackson, Sr., Joe Jackson Jr., Jimmy Valdair, Mel Hall, The Yokoi Troupe, Paul Gordon, Bobby Whaling and Yvette, Grover O'Day, The Cycling Kirks, Jess Monefeldt (stage-names of acts included LeBrac and Bernice, Maysy and Brach, and Jim Dandy), The Cyclonians, Michelletty, Mario Royas, Boy Foy, The Shyrettos, The Goetche Brothers, The Volantes, Walter Nilsson, Steve McPeak, Barry Lappy, Bruskis, The Esquedas, Navarros, Kolmedys, and Kenny Sherburne, as well as hundreds of others, have accomplished an unbelievable array of stunts.

Boy Foy is famous for his juggling while riding a unicycle. In 1933 at the age of 14 he balanced five balls and juggled four hoops while one-foot riding a unicycle.

The Shyrettos, which included Alfred Shyretto, Walter Shyretto, and Honey Shyretto (Fig. 14-26), performed both on unicycle and circus or artistic bicycles.

Fig. 14-25. In 1902 Albert H. Minting, who rode a unicycle on a 20-inch wide spiral track to a summit sixty feet above, then descended, was billed as the "Only Unicycle Ascensionist in the World" (courtesy Hertzberg Circus Collection, San Antonio Public Library).

Fig. 14-26. Honey Shyretto (photo courtesy Fred Pfening, Jr.).

Frank Kirk of The Cycling Kirks and Paul Gordon were both top performers on both bicycles and unicycles. Paul Gordon rides a unicycle in the movie "Showboat."

The Goetche Brothers became famous for performing a standing three-high pyramid with the bottom man riding a unicycle.

The Cyclonians began mainly as a troupe-type act. Charley VanBuskirk started in the act when he was only three years old. He later performed a single act, and presently performs "Adagio on Wheels" with his wife Joyce.

Jess Monefeldt, who performed with others as Maysy and Brach and later as LeBrac and Bernice and solo as Jim Dandy, was outstanding at adagio, balancing, and spinning feats, including spinning 16 hoops in different directions while riding a 9-foot, gold-plated giraffe unicycle. Jess Monefeldt continued to perform until his death at age 70 in 1977.

Mel Hall is often mentioned by other professionals as having been the greatest all-around unicycle performer. Mel Hall presently has a baboon act and the baboons even ride giraffe unicycles. In his own performing days, Mel Hall did many outstanding tricks, and is perhaps best remembered for riding a giraffe unicycle that had what appeared to be two saddles parallel to each other in a shoulder-stand while pedaling with his hands. To my knowledge, no one else has ever duplicated this feat. It is also interesting to note that Mel Hall's youngest daughter learned to ride a unicycle when she was about 18-months old, and this is perhaps a record for the youngest to learn to ride.

Barry Lappy of Hastings, England, started unicycling at the age of seven when his father, who owned a bicycle shop, made him a unicycle. By the age of nine, he had already performed in the Billy Smart Circus and the Hungarian State Circus. He next came to the United States and performed for two years with The Greatest Show on Earth.

I had the opportunity to meet Barry Lappy and his father and mother when Barry performed in San Diego, California, at the age of ten. I was extremely impressed. For his age, he was by far the most skilled unicyclist I have ever seen.

Barry Lappy continues as a star professional performer, appearing in circuses in England, Romania, and elsewhere. He performed at the Monte Carlo Festival in Monaco in 1979 and won an award and a medal. Latest report is that he is the star of "Tom Courtney's Circus World" and is billed as "The Wizard on Wheels."

Walter Nilsson and Steve McPeak, famous professionals who also established records, are covered below in this chapter.

THREE FAMOUS UNICYCLISTS

Three famous unicyclists who have set new standards for unicycling are Walter Nilsson, Steve McPeak, and Wally Watts. Each of these unicyclists set one or more world records, which are described below and summarized again in Chapter 15.

Walter Nilsson

Walter Nilsson, now deceased, was already famous as a vaudeville performer who used many types, styles, and sizes of unicycles and was called "The King of the Unicycles" when in 1933 he set out on an incredible journey. His goal, to ride an 8-foot unicycle across the United States. He was 33 years old at the time.

He started from the George Washington Bridge in New York. One hundred and seventeen days later, after covering a distance of 3,306 miles, he pedaled into San Francisco. The feat earned him a hero's welcome and Ripley's award for "The Most Unbelievable Feat of the Year."

Walter Nilsson and the 8-foot unicycle he used to ride from New York to San Francisco are shown in Figure 14-27. To my knowledge, no one else to date has ridden a unicycle that is 8-feet or taller such a long distance. If this is true, he also holds the time record of 117 days for covering the 3,306 miles on an 8-foot giraffe unicycle, with an average of over 28.2 miles per day.

Other information that I have been able to uncover about Walter Nilsson is that he had a collection of over 50 unicycles at his home in Closter, New Jersey, had a "Funi-Cycle" booth at Coney Island, and later had a bicycle shop in Santa Monica, California. One of the

Fig. 14-27. Left to right: Alvin Drysdale, Walter Nilsson (holding the eight-foot unicycle he rode from New York to San Francisco in 1933), and Tom Simmons in photo taken in 1931 or 1932, prior to Nilsson's cross-country trek (photo courtesy Alvin Drysdale).

giraffe unicycles that Nilsson used is now owned by Dr. and Mrs. Miles S. Rogers, who for a number of years performed with their son and daughters as the Wonderwheels (detailed later in this Chapter). Walter Nilsson also once built a standard unicycle in his shop in Santa Monica for Dr. Rogers.

A promotion booklet that has a copyright date of 1932 (before he made his cross-country ride) has a number of interesting photos from around the world of Walter Nilsson riding 8-foot giraffe unicycles, including one of him riding the unicycle on the edge of a building and another of him riding on top of a pyramid.

Various newspaper and magazine articles from later years show the motor-driven monocycle (described previously in this chapter), a walking pedal cycle, and a variety of novelty pedal cycles from his collection.

Steve McPeak

Steve McPeak not only holds a number of world unicycling records, but also must surely hold the record for breaking unicycle records. This seems even more remarkable when you realize that he did not learn to ride a unicycle until he was 20 years old.

It all started in 1965 when Steve McPeak was a 20-year-old freshman at Asbury College in Wilmore, Kentucky. Walking aimlessly across campus, he noticed a student riding a unicycle. Steve's interest increased considerably when the rider stopped to talk to a girl, rocking the unicycle back and forth in one place. Recalling the incident, Steve said, "It was so neat I couldn't believe it. Right then I decided to learn to ride a unicycle myself."

It happened that Steve was watching one of the three unicyclists on campus, and they wanted another collegiate to learn so that they would have a four-man act for the college gym show.

With six inches of snow on the roadway, Steve first attempted to ride a standard three-foot unicycle. That first day he managed to stay up long enough to have his picture taken. A month later, when he performed in the college gym show, he rode a six-foot high, chain-driven giraffe unicycle. Already he had become the best unicycle rider on campus.

Although he had no idea what the current record was, Steve decided that he wanted to ride a taller unicycle than anyone had ever done before. Even when he heard that someone had ridden a

15-foot unicycle, he did not change his goal. In my research, I have not been able to find any evidence of unicycles taller than this having been ridden up to that time. A photo that appeared in **Acrobat** magazine showed Walter Syretto of The Syrettos riding a 14-foot giraffe unicycle a number of years before this.

To make up for his late start and the fact that he was not born in a circus family, Steve practiced constantly, riding his unicycle from class to class and to his meals. In fact, he unicycled everywhere. On weekends he often worked out on unicycles at the gym. Sometimes he went for long unicycle rides in the hills with his three unicycle companions.

For summer vacation Steve returned to his home in Hoquiam, Washington, and started working his way upward. First he designed, built, and learned to ride a nine-foot chain-driven unicycle. Then he moved up to a 12-footer.

When he returned to Asbury College in the fall, he took the 12-foot unicycle along with him. In the college gym show that spring he not only rode the 12-footer forward, but also rode it backwards and rocked it back and forth in one place.

Back in Hoquiam the next summer Steve built and mastered other unicycles, including a 13-footer, just two feet shorter than the record for the tallest unicycle that had ever been ridden that Steve had heard about. Another was a three-wheeled model in which two wheels drove the main motion wheel. He also started riding unicycles on a seven-foot high tightwire. He removed the tire from a three-foot unicycle and, holding a long pole to help maintain balance, learned to ride it across the wire. Before long he moved up to a wire suspended 35 feet above the ground.

In September Steve transferred to Seattle Pacific College in Seattle,

Fig. 14-28. Steve McPeak riding a 20-foot unicycle (photo from **The Seattle Times,** by permission).

Washington. In October he finished building a 20-foot unicycle, which Steve believed was five feet taller than any unicycle that had ever been ridden up to that time. In November 1966 Steve used a ladder connected to a tightwire for mounting the 20-foot unicycle (Fig. 14-28). Then he pedaled away from the ladder, made a large circle, and returned to the ladder. The record was his.

The feat is even more remarkable when you consider that it was accomplished less than two years from the time when Steve had first tried a three-foot standard unicycle.

In February of 1967 Steve traveled to New York, where he appeared on I've Got a Secret. His secret was that he rode the tallest unicycle in the world, which the panel failed to guess. Steve then rode the 20-foot unicycle before the TV cameras.

After the spring semester Steve quit college to become a professional performer. At the time he did two acts--one on the ground, the other on a 35-foot high tightwire. His ground act included riding the tallest unicycle in the world. For a finale on the 35-foot high wire, he rode a 10-foot unicycle across without a net below. The best anyone else had ever done was a six-foot unicycle, and that had been on a wire six feet above the ground. For over a year Steve performed with small circuses along the West Coast.

In 1968, as a publicity stunt, Steve unicycled from Chicago to Las Vegas, making most of the distance on a 13-foot unicycle (Fig. 14-29 and Fig. 14-30). Several times, because of high winds, he was forced down to a standard unicycle. It was on the small unicycle that he made what he believed was the longest one-day ride up to that time. To date, I have not found any evidence to dispute this. The possibility exists that longer one-day rides had been made on "big-wheel" unicycles, perhaps before the turn of the century, but I have not found any records of this. Steve rode the standard unicycle, which has a shorter tracking distance than a "big-wheel" unicycle, for 23-1/2 hours and covered a distance of 186 miles. Except for four brief rest stops, he rode continuously.

In all, the trip from Chicago to Las Vegas covered 2,311 miles and took six

weeks and one day. He averaged over 53 miles a day. The only longer ride up to that time had been made by Walter Nilsson in 1933 on an 8-foot unicycle, as detailed above in this chapter. Steve sent me a map of the route that he took with the sections marked where he was forced to use the small unicycle. It is my estimate from this that he made about 1,500 miles on the 13-foot unicycle and

Fig. 14-29. Steve McPeak juggles three clubs while riding the 13-foot unicycle he used for most of his Chicago to Las Vegas ride (photo courtesy Steve McPeak).

Fig. 14-30. Steve McPeak on 13-foot unicycle with his brother, John McPeak, on his shoulders spinning plates on sticks (photo courtesy Steve McPeak).

800 miles on the small unicycle. I believe that this is the longest distance ever covered on a 13-foot unicycle in a period of six weeks and one day. A number of newspaper articles indicated the distance of the ride as 2,200 miles, but Steve said that the speedometer on the car that accompanied him on the journey gave a reading of 2,311 miles.

For a time Steve performed at Circus Circus Casino in Las Vegas. The low ceiling limited him to doing a ground act, but he set up a 35-foot high tightwire on a ranch just outside of Las Vegas and continued riding unicycles on the wire.

It was on this wire that Steve performed his greatest feat up to that time. He had constructed a special 20-foot unicycle--equal in height to his then tallest-ever-ridden-on-the-ground unicycle. Then on December 15, 1968, he rode it across the 35-foot high tightwire (Fig. 14-31). Steve used safety cables but

did not have a net below.

Steve continued to work his way upward, this time riding on the ground again. On February 2, 1969, in the parking lot behind Circus Circus Casino, he climbed a ladder to a special platform. Then he mounted a 31-foot tall unicycle, which towered almost to the height of an Olympic 10-meter diving platform (Fig. 14-32). Thirty feet away was a second platform. He hesitated, working the pedals back and forth, which in turn moved the wheel far below.

Then Steve pedaled away from the support. Those watching strained their necks to look upward at Steve pedaling at the top of the long unicycle frame. After what seemed a long time--actually it was about a 30-second ride--Steve reached the second platform. With this he had added eleven feet to his old record for riding the tallest unicycle.

Steve rode the 31-footer a total of four times, all on that same day. The longest ride was 100 feet.

For a time after that, Steve concentrated on his high-wire act. The 31-foot unicycle was placed on display in the American Bicycle Hall of Fame in Richmondtown, Staten Island, New York, where it was suspended in a horizontal position. There wasn't room to stand it up.

In his high-wire act, Steve included not only the 20-foot unicycle, but also a 10-foot zigzag unicycle (Fig. 14-33) and a tandem giraffe unicycle (Fig. 14-34).

But Steve was by no means through with breaking unicycling records and performing unusual unicycling feats. On November 8, 1975, he gained access to a 1,500-foot cable that is suspended 700 feet above Hoover Dam and rode a specially-constructed unicycle across. Since Steve did not have permission to do this stunt and he was trespassing on government property, he was fined $200. This escapade was shown on TV on "To Tell the Truth."

Steve McPeak no longer had the record for riding the tallest unicycle on the ground on October 28, 1976, when he regained the record for the tallest unicycle, not by riding on the ground but on a tightwire. With David Frost interviewing him for the "Guiness Book of

Fig. 14-31. Steve McPeak riding 20-foot unicycle across tightwire suspended 35 feet above the ground (photo courtesy Steve McPeak).

Fig. 14-32. Steve McPeak riding 31-foot unicycle (photo courtesy John McPeak).

Fig. 14-33. Steve McPeak riding 10-foot zigzag unicycle across high wire (photo courtesy John McPeak).

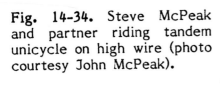
Fig. 14-34. Steve McPeak and partner riding tandem unicycle on high wire (photo courtesy John McPeak).

World Records" show, Steve rode a 41-foot unicycle across a tightwire suspended 40 feet above the ground to set a new official world's record.

I watched Steve McPeak perform this spectacular feat when the "Guiness Book of World Records" was televised. On the same program, his brother John McPeak, also a professional performer, broke another world's record by juggling for 6 hours and 45 minutes.

It is perhaps surprising that Steve chose to ride the unicycle on a wire rather than on the ground. No one had even approached his old record for riding a 20-footer on the high wire.

Other people were to ride unicycles taller than 41-feet on the ground, however (see Chapter 15). The record had worked its way up to a 72-foot unicycle when on November 21, 1980, Steve McPeak rode a 100-foot unicycle that weighed 1,400 pounds and cost $21,000 and took two years to complete. Steve used a safety harness suspended from a crane. This amazing feat was shown on national television on an NBC special called "Daredevils."

Latest word is that Steve has added an additional 100 feet to this unicycle, and plans to ride the 200-foot unicycle "one of these days."

Wally Watts

Unlike Walter Nilsson and Steve McPeak, Wally Watts is not a professional unicycle performer. He earns his living doing other things, and has in fact spent a great deal of this money doing some amazing things on one wheel.

Wally Watts of Edmonton, Alberta, Canada, decided that he wanted to ride a unicycle across Canada from the Pacific Ocean to the Atlantic Ocean. Unlike most other people who have made long rides on unicycles, Wally Watts decided that a "big wheel" with its longer tracking distance would be a real asset. Since no manufactured unicycles were available with "big wheels," Wally designed and built his own. The unicycle had a 42-inch wheel with a solid rubber tire.

On May 27, 1973, Wally started his journey from English Bay in Vancouver on his 42-inch wheel unicycle. Three months and one day later, on August 27, 1973, he completed his 4,550-mile ride when he reached the Atlantic Ocean in Halifax, Nova Scotia.

With this ride, Wally Watts had made the longest journey ever up to that time on a unicycle, breaking Walter Nilsson's record that had stood since 1933 by over a thousand miles. Wally's journey took 93 days and he averaged over 48 miles a day.

As incredible as Wally's unicycle ride across Canada was, it seems like only a "practice run" in comparison to what was to follow. People had made round-the-world journeys by pedal power on a variety of devices, including penny farthings, regular bicycles, and tandem bicycles, but no one had attempted it on a unicycle until Wally Watts set out to accomplish this feat. He left New York by plane on April 19, 1976, and flew to Scotland, where he began unicycling his way south and east.

He used a unicycle similar to the one he used for his trans-Canada ride, except it was of sturdier construction and had a 43-inch wheel instead of a 42-inch wheel.

On October 8, 1978, a little over 28 months after he started, he pedaled across the George Washington Bridge and on to the Guinness Museum, where he received official recognition for being the first person to unicycle around the world.

He had pedaled 12,000 miles and logged from 50 to 70 miles a day, which is a grueling pace even on a bicycle. Along with the vagaries of terrain and weather, Wally endured a pulled Achilles tendon in Greece, a broken arm when forced off the road in Turkey, a robbery in Afghanistan, and a terrible case of "Delhi Belly" in India. After these adventures, the last part of the journey from California to New York was, in Wally's words, "a piece of cake." In all, he traversed 16 countries, breaking the journey several times to earn money to continue or wait out winter storms or monsoon rains. He spent $15,000 to make this incredible journey. Perhaps someone else will someday also unicycle around the world, but Wally Watts will always be the first person to do so.

Wally Watts has been in the process of constructing a geared-down unicycle with a 10-foot wheel, which he plans to ride, but to my knowledge, he has not yet completed this cycle.

MODERN UNICYCLING

For many years the unicycle remained largely the vehicle of professional riders. Then very slowly it was discovered as a recreational and hobby device. A few bicycle companies started manufacturing unicycles on a limited basis. Since that time the demand has increased and a number of companies, both domestic and foreign, have manufactured unicycles.

In this section, I will attempt to trace the development of modern unicycling as a recreational activity, performing art, and competitive sport.

Judge Edison Hedges

One of the most interesting unicyclists was the late Judge Edison Hedges of Atlantic City, New Jersey. His outstanding career as a jurist and assemblyman in New Jersey belied the fact that he was the same Eddie Hedges who broke many world speedboat records, who was an accomplished cellist, and who during World War II participated in benefit performances for GIs at the Atlantic City Steel Pier as a vaudeville unicyclist and trick rider.

The unicycling first started when he saw Willie Richie perform on Steel Pier in the vaudeville show as a tramp cyclist. Hedges decided then that he wanted to perform like that. He became friends with Willie Richie, who taught Hedges the act. Willie Richie died shortly after that and Hedges purchased all of the cycle equipment, which amounted to a huge truckload, from Richie's widow.

Hedges practiced Willie Richie's act until he had it down pat. He was later booked for 18 shows at Steel Pier, the proceeds of which were contributed to the War Fund.

My Unicycling Experiences

When I first started unicycling in 1949 at the age of 13, I had seen unicycling in circus and stage acts, but I don't remember having seen anyone ride on the streets.

I was already heavily involved in gymnastics both at school and the YMCA when a friend showed me the remains of a unicycle that had belonged to his uncle, a former professional stage performer. The unicycle had been in a fire. In fact, there was only the fork, hub, pedal arms, and seat post, only enough so that you could tell that it had once been a unicycle.

Apparently my friend didn't consider it a treasure. He quickly accepted my one dollar offer. In fact, he seemed to think I was crazy to pay that much. Little did he know that I would have gone much higher.

With the help of a man at a bicycle shop, I built the unicycle back up, spoking a rim to the old hub, then attaching a leather racing saddle to the post. There were many difficulties. Standard bicycle parts had to be adapted to fit. The original unicycle had obviously been handmade.

I had no idea about how to learn to ride it. I held onto the fence by our house and managed to mount. Then quickly my first spill. Somehow, by trial and error, I

learned to ride it. First it was from the fence a short distance across a driveway to the house. Before long it was around the block and beyond. Figure 14-35 shows me riding that first unicycle.

I was surprised to learn that my grandfather had also ridden unicycles. When I showed my first unicycle to my grandfather, he said that they had built and ridden unicycles when they were boys. That would have been sometime before 1910. I had always believed what my grandfather told me he had done. For

Fig. 14-35. The author riding his first unicycle at age 13.

example, I believed he had ridden those long distances on a bicycle and had not thought much about it. But I couldn't quite believe the part about the unicycling. My grandfather was getting along in years, and I had never seen him ride even a regular bicycle. So I was more than a little worried when he took the unicycle and, using a tree as a support, mounted it. Then in complete control he pedaled over to another tree. He dismounted, handed me the unicycle, and took a seat on the yard-swing chair. "Better not tell your grandma I did that," he said. He later explained that he and various friends of his had built their own unicycles and learned to ride them. As so often happens, I didn't ask more questions when I had the chance before he died.

A friend came over and learned to ride on the same unicycle. This was a good motivator. When one of us learned a new skill, the other had to learn it too, even if it meant hours of extra practice "in secret."

With some adult help, I built a giraffe unicycle and a handlebar unit. The friend who had learned on my first unicycle and I started riding unicycles in parades. We worked up an amateur act and performed in a number of shows in and around Fresno, California. The big even of the year for us was always the Annual YMCA Circus.

This was how I got hooked on unicycling. Through the years I built unicycles of every description and taught unicycling in various YMCA programs. The first magazine article that I sold was "How To Build and Ride a Unicycle." It was published in the September 1964 issue of **Mechanix Illustrated**.

Still, up until 1970 when I was researching my first unicycle book, I seldom encountered another unicyclist that wasn't a professional performer or someone that I had taught to ride. I did see some articles in magazines that mentioned other individual riders and riding groups, but I did not know that unicycling was already in the process of being organized. I kept seeing the name William Jenack mentioned as a

Fig. 14-36. The author is shown at an early age practicing for a YMCA circus.

promoter and teacher of unicycling, but it wasn't until November 20, 1972, that I finally managed to find his address and write to him. Bill Jenack answered with a letter dated November 28, 1972, that was to be the first of hundreds that we exchanged over the next ten years until his death on February 24, 1982. The last letter I received from him was dated February 9, 1982.

The first letter from Bill in 1972 was five single-spaced typewritten pages packed with information about unicycling. I was surprised to learn that, unknown to me, there were actually, in addition to professional performers, thousands of amateur unicycle riders, not only in this country but also in other parts of the world as well. I was then in contact with the person who probably knew more about unicycles and unicycling than anyone else in the world.

William M. Jenack

One of the first and most ardent promoters of unicycling for everyone was William M. Jenack, who lived the later part of his life in Westbury, New York. He became interested in unicycling at an early age and worked his way through college as a magician, acrobat, and unicyclist--somehow blending them all together in an act. During the years that I corresponded with Bill he was a computer technician at the Republic Division of Fairchild Industries. Bill remained enthusiastic about unicycling all through his life. All members of his family learned to ride. One of his sons, John (Jean Paul) Jenack, is an outstanding unicyclist today and is carrying on the work of promoting and developing unicyling started by his father.

However, Bill did not by any means limit his unicycling instruction to his own family. In fact, he probably taught more others to ride than anyone else in the world. He taught four-year-olds, a 66-year-old man, and all ages inbetween--boys and girls and men and women alike. He even taught a totally blind man, John Lizza, to ride a unicycle (Fig. 14-37).

Bill Jenack put together one of the

Fig. 14-37. Bill Jenack (on right) taught John Lizza, who is blind, to ride a unicycle.

largest collections of unicycles and special bikes anywhere (this collection is now in the possession of his family). Included in the collection are a dozen regular-size commercial model unicycles, several manufactured giraffe models, and half a dozen custom-built unicycles that were used by professional performers, five circus-type bikes, two of which break apart to become unicycles, four regular unicycles built and used by performers in the 20s, and a couple of ultimate wheels of special double-wheel design. There are also a couple of small unicycles for use by four to six-year olds, four regular unicycles used by his family, six other training unicycles which are 20 and 24-inch wheel models with balloon tires and special saddles, a special three wheel (on top of each other) six-foot unicycle, and two pony saddle unicycles. And then there are a number of regular and special bicycles, including two penny farthings and two tiny vaudeville bicycles. Also, there are a couple of bicycle trailers, which work behind unicycles as well. This was basically the collection that Bill Jenack had in 1972. Regarding the collection at the time, Bill said, "And I must say, I've almost reached the saturation point as far as room is concerned."

However, Bill continued to add cycles to his collection over the years, so the number and range of cycles was probably even greater at the time of his death in 1982.

By 1972, Bill had taught over 500 neighborhood children how to ride and had formed the Jenack Cyclists, a group that performed in parks, parades, and civic events (Fig. 14-38). The number of performers at these events was often fifty or more.

Bill Jenack also did sky diving.

In 1967, after talking with a number of unicyclists about the country, he formed the Unicyclists Association of America, a non-profit, no dues, organization that was open to anyone who wished to correspond and swap ideas and information on the sport of unicycling. Through this organization, Bill corresponded with unicyclists throughout the world.

Bill Jenack was also the founder and main thrust in the formation of the Unicycling Society of America, Inc., a national non-profit organization that is devoted to unicycling and is still thriving today.

Bill Jenack also had an active Lunch Hour Unicycle Group at the Republic

Fig. 14-38. Bill Jenack leading a group of young unicyclists.

Fig. 14-39. Lunch-hour unicycle group was led by Bill Jenack (on right) at the Republic Aviation Division of Fairchild Industries in Farmingdale, L.I., New York (photo courtesy Fairchild Industries).

Aviation Division of Fairchild Industries in Farmingdale (Fig. 14-39). At one time there were some 40 adults who had their own unicycles and it was not an uncommon sight to see a dozen unicyclists practicing in the parking field during lunch hours.

I only met Bill Jenack in person one time when he came to California with his wife, Mary, and their son, John. That memorable visit lasted only a few hours. Part of the time we spent unicycling and juggling. Bill Jenack probably knew (and in my opinion did know) more about unicycles and unicycling than anyone else in the world.

Rudy Yung

Rudy Yung, who died in 1971, was one of the outstanding early promoters of unicycling. A machinist by trade, he first started building and riding unicycles in the early 1930s. He built many novelty cycles, including the motor-driven monocycle detailed previously in this chapter, the big-wheel unicycle shown in Figure 14-40, and all of the cycles shown in Figure 14-41. He taught boys and girls how to ride unicycles and formed a unicycle riding group that was first called

Fig. 14-40. Rudy Yung rides a unicycle that he built from a wagon wheel (photo courtesy Herman Yung).

Fig. 14-41. The Cycl-O-Trons, a unicycle group started by the late Rudy Yung, performing in a parade (photo courtesy Herman Yung).

the "Wheelits" and later renamed "Cycl-O-Trons." They performed in parades, State Fairs, and charity benefits on the west coast. Some of the unicyclists that he taught went on to perform professionally.

Cycling Hujos

The Cycling Hujos (Fig. 14-42) of Ogden, Utah, started some 18 years ago when Joseph W. Stegen, Jr., and Hugh Taylor got together when they were about 50 years old. They worked up an act that featured not only unicycling, but also juggling, clowning, and acrobatics.

Over the years, they performed over 650 free charity shows and rode in numerous parades. Joseph W. Stegen, Jr., who did not start unicycling or juggling until he was 48 years old, is shown riding a unicycle and juggling balls (Fig. 14-43), juggling rings (Fig. 14-44), balancing ball on stick and spinning rings on wrists (Fig. 14-45), and performing as "JOSCO THE CLOWN" at the big Utah State Fair (Fig. 14-46). His performances are truely amazing for someone who did not take up

the circus arts until he was 48 years old. He also has hobbies collecting circus programs from all over the world and building scale-model circuses.

Fig. 14-42. The Cycling Hujos--back row, Gay Taylor, Mel Thompson, and Dean Claxton; front row, Gil Claxton, Hugh Taylor, Joseph W. Stegen, Jr., and DeAnn Thompson (photo courtesy Joseph W. Stegen, Jr.).

Fig. 14-43. Joseph W. Stegen, Jr., juggling balls while riding unicycle (photo courtesy Joseph W. Stegen, Jr.).

Fig. 14-45. Joseph W. Stegen, Jr., balancing ball on stick and spinning rings on wrists (photo courtesy Joseph W. Stegen, Jr.).

Fig. 14-44. Joseph W. Stegen, Jr., juggling rings while riding unicycle (photo courtesy Joseph W. Stegen, Jr.).

Fig. 14-46. Joseph W. Stegen, Jr., performing as "JOSCO THE CLOWN" (photo courtesy Joseph W. Stegen, Jr.).

Figure 14-47 shows two talented younger members of the Cycling Hujos. Mel Thompson is shown riding a unicycle with Dean Claxton on his shoulders juggling in Figure 14-48 and Mel

Thompson is shown juggling clubs on a 6-foot unicycle in Figure 14-49. Although most all the members of the Cycling Hujos are now married and they no longer perform regularly as the Cycling Hugos, they still get together occasionally and put on a performance.

Fig. 14-49. Mel Thompson on 6-foot unicycle juggling clubs (photo courtesy Joseph W. Stegen, Jr.).

Fig. 14-47. Gil Claxton and DeAnn Thompson are a pair of talented younger members of the Cycling Hujos (photo cortesy Joseph W. Stegen, Jr.).

St. Helen Unicyclists

One of the most successful unicycling programs was that of Father James J. Moran, now deceased, at St. Helen, a Roman Catholic parochial school in Newbury, Ohio. It all started in the late 1960s when Father Moran went to a bicycle shop to purchase a bicycle-built-for-two for use in the school recreation program. While there, he saw a unicycle and bought it too. The unicycle gathered dust for some time, until one of the students said he wanted to learn to ride it. So Father Moran taught him.

After that, more and more of the students wanted to learn, so more unicycles were purchased (by 1972, the school owned over sixty of them) and many students bought their own. Because of the popularity, unicycling was added to the physical education program. Soon every student at St. Helen School, which had grades four through eight, had learned to ride a unicycle. By 1972, counting graduating classes, more than 200 had learned.

No place at the school was off-limits to unicycles. Students rode from home to the school and then, once at school, in the gymnasium, hallways, and in and out of the classrooms.

A special demonstration team was

Fig. 14-48. Mel Thompson riding the unicycle with Dean Claxton on his shoulders juggling (photo courtesy Joseph W. Stegen, Jr.).

Fig. 14-50. The St. Helen Unicyclists performing in a parade under the direction of Father James J. Moran (photo courtesy Father James J. Moran).

formed. Unicycles from three to eleven feet tall were used to perform drills and for ramp-to-ramp jumps and riding obstacle courses and across narrow beams. They also played games, such as softball and basketball, on unicycles. The St. Helen Unicyclists have performed in many parades (Fig. 14-50) and shows, including national television appearances before millions of viewers.

Father James J. Moran continued to be active with the St. Helen Unicyclists even after he retired right up to the time of his death in 1979.

Wonderwheels

Unicycling is an ideal activity for a family to do together, as the Rogers family of Cerritos, California, demonstrated when they formed a well-balanced group called the Wonderwheels.

It started in 1964 when Dr. Miles S. Rogers, a research psychologist, thought his two older children might be big enough to start learning to ride a tiny unicycle that had been built for him by the famous unicyclists Walter Nilsson. Dr. Rogers also owned a larger Nilsson-built unicycle and was anxious to brush up on his own long-dormant unicycling skills. He had learned to ride a unicycle as a junior

high school boy.

Soon Dawn, then seven, and Craig, nine, learned to ride. Other neighborhood children soon bought unicycles and a team was formed. Thirty different youngsters were involved before the Wonderwheels became strictly a family team at the end of 1968.

The team consisted of Dr. Rogers, who earned his Ph.D. at Princeton; Mrs. Charlotte Fox Rogers, a former clinical psychologist; and their children Craig, Dawn, Bruce, and Valerie (Fig. 14-51 and Fig. 14-52). Dr. Rogers and the children all rode unicycles. Mrs. Rogers was not a unicyclist; she rode an adult tricycle covered with flamboyant tissue paper flowers color keyed to the costumes worn.

For a small, strictly amateur, family organization, the Wonderwheels reached some startling heights. Before the group disbanded on August 31, 1974, they put on 155 costumed appearances, which included halftime shows for professional sports events, a Halloween program for the children of Watts, a show for a foster children's picnic, and numerous parades. One of the highlights was performing at Expo 67 in Montreal. Another interesting experience was taking their unicycles to Baja California in a four-wheel-drive land cruiser. Mexican children quickly gathered in the plazas to watch their impromptu performances.

They participated in 92 Southern California competitive parades in the Novelty category and won a sweepstakes trophy, a special award, and 48 first-place, 21 second-place, and eight third-place trophies.

The Wonderwheels have vividly demonstrated what a family, properly balanced, can do on unicycles.

Fig. 14-51. The Wonderwheels--left to right, Dr. Miles S. Rogers, Dawn Rogers, Craig Rogers, Valerie Rogers, Charlotte Fox Rogers, Bruce Rogers (photo by Bob Shumway and courtesy Charlotte Fox Rogers).

Fig. 14-52. The Wonderwheels performing a colorful unicycle routine.

Franz Karrenbauer

Franz Karrenbauer of Germany, who has been living in Luxembourg for the past 25 years, has been a unicycling fan for 30 years. He now performs a very interesting 20-minute act as a hobby for charity shows (Fig. 14-53). His act makes use of a variety of novelty cycles.

Clubs and Riding Groups

Many clubs and riding groups are presently active or have been active in the past, including Jenack Cyclists (covered previously in this chapter), Arnold Wheels in Tempe, Arizona, the Paul Fox Unicycle Club, Inc., in Marion, Ohio, the Concord Unicycle Club in Concord, California, the Pontiac Unicyclists in Pontiac, Michigan (the name was retired in honor of the director of this group, Bernard Crandall, when he died in 1978), the Pontiac Group (directed by Floyd Crandall, son of Bernard Crandall), the Wonderwheels (covered previously in this chapter), the San Diego Unicycle Club in San Diego, California, the St. Benedict Unicycling Team in Cleveland, Ohio, the Redford Township Unicycle Club, Inc., in Redford, Michigan, The Uniques in Lynnwood, Washington, Las Cruces Unicycle Club in Las Cruces, New Mexico, the Mobile Unicycle Club in Mobile, Alabama, the Oak View Elementary School Exhibitional Activities Club in Fairfax, Virginia, the Smiling Faces of Findlay, Ohio, Uni-Gang in Spring, Texas,

Fig. 14-53. Franz Karrenbauer performing his cycle act (photos courtesy Franz Karrenbauer).

Kokomo Road Runners Unicycle Club in Kokomo, Indiana, Athens Unicycling Society in Athens, Ohio, the Waukegan One Wheelers in Waukegan, Illinois, and the Sacramento Unicycle Club in Sacramento, California.

A number of youth and college circuses have featured unicycle acts as part of their shows, including the famous Sailor Circus of Sarasota, Florida, the Hamilton Mini Circus in Hamilton, Ohio, the Florida State University "Flying High" Circus, and the Great Y Circus in Redlands, California.

Joe Mole, who was known as "The Professor of Cycles" in his vaudeville performing days, was still actively promoting and teaching unicycling at a Boy's Club in Westminster, California, when he was 86 years old in 1975. This great man has made an important contribution to the sport of unicycling.

Competition and Organizations

Unicycling competition dates back to at least 1888, when one- to 14-mile races were held. The Festival of Cyclists in London's Crystal Palace in 1896 was perhaps a form of competition, with the cyclists attempting to outdo each other.

I have been unable to document any organized competition between this time and 1965, although I believe there probably was competition at various times.

In 1965, unicycling competiton called "First Unicycle Rodeo" was held in San Diego, California. The competition was sponsored by the San Diego Unicycle Club, Inc., which started in 1961. Events included hula-hooping, golf ball pick-up, ball bouncing, relay racing, standing still, and rocking.

Stelber Industries, Inc., who manufacture bicycles and unicycles, and the New York City Department of Recreation jointly sponsored "The World's First Unicycle Invitational." It was held on Saturday, October 2, 1971, in New York City's Central Park. The idea for this event came from Ms. Monica C. de Hellerman of Bass and Company, Inc., public relations firm for Stelber. The events included sprint and distance races and individual and team trick riding. In spite of poor weather, the event drew 61

unicyclists and 250 spectators.

This event seems to have established unicycling as a competitive sport. Other competitions followed. For example, on Saturday, July 15, 1972, a Rockathon, sporsored by the Paul Fox Unicycle Club, Inc., was held in Marion, Ohio. The contest was basically to see who could rock a unicycle back and forth in one spot for the longest time.

On September 24, 1972, the Paul Fox Unicycle Club, Inc., sponsored a Rideathon. The competition was to see who could continue riding the longest. Fifty-three riders entered.

On Sunday, October 22, 1972, the Pontiac Unicyclists in Pontiac, Michigan, sponsored a Unicycle Round-Up. The program included separate events for boys and girls in racing for short unicycles with 20-inch wheels, 24-inch wheels, and for giraffe unicycles, relay races, backward and one-leg races, and individual and team trick riding. In addition, there was the selection of Mister Unicycle 1972. The event was reported to have been a complete success.

In order to hold competition on a national level, a national organization had to first be formed. This organization, the Unicycling Society of America, Inc., was founded in July, 1973, largely through the efforts of William M. Jenack, as detailed previously in this chapter. The founder members were Bernard Crandall, Paul Fox, Nancy Fox, Peter Hangach, Patricia Herron, Bill Jenack, Gordon Kruse, Steve McPeak, Father James J. Moran, Dr. Miles S. Rogers, Charlotte Fox Rogers, Andy Rubel, Dr. Claude Shannon, Jim Smith, and Dr. Jack Wiley.

Since I was one of the founder members, I have some recollections of how and why this came about. Bill Jenack was anxious to get a national organization started. He talked to other people who were also interested in unicycling. Then he somehow put it all together.

Since its establishment, the organization has published a quarterly newsletter and sponsored an annual National Unicycle Meet, which has been held in various parts of the United States.

The Unicycling Society of America, Inc., has done an outstanding job of promoting unicycling in this country. This has been made possible by the volunteer help of unicyclists, parents, and others interested in the sport of unicycling.

Unicycling has also become an organized sport in a number of other countries, including Japan, where Jack Halpern has done an excellent job of organizing and promoting the sport; Germany, where Hans Born, a world authority on the sport of artistic bicycling, has also promoted unicycling; Sweden, where Goran Lundstrom has organized and promoted unicycling; and Denmark, where the Danish Unicycling Federation has been formed.

On June 1, 1982, the International Unicycling Federation was officially established. Bill Jenack had the idea for such an organization even before he started the Unicycling Society of America, Inc. Jack Halpern wrote a detailed proposal for such an organization in 1980. John Foss, Kenneth Fuchs, and John (Jean Paul) Jenack, all champion unicyclists and active promotors of unicycling, were instrumental in helping to get this organization started. The First International Unicycle Convention is scheduled for July 1984.

Chapter 15

FEATS AND RECORDS

Unicycling feats and records fall into a number of categories, including longest journey, tallest unicycle ridden on ground, tallest unicycle ridden on tightwire, endurance records, speed records, riding smallest unicycle, riding unicycle with smallest wheel, riding unicycle with largest wheel, most times for performing a particular skill, longest time for performing a particular skill, youngest to learn to ride, oldest to learn to ride, unusual and/or difficult to ride unicycles, and so on. Some of the feats and records have been detailed in Chapter 14. These will be summarized again in this chapter.

In many cases, it is very difficult to document and/or varify the records. In most cases, I was not there when the records were broken or the feats performed. There may be cases where people have already broken the records that I have listed here. If so, I would like to hear about them for possible listings in future editions of this book.

LONGEST JOURNEY

As early as 1888, speed records were listed for from one to 14 miles with the riders on unicycles with large wheels, but I have not found any evidence to indicate the early use of unicycles for making longer rides, although it is quite possible that some early unicyclists made journeys of 100 miles or more.

The first person known to have ridden a unicycle across the United States was Walter Nilsson. In 1933, he rode from the George Washington Bridge in New York to San Francisco, covering a distance of 3,306 miles in 117 days. His average speed was over 28.2 miles per day. He used an 8-foot giraffe unicycle, which is perhaps

surprising, since no one had claimed to have done it on a standard unicycle.

Walter Nilsson's journey seems to have set a standard, although it is interesting to note that in recent years a number of people have made shorter journeys claiming the distance record without apparently even knowing about Walter Nilsson's ride.

The next long journey to receive much publicity was Steve McPeak's Chicago to Las Vegas ride which covered 2,311 miles and took 43 days. While his ride was shorter than Nilsson's, Steve covered perhaps 1,500 miles on a 13-foot unicycle, which to my knowledge is the longest distance ever ridden on a unicycle this tall in such a short time period.

In 1970 at the age of 21 Jacquie Douglas rode a unicycle north from Costa Mesa, California to Cambria, California, a distance of over 200 miles in two weeks, averaging 15 miles a day. She chose the unicycle for a chance to "see the beautiful scenery you miss in an automobile" rather than to break any record. However, I know of no other girl or woman who has ridden further or made a two-week journey on a unicycle.

In 1973, Wally Watts rode a unicycle with a 42-inch wheel from English Bay in Vancouver to Halifax, Nova Scotia, covering a distance of 4,550 miles in 93 days, averaging over 48 miles a day and setting a new world record.

On October 8, 1978, Wally Watts completed an incredible around-the-world journey on a unicycle with a 43-inch wheel, covering a distance of 12,000 miles. This journey is described in Chapter 14.

Wally Watts is still to my knowledge

the only person to have ridden a unicycle around the world. However, on November 7, 1983, Pietro Biondo of Montreal, Canada, completed a 15-month tour around North America that covered a distance of 12,193 miles, which is longer than the 12,000 miles claimed by Wally Watts. Pietro Biondo used a home-built giraffe unicycle with saddle bags and spare tire mounted near the ground to make his incredible journey--the longest by far in a 15-month period.

Wally Watts has probably ridden the longest distance over a six year period. His trans-Canada distance added to his around-the-world ride total 16,550 miles.

Other unicyclists who have made long rides include Kevin Erskine, who pedaled 3,000 miles in the western U.S. on a giraffe unicycle; Brad Armstrong, who completed ride across the United States to Imperial Beach, California, on March 17, 1978; and Bob McIntyre, who rode a giraffe unicycle from Portland, Oregon, to Washington, D.C., covering a distance of 3,200 miles, in 1978.

John (Jean Paul) Jenack reported seeing a man named Joe Faul or something similar who was riding a unicycle around the world at the Olympics in Montreal in 1976, but I have not been able to get any further information on this.

TALLEST UNICYCLE RIDDEN ON GROUND

I am somewhat surprised that the early professional unicyclists did not try to outdo each other by constructing and riding taller and taller giraffe unicycles, but I find no evidence of this. In fact, until Steve McPeak came along, no one seemed to know exactly what the record was. Walter Syretto was known to be riding a 14-foot giraffe unicycle in the early 1960s and perhaps much earlier than this, but I do not know if this was the record.

Steve McPeak seems to have started the competition for riding the tallest unicycle on the ground when he rode a 20-footer in November 1966 (see Fig. 14-28).

On February 2, 1969, before anyone had broken his 20-foot record, Steve McPeak rode a 31-foot unicycle in the parking lot behind Circus Circus Casino in Las Vegas.

On August 22, 1974, Danny Haynes, then 17 years old, established a new world record when he rode a unicycle that was 34 feet 5 inches tall.

In late 1976 Jim Petty, then age 29, of Grand Junction, Colorado, rode a unicycle that was 39 feet 10 inches tall. This was a new world record for riding on the ground (Steve McPeak had already rode a 41-footer on the high wire by this time).

Brett Shockley rode a unicycle that was 53 feet 9-1/2 inches tall on July 15, 1977. By this time, all riders were using safety wires and/or safety harnesses when riding these extremely tall unicycles. In my opinion, if these heights are attempted, safety devices should always be used.

On March 25, 1980, Sem Abrahams rode a 72-foot unicycle a distance of 7.32 meters with a safety harness in Tokyo, Japan (Fig. 15-1).

On November 21, 1980, Steve McPeak regained the world record for riding the tallest unicycle on the ground by riding a unicycle that was 100 feet tall with a safety harness.

TALLEST UNICYCLE RIDDEN ON TIGHTWIRE

Lou Lacher, who died at the age of 82 in 1965, is reported to have been the first person to ride a unicycle on a tightwire and that he did this in New York City before the "turn of the century."

In recent years, no one seems to have even challenged the records set by Steve McPeak (see Chapter 14). His record is currently a 41-foot unicycle on a wire 40 feet above the ground, which he set on October 28, 1976.

Steve McPeak has also ridden a variety of other unicycles on the high wire, including a 10-foot zigzag unicycle and, with a partner, a tandem giraffe unicycle.

SPEED AND ENDURANCE RECORDS

In 1888 W. H. Barber used a big-wheel unicycle to set a 3 minute and 27 second record for the mile, breaking the then existing world record by 10 seconds.

LeGrand is listed as having set a new endurance record at Maubeuge, France, by riding a standard unicyle for 11 hours 21 minutes and covering 83.4 miles.

On September 5, 1977, Frank Williams rode 100 miles from Austin to Wasco, Texas, in 12:50:00. On May 4, 1980, Jack Halpern rode 100 miles in 11:26:07 in Tokyo, Japan. Cathy Fox of Marion, Ohio, topped this on June 7, 1980, by riding 100 miles in 10:37:10. Earlier, Cathy Fox had made a 48-mile ride on a unicycle with a 42-inch wheel in 4:20:00. On January 10, 1981, Johnnie Severin of Atwater, California, made a 100-mile ride in 9:20:53 for a new world record.

Floyd Crandall set a 100 meter sprint record of 14.89 seconds on March 24, 1980, in Tokyo, Japan.

Bill Loden of Booneville, Mississippi, rode a unicycle backwards for 14.8 miles in 40 minutes (in 1983?).

MULTI-WHEEL UNICYCLES WITH MOST WHEELS

Megumi Tsukahara of Japan is shown in Figure 15-2 riding an 8-wheeler that was built by her dad, who is an enthusiastic builder of unusual unicycles.

Figure 15-3 shows Jack Halpern riding a 13-wheeler that was built by Masahiko Hayashi of Nagoya, Japan.

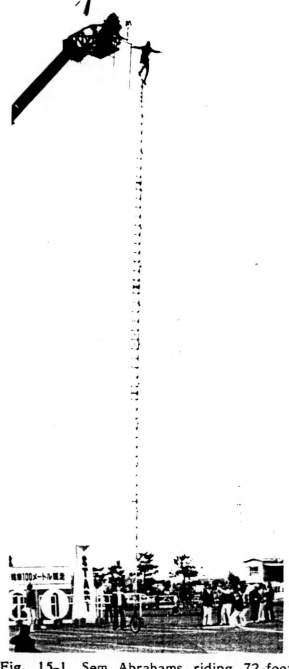

Fig. 15-1. Sem Abrahams riding 72-foot unicycle with safety harness in Tokyo, Japan, on March 25, 1980 (photo courtesy Unicycling Society of America, Inc.).

Bert Myers reportedly broke all records for distances from 2 to 14 miles that same year. He rode 13 miles and 5,098 feet in one hour; and 14 miles in one hour and 7 seconds.

On September 12, 1955, Raymond

Fig. 15-2. Megumi Tsukahara of Japan is shown riding 8-wheeler (photo courtesy Unicycling Society of America, Inc.).

Fig. 15-3. Jack Halpern riding a 13-wheeler (photo courtesy Joyce Jones and the Unicycling Society of America, Inc.).

Fig. 15-4. Goran Lundstrom is shown holding his son on his 63-1/2 inch wheel unicycle (photo courtesy Unicycling Society of America, Inc.)

Several backwards-forwards 4-wheelers and at least one 6-wheeler have reportedly been built and ridden in Japan.

UNICYCLE WITH LARGEST WHEEL

In 1980 Goran Lundstrom of Sweden built and successfully rode a unicycle with a 63-1/2 inch wheel (Fig. 15-4). The unicycle weighs 14 kilograms. This is the largest-wheel unicycle that I know of that has been built and ridden with the rider mounted above the wheel. Some early writings mention a monocycle with the rider inside the wheel with a 20-foot wheel, but I do not know if this was actually constructed and ridden. Wally Watts has reportedly been in the process of building a geared-down unicycle with a 10-foot wheel, which he intends to ride.

UNICYCLE WITH SMALLEST WHEEL

Walter Nilsson was riding a mini-wheel giraffe unicycle with a 4-1/4 inch wheel in the 1930s. I have heard of several similar unicycles with even smaller wheels that have been constructed and ridden since that time.

John (Jean Paul) Jenack is reported to have set a world record for riding the unicycle with the smallest wheel on September 26, 1983. The unicycle was built by Al Hemminger, present Secretary of the Unicycling Society of America, Inc. The unicycle stands about 14-inches high and has an 11/16-inch diameter wheel. John Foss, present Newsletter Editor of the Unicycling Society of America, Inc., has also ridden this unicycle. He has also ridden Goran Lundstrom's 63-1/2 inch wheel unicycle and is reported to be the only person in the world to have ridden both the unicycle with the smallest wheel and the unicycle with the largest wheel.

MISCELLANEOUS FEATS AND RECORDS

One of the most unusual unicycles that has been built and ridden was unveiled by Jack Halpern in 1982. It's a forwards-backwards multi-wheel, except it has only half a wheel for the upper wheel. When the upper-wheel is turned so that it does not contact the lower wheel, the lower wheel is free-wheeling. Jack Halpern demonstrated that he could ride this unicycle at the 1982 National Unicycle Meet.

Sem Abrahams has successfully performed coasting on a wheel with foot-pegs (Fig. 15-5). These wheels are sometimes called "Impossible Wheels."

185

Fig. 15-5. Sem Abrahams is shown riding an "Impossible Wheel" (photo by John Foss and courtesy Unicycling Society of America, Inc.).

Mel Hall's youngest daughter learned to ride a unicycle at the age of 18 months. I do not know if any child younger than this has ever learned to ride.

Charles Berry of Watsonville, California, learned to ride a unicycle when he was sixty years old. Bill Jenack told me that he taught a 66-year-old man how to ride a unicycle. It is quite possible that someone even older than this has learned to ride.

In 1974 Floyd Crandall rode a unicycle up a ramp and leaped over seven people who were prone in front of the ramp. In 1980 Randy Barnes leaped 11 feet 8 inches from a ramp on a unicycle. On May 8, 1982, he made a ramp-to-ramp jump of 10 feet 6 inches.

Another notable unicycling feat was that of Bernard Munier of France. In 1971 at age 20 he rode a unicycle down the 1,700 steps and landings of the Eiffel Tower non-stop without touching a rail with his hands or a step with his feet. Stirrups held his feet to the pedals.

Jess Monefeldt is reported to hold a world record for spinning 16 hoops in different directions while mounted on a giraffe unicycle. It took 27 years of practice to accomplish this feat.

Steve McPeak's unicycle ride across a 1,500-foot long cable suspended 700 feet above Hoover Dam, I believe, is one of the most spectacular feats ever performed on a unicycle.

Floyd and Clyde Crandall rode a unicycle with a large saddle, each with a person on shoulders, making four on one unicycle. I've seen a standing three-high performed on a unicycle, but this is the only time I have heard of four people on one unicycle.

On September 19, 1981, Carol Bahorich and John Foss had an informal contest to see who could mount giraffe unicycles the most times in a row without a miss. They called it a draw at 130 because they both wanted to go to dinner.

Similar problems have resulted in idling, juggling while riding or idling on a unicycle, and other similar contests. There are a number of people that can do these skills for many hours.

A number of unicycles have been built and ridden with two riders, but to my knowledge, a unicycle for three riders has not yet been built and ridden.

Jess Monefeldt used a zigzag giraffe unicycle that had the zigzag to the side rather than forward and backwards in his 1932 cycling act "Maysy and Brach." This is the only unicycle of this type that I know was actually built and ridden.

APPENDIX

SOURCES FOR UNICYCLES AND OTHER EQUIPMENT

JIM BAYLISS
2409 East Side Drive
Austin, TX 78704
(artistic bicycles)

BRIAN DUBE, INC.
520 Broadway
New York, NY 10012
(unicycles and juggling equipment)

BUTTERFINGERS
Unit 11A, Church Farm Business Park
Corston, Bath, BA2 9EX
England
(unicycles and juggling equipment)

JENACK CIRCUS CORPORATION
67 Lion Lane
Westbury, NY 11590
(unicycles and juggling equipment)

MORE BALLS THAN MOST LTD.
14-15 Leathermarket
Weston Street
London SE1 3ER
England
(unicycles and juggling equipment)

SEMCYCLE, INC.
P.O. Box 40353
Redford, MI 48240
(unicycles and juggling equipment)

CUSTOM UNICYCLE BUILDERS

ARNOLD WHEELS
Larry Chebowski
1310 E. 8th Street
Tempe, AZ 85281

JUAN WALDEMAR HALL
Jagtuej 23A
2200 Kobenhavn N
Denmark

D.M. ENGINEERING
David Mariner
R/O 59, Fairmile
Christchurch, Dorset BH23 2LA
England

THE UNICYCLE FACTORY
Tom Miller,
2711 N. Apperson
Kokomo, IN 46901
Phone (317) 452-2692

ORGANIZATIONS

INTERNATIONAL INDOOR CYCLING COMMISSION (COMMISSION INTERNATIONALE DE CYCLISME EN SALLE)
Gaustr. 77, D 6520 Worms
West Germany
(artistic bicycling)

INTERNATIONAL JUGGLERS ASSOCIATION
Post Office Box 3707
Akron, OH 44314-3707
(juggling)

INTERNATIONAL UNICYCLING FEDERATION, INC.
John Foss
P.O. Box 96
Levittown, NY 11756

JAPAN UNICYCLE ASSOCIATION
6-21-39 Nobidome
Niizashi, Saitama
352 Japan

UNICYCLING SOCIETY OF AMERICA, INC.
P.O. Box 40534
Redford, MI 48240

PUBLICATIONS

SOLIPAZ PUBLISHING COMPANY
P.O. Box 366
Lodi, CA 9524
(Publishes books on unicycling and circus skills. Write for free brochure).

ABOUT THE AUTHOR

Jack Wiley has had a varied career. He traveled overland by buses and trains from the United States to Buenos Aires, Argentina, and returned by way of the Amazon; received his Ph.D. from the University of Illinois in 1968; did physiology research at the University of California at Santa Barbara; and lived aboard a sailboat for a number of years.

Dr. Jack Wiley first became interested in unicycling when he was in the seventh grade. A friend showed him the remains of a unicycle that had belonged to his uncle, a former professional stage performer. Jack Wiley purchased the unicycle and restored it with the help of a man at a bicycle shop.

He then learned to ride the unicycle, built other cycles, and worked up an amateur act. He performed in many shows in and around Fresno, California, including the Annual YMCA Circus.

Unicycling has remained an important part of his life since that time, and he has written a number of books on the subject, including *The Complete Book of Unicycling, How To Build Unicycles and Artistic Bicycles,* and *Unicycles and Artistic Bicycles Illustrated.*

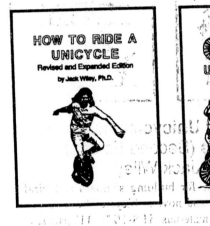
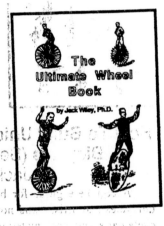

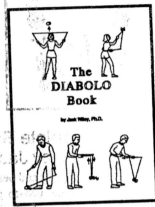

UNICYCLING, CIRCUS SKILLS, DIABOLO, AND TUMBLING

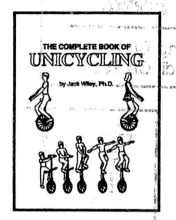 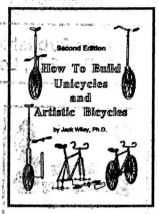  

The Complete Book of Unicycling
by Jack Wiley

The most popular and best selling unicycling book in the world. A complete how-to guide for learning to ride and performing all levels of artistic skills on a variety of standard and giraffe unicycles. Also covers the history and development of unicycling and records and feats. 187 8-1/2" x 11" pages, 321 photo and line illustrations. Paperback.

The Complete Book of Unicycling **$27.95**

Basic Circus Skills (Third Edition)
by Jack Wiley

A revised and updated edition of the popular guide to performing circus skills, including juggling, balancing, devil stick, diabolo, stilts, unicycling, tumbling, acrobatic balancing, ladders, pyramids, and clowning. Also covers how to stage amateur acts and circuses. 61 8-1/2" x 11" pages, 134 photo and line illustrations. Paperback.

Basic Circus Skills **$12.95**

How To Build Unicycles and Artistic Bicycles (Second Edition)
by Jack Wiley

A complete guide for building standard and giraffe unicycles and artistic and novelty bicycles from bicycles, cycle parts, and stock materials. 81 8-1/2" x 11" pages, 131 photo and line illustrations. Paperback.

How To Build Unicycles and Artistic Bicycles **$15.95**

Individual Tumbling, Balancing and Acrobatics
by Jack Wiley

A complete guide to individual tumbling, balancing and acrobatics, from basic rolls to the most advanced skills and routines ever performed. Also covers history and development and competition rules. 61 8-1/2" x 11" pages, 104 photo and line illustrations. Paperback.

Individual Tumbling, Balancing and Acrobatics **$12.95**

ORDER FORM

Solipaz Publishing Company
P.O. Box 366
Lodi, California 95241

OUR GUARANTEE: If you are not completely satisfied with any item, you may return it for a full refund.

Qty.	Description	Item Price	Total Price
	SUBTOTAL •		
	CA residents add 7% sales tax •		
	Shipping and Handling •		$2.00
	TOTAL •		

Name _____

Address _____

City_____ State_____ Zip _____

THANK YOU FOR YOUR ORDER   (Enclose Check or Money Order)